Graphics by Phannavit Samphanprat

There are no wrong turnings. Only paths we had not known we were meant to walk - Guy Gavriel Kay

To Frank, for all your great friendship which is so special to me. Also for the dedication with which you have made all things possible.

To Jazz, a beautiful lady, for all your patience and understanding whilst this book was being written.

To Steven, my godson, so that I can prove to him that the old girl wasn't always old. And finally to Thomas and Matthew, his two sons, in the hope that they can discover a time when life was so different.

CONTENTS

FOREWORD

When I first met Eunice Musgrave some fifty years ago I was struck by her sense and depth of humour, a formidable virtue that has come to her rescue on numerous occasions on her journey through life. And what an amazing life: Cordon Bleu chef; state registered nurse and lecturer in clinical hypnotherapy; air hostess during the "golden years" of flying; writer, producer and actor in musical productions and pantomimes, and a last bastion of hope for animals in need.

From an early age she showed determination to succeed in anything she turned her hand to; driven, she will tell you, by fate...destiny...karma...kismet or whatever exemplifies a person's inner sense of purpose and understanding; something Eunice refers to as her spiritual navigator.

As a small child Eunice sensed the need to go along with her gut feelings, reinforced by her staunch belief in life after death – another characteristic that amazed her parents at the time.

Faith has sustained her throughout, though there were times she wanted nothing more than to lie down and die. But there was always a path to follow; a journey to fulfil that drove her forward. Eunice believes that choices made along the way are predestined even though her own journey was difficult at times and tested her to the limits. At such times her innate sense of humour, largely attributable to her upbringing, came to her assistance. Laugh and the world laughs with you; cry and you cry alone! A worn out cliché perhaps, but still valid many people would agree.

"Think of the millions of people there are in the world yet we meet but a handful in the course of a lifetime," Eunice reflected on one occasion. "Some folk make us question ourselves; some give us strength when we need it most; some are there because they have been through many lifetimes..." As we journey along life's path, she maintains, lessons must be learnt to help us assess our self-worth and strengthen our spiritual resolve to guide us to a safe destination.

Though Eunice dreamt of becoming an air hostess from an early age other people influenced the path she followed before she could realise her dream. Indeed her parents were her guiding light – something pointed out more than once in the annals of her memoirs. Clearly she owes so much to the wise counsel provided by her mother and father.

Eunice also owes much to Bill, her husband and soulmate. For many years in their relationship he brought great joy into her life. Later he brought abject misery that left her dejected in a way she could never have imagined when he left the marital home for another woman. Heartbroken, Eunice had to pick up the pieces, confront her dilemma head-on, and get on with life. She rose to the challenge and emerged stronger than before because she refused to abandon her fundamental beliefs.

Life's journey has taken her from catering to nursing to flying to acting to caring for stricken animals in the United States and in her beloved Yorkshire Dales.

"My Date with Destiny" is an unvarnished memoir of one woman's extraordinary journey through life that will inform, amuse and, hopefully inspire others never to give up when faced with life's many challenges.

It has been a profound pleasure participating in the preparation of this book and great joy to be able to strengthen my relationship with a lady I hold dear as a wonderful lifelong friend and cherished member of our family.

Frank W. Skilbeck [Ed]

INTRODUCTION

The Real World of Flying

The 1960s fell smack in the middle of the "golden age" of air travel, generally accepted to have started in 1935 and to have lasted for around forty years. It was an inspiring era and a time when many of the first commercial airline pilots were war veterans including heroic aviators who saw action during the Battle of Britain. Others saw service ferrying life-saving supplies in the 1948-9 Berlin Airlift when the Soviet Union blocked Western Allies' rail, road and canal access to Allied-controlled sectors of Berlin. They were magnificent men whose flying machines became a vital part their lives. For me, it was a privilege to become acquainted with both.

It was also a period when air hostesses were identified and identifiable as models of the skies and a time when a few, fortunate passengers were treated like royalty or heads of state sipping cocktails and savouring seven-course gourmet meals at twenty-five thousand feet. These were golden years.

What was it really like to travel the world in the sixties working in a pressurised tube almost five miles above the ground? Well, I can tell you from personal experience that stylish, sexy and immaculately groomed air hostesses were up there with the top models of their day. They were the stars of the skies.

Yet becoming an air hostess wasn't easy. To begin with, the interview process was a rigorous test; a nerve-wracking experience often in front of a panel of frosty-faced, senior airline representatives.

With a withering look or a cutting remark, any one of them could reduce the strongest girl to jelly, making her feel she was something that had just crawled out from a hole in the ground and wished she could get right back into it. Even more daunting were the constant reminders that only one in a thousand applicants made the grade. Yet every attempt to intimidate us failed because all we could see ahead was a glamorous and exciting job – and that's what spurred us on.

During the early days of commercial air services, long-haul flights took a lot longer to reach destinations than now -- days longer in fact. And the more time passengers and crew spent together the more relaxed the on-board atmosphere became. Without doubt crews gradually unwound the further they travelled from base. Passengers, in those days, were always most respectful towards cabin staff; something I put down to our on-board role as PR representatives as well as the ones attending to passengers' personal safety, needs and comforts.

There was time to interact with passengers on a more personal and professional level. Life was filled with fun and the fun didn't stop when the plane touched down in a foreign land. We enjoyed the most amazing crew parties, especially on long-haul flights. We socialised in romantic settings in tropical climes, accommodated in the best hotels for long enough to get to know a place really well and savour the experience. We greeted well-known celebrities as our on-board guests – even royalty on several occasions in my personal experience. Those of us lucky enough to take to the skies in the sixties and seventies really did have the very best of everything. We were the envy of so many, proudly representing flying at its best.

Former RAF jet pilot and bestselling English author Frederick Forsyth observed that "...air hostesses were certainly among the sexiest girls in the world, partly because they were unapproachable and unwinnable". How true. We were everything to everyone, but at the same time we meant nothing to anyone in particular.

In this publication of my personal recollections of the real world of flying, it's a privilege to offer you a peek into my working life that started in catering in the fifties, went on to nursing and then flying (my true calling) and my life after retiring from flying. For readers to understand what I mean by "the real world of flying" I think the following may help...

The Real World of Flying

Those were the good old days. Pilots back then were men that didn't want to be women or girly-men. Pilots drank coffee, whiskey, smoked cigars and didn't wear digital watches. They carried their own suitcases and brain bags like the real men they were. Pilots didn't bend over into the crash position multiple times a day in front of passengers at security so that some government agent could probe for tweezers or fingernail clippers or too much toothpaste.

Pilots did not go through the terminal impersonating a caddy pulling a bunch of golf clubs, computers, guitars, and feed bags full of tofu and granola on a sissy trailer with no hat, and granny glasses hanging on a pink string around their pencil neck while talking to their personal trainer on the cell phone!

Being an airline captain was as good as being a king. All air hostesses, aka stewardesses, aka flight attendants, aka cabin attendants were young, attractive, single women who were proud to be combatants in the sexual revolution. They didn't have to turn sideways, grease up and suck it in to get through the cockpit door. They would blush and say thank you when you told them they looked good, instead of filing a sexual harassment claim. They talked about men with no thoughts of substitution.

Passengers wore nice clothes and were polite. They could speak and understand English. They didn't speak gibberish or listen to loud gangsta rap on their iPods. They bathed and didn't smell like a rotting pile of garbage in a jogging suit and flip flops. Children didn't travel alone.

If the captain wanted to throw some offensive, ranting jerk off the airplane, it was done without any worries of a libel suit or getting fired.

Axial flow engines crackled with the sound of freedom and left an impressive black smoke trail like a locomotive burning soft coal. Jet fuel was cheap and once the throttles were pushed up they were left there. After all it was the jet age and the idea was to go fast. Economy cruise was something in the performance book, but no-one knew why or where it was. When the clacker went off no-one got up tight and scared because Boeing built it out of iron; nothing was going to fall off, and that sound had the same effect on real pilots then as Viagra does now for those new age guys.

There was very little plastic and no composites on the airplanes....or the hostesses' pectoral regions. Aircraft and women had eye-pleasing symmetrical curves, not a bunch of ugly vortex generators, ventral fins, winglets, flow diverters, tattoos, rings in their nose, tongues and eyebrows.

Airlines were run by the likes of C. R. Smith [CEO of American Airlines from 1934 to 1968 and from 1973 to 1974] and Juan Trippe [founder of Pan American World Airways] who had built their companies virtually from scratch, knew many of their employees by name and were lifetime airline employees themselves not pseudo financiers and bean counters who flit from one occupation to another for a few bucks, a better parachute or a fancier title while fervently believing they are a class of beings unto themselves.

AND SO IT WAS BACK THEN ...AND NEVER WILL BE AGAIN.

PART 1

FOLLOW YOUR STAR

But have a back-up plan

On a cold, rainy and windswept November day in 1960 I looked back on my time as a nurse and the rigours and disciplines that had governed my hectic life from the very start of training and for the three years that followed. My ever-caring mother, erudite as always, had counselled me upon leaving school, "…no matter which star you choose to follow Eunice my dear, if I were you I should first consider a reliable profession so you will have something to fall back on should the need arise."

It was sound advice of course, reminding me of another occasion when mother suggested I should at all times carry a large safety-pin on my person just in case my knickers-elastic broke. Fortunately for me, plan B was never enacted.

Whenever discussing or considering my career path, mother acknowledged only three "fail-safe" professions: funeral directors, who could never go out of business; cooks, because everybody has to eat; and nurses because the world always has sick people in need of care. It was difficult as a young daughter to argue with such impeccable logic.

My parents, both consummate professionals, lived life to the full, whilst assiduously extolling the disciplines and restraints emblematic of Britons born in the early part of the 20th century. Mother trained as an opera singer and also as a violinist. She was an accomplished musician and I well remember her beautiful rich mezzo soprano voice, sometimes likened to liquid gold. She was trained by a protégé of Paulo Tosti. The violin, her second instrument, served her well in later life with the Singapore Symphony Orchestra.

Whenever she discussed the music business mother maintained that a true artist should always retire from his or her career whilst on a high to be remembered for their best performances. Is it not the case nowadays, she would ask ruefully, that some singers will go beyond that high point and leave an audience with less-worthy memories?

This was so true in relation to Maria Callas one of the more outstanding singers of her time. Her voice was such a wonderful gift that brought great pleasure to so many people. It broke my heart to witness her last performance in concert. She had been so ill, and like so many artists her gift and love of music was her one consolation. Shunning good advice from friends she performed when, to my mind, her voice was barely recognisable as that of a great diva. All the emotional stress which broke her heart, and made her so ill, resonated in every note, and her top notes were barely recognisable as those of Maria Callas. Mother always said that the voice was the window of the soul, and that was truly illustrated not only by Callas' greatest performing years but also at that final concert. In that moment she truly was Giselle, the dying swan.

Mother, true to her beliefs, successfully migrated from the singing phase of her life into the orchestral part, sustaining her musical passion until she became elderly, stricken by arthritis in both hands and unable to perform.

An important part of mother's musical endeavours, particularly in the earlier years, was her circle of close friends including English contralto Kathleen Ferrier, a very attractive lady who did not begin her career as a singer. At first, she was an accomplished pianist though she also sang in choirs, her voice so powerful she was obliged to sing from the rear of the choir. In 1937, when she competed as a pianist in the prestigious Carlisle Festival, she was dared by her husband to take part in the singing competition at the same venue. She accepted the challenge and stunned everyone by walking off with the Rose Bowl, the highest award for singing. Afterwards, her singing career took off. Acknowledged as one of the world's greatest contraltos -- then and now -- Kathleen Ferrier died in 1953 after succumbing to cancer. She was only forty-one years old. We were in Singapore at the time and, of course, the news was most upsetting especially for my mother as they were firm friends.

Ena Mitchell was another distinguished singer and friend of mother's who, like mother, was born and raised in Carlisle. Specialising in concert work, mainly oratorio, she went on to become a famous soprano performing with the Halle and Bach Choirs at London's Royal Albert Hall. A sought-after coach and teacher of music she used to say to her students, "Never sing louder than lovely!" She died in Carlisle in 1979.

As a small child during the war years I, and my parents, lived with my grandparents and I well remember the musical evenings spent there. My grandfather was a well-known church organist and the first man ever to play the organ in the All Saints' Cathedral of Cairo. He taught my father to play the piano and thereby hangs a tale. Father was serving in the army at that time stationed at Carlisle Castle and had fallen hook, line and sinker for my mother after hearing her singing in concert. He approached my grandfather to ask him if he would teach dad to play the piano…a thinly-disguised ruse to get to meet my mother. As it turned out, grandfather liked my father at first sight and realised what was going on in the background. He suggested that if my father, a well-known fencing champion, instructed my mother in the art of fencing, he would teach him to play the piano. It seemed an honourable quid pro quo. But it didn't work out as planned. Mother never learned to fence, but father became a splendid pianist and derived much pleasure accompanying my mother when she sang at home or played the violin at some of our wonderful alfresco musical evenings. The venue would be filled with neighbours and friends, and everyone would "do a turn" as we say. When it was my turn I always refused to sing unless somebody gave me sixpence. Once incentivised to perform I would go on and on and on until they paid me to shut up; I was mercenary to the end!   I also queued up with soldiers at the garrison on pay day. The paymaster would duly give me one penny. I would disappear from the garden only to be found standing in line – again and again. The paymaster would then take me home – again and again.

Happily married for fifty-one years, my parents spent a lot of time travelling overseas. Starting his army career as a young apprentice in the Coldstream Guards, Charles William Victor Hankinson had a passion for sports particularly gymnastics and fencing. Father had the distinction of being the British Army's undefeated fencing champion for forty years. A keen horseman, as well as a gymnast, he was responsible for training army gymnasts for Olympiads and for organising various aspects of the Royal Tournament in the early days. Father's army career started in the Guards but he was soon seconded to the Army Physical Training Corps (APTC) because of his sporting prowess and that's where he spent most of his post-war service achieving the rank of lieutenant colonel. His OBE was awarded for services to the army during his time with the Corps.

Held in high regard by his men who considered him kind, fair and caring, father treated everyone with respect making it clear to those in his ambit that his men were part of his "family" – an officer quality that many Sandhurst-trained officers failed to comprehend or practise.

When he died, father's funeral attracted former army personnel, some still serving, some retired. One man came from Malaya (now Malaysia) and draped a Union Jack flag over the coffin as a lone trumpeter sounded the last post. Father was loved beyond words and I was extremely proud to have been his daughter. My mother, Hannah Eileen Whitaker, staunchly supported my father's military career and travelled the world with him.

This of course meant that mother only ever performed in concert after getting married and when musical opportunities arose. She did sing with Radio Malaya on occasions and played the violin in the Singapore Symphony Orchestra. Mother was very happy with this arrangement as her life as the wife of an army officer in those days was a great adventure in itself.

They were a very handsome couple who brought great pleasure to so many others and, as parents, were the most wonderful people in the world. I was truly blessed to have them as my mother and father. They were married in 1930, and I was born eight years later. Sadly, my mother lost two boys before my arrival, so it's not difficult to understand how I was a very much longed-for and beloved only-child. However this didn't mean I was spoilt or indulged as an only child as so many are. I went to boarding school so that as an only child I would learn to stand on my own two feet from an early age, and enjoy the companionship of other children. That sacrifice cost my parents a great deal emotionally as they hated to say goodbye every time I had to return to school. I enjoyed the most wonderful childhood and the person that I have always been -- and still am -- I owe to their generous love and support.

Father's sporting abilities had not gone unnoticed by folks in the motion picture industry. For example, he was asked to arrange fencing sequences for various films including *Scaramouche*. I remember as a small child being taken onto the film set to meet Margaret Lockwood and Stewart Granger, stars of the film, who invited me to be one of the ragamuffin children in the movie. I was thrilled. Could it be the start of a career in acting?

Both King Farouk and David Bowes Lyon were taught to fence by my father and we met many other interesting dignitaries as a result of his career. Field Marshall Montgomery, one of Britain's most inspirational military commanders during World War II, was a friend of my parents. Wherever we were stationed Monty always insisted on staying with us when making an army inspection. "I like coming to Hank's," I recall him saying, "because Eileen always tells me the truth." Certainly life was never dull in our family.

On one of the many occasions I attended the Sandhurst Military Ball that followed passing out parades I found myself in a group that included the future King Hussein of Jordan. I thought at the time that he was such a handsome and delightful young man.

The present Duke of Kent attended one of the pentathlon courses organised by my father whilst he was stationed in Aldershot in the south of England. The Duke was a very young man at the time and there were many enjoyable evenings spent at the officers club at Farnborough when all the young officers would let off steam jousting like knights on bicycles with mops at the ready. It was all so very long ago yet still constitutes a legacy of happy memories.

During quiet moments I mulled over my mother's well-meaning advice to find a "proper job" knowing full well she expected me to keep my feet firmly on the ground – understandably so, as I was a much-loved and only-child. This was compounded by the fact that my mother, who had always been aware of my childhood dream to become an air hostess, was terrified of flying. "It's strictly for the birds dear," she would proclaim unequivocally. Unless she was offered a parachute, accompanied by a cast-iron guarantee that she would each time return to earth in one piece, not even the Almighty could get her onto an aircraft.

Many years later I recalled with deeper understanding, and profound appreciation, my darling mother's advice to "…consider a reliable profession…" as I developed a passion for cooking and eating good food. Later, on reaching middle age, and after a rollercoaster ride on the sea of life, I returned to the time-honoured profession of nursing and taking care of people until I retired.

But there was no getting away from my childhood dream to be an air hostess. As part of a military family I was accustomed to journeying far and wide, though always by sea aboard a British troopship. I found it all very inspiring but I yearned to join what I perceived to be an exclusive band of professional airmen and airwomen blazing trails across the skies.

I left school at seventeen, four years short of the acceptance age for joining an airline. So, I had plenty of time to fulfil my mother's wish to get a proper job while waiting for that magical coming-of-age moment and a passport to a life of adventure and the realisation of my dream.

On my mother's part, she thought that as time passed by I would either morph into a modern-day Florence Nightingale or marry a handsome young doctor who would anchor my flights of fancy. Yes, I had my dream but I also had a tremendous respect for mother. Some form of compromise was essential.

With a certain amount of reluctance on my part at the time, I signed up for a Cordon Bleu course and learnt to cook food to the highest standard. I went further and became a student nurse at

London's famous Charing Cross Hospital. Neither my mother nor I appreciated that both career paths would later augment my chances of becoming an air hostess – a collision course that would not lack irony. But more about that later.

So, for four years I buckled down and, to my surprise, experienced a blend of great fun and hard work. Learning to cook Cordon Blue style started me on a fascinating and satisfying journey through the world of culinary skills. In six months I had learnt to cook everything from poached eggs to filet mignon with style and panache. Whether cooking for formal dinners, banquets or buffets, the course was designed to create the flawless hostess. This was for me, and I lapped it up.

Presentation was a crucial element, and in time, along with fellow members of the course, I could hold my head high if called upon to deliver catering to a high standard. In later life my experience was tested when I ran the household of English aristocrats during the course of which my life was enriched by the company of so many interesting personalities. All this thanks to my Cordon Bleu course. Mother wasn't wrong.

NURSING IS A WORK OF HEART

The very first requirement in a hospital is that it should do the sick no harm – Florence Nightingale.

I joined Charing Cross Hospital in London.

A British hospital in the fifties was the unquestionable domain of Matron; a powerful and vastly experienced iron-lady of nursing who knew everything that went on in her sphere of interest. Nothing escaped their gaze. A 1950-era hospital Matron was a force to be reckoned with - even doctors held their breath when she did her rounds. Any nurse unfortunate enough to be paraded before Matron, even for a minor infringement, often suffered an involuntary loosening of the bladder. Obedience was the order of the day; daily life in the wards was conducted under a strictly imposed regime of self-discipline. There were no exceptions, no arguments and lives were saved – in most cases anyway.

I recall one particularly serious but humorous occasion concerning a young student nurse, a slightly-built Chinese lad called David, who found himself for the first time assigned to Male Medical. This was a ward where, regrettably, there were often nightly occurrences of patients dying. Superstitious about death and dying, like most Chinese, David was terrified he may have to cope with someone's death on his watch, something he had never experienced before. It is fair to say he was a fairly green student.

During this particular shift, when the night Sister did her rounds of the wards (one senior Sister patrolled the entire unit at night with a couple of staff nurses for back-up) she came across David kneeling by the bed of an elderly gentleman. The poor man was definitely in his final moments. David was pleading with the unfortunate fellow, "…please don't die until the day staff come on duty!" His pleas went unanswered. The poor man passed away that night and it was down to David to prepare him for the mortuary. Our young student nurse suffered a panic attack.

I should point out that any hospital, at night-time, can be a very lonely place with few people moving around. David, realising he had a task to perform, pulled himself together and dutifully wheeled the trolley to the mortuary pushing it across a cobbled area outside the hospital. Through sheer bad luck a caster wheel came adrift and the trolley tipped forward ejecting the unfortunate corpse…akin to a burial at sea. David was alone, utterly dejected and beside himself with grief.

The next morning he appeared before Matron. Before she could utter a word, David blurted out, "Me velly solly body fell off trolley!"

Matron and assembled staff manage to stifle the urge to laugh out loud; after all, the situation was much too serious. But it was impossible not to see the funny side of David's outburst. Soon afterwards he quit nursing because his English language skills were not up to the standard required to continue further studies. And to this day, nobody knows what became of him.

Nurses' working hours in the 1950s were long and the pay minimal, yet it was an era during which self-discipline guided patient care. First name familiarity, practised in today's hospitals, was frowned upon. Colleagues were addressed as Mr, Mrs or Miss irrespective of rank. There was no "love", "dear", or "darling" in those days; affectations which today I still find unprofessional, even demeaning.

Hospital work could be gruelling at times and those who stuck it out earned every penny. Even so, most of what we earned went on accommodation in the nurses' quarters. Student nurses, in those days, had to be residential. Other inescapable expenses included laundry bills for our uniforms that had to be crisp and white and accompanied by pleated caps on heads. There were text books to purchase and miscellaneous personal care items to buy. Little money was left for anything else. I had about thirty pounds a month of spending money in my pocket – call it a pound for each day of the month.

House rules were also very strict. We had to be in by 10 p.m. every night apart from one night a week when we could stay out till midnight. We were given a key that had to be deposited in a box on our return. Doors to the nurses' quarters were locked at 10.30 p.m. but it was amazing how adept we became at finding other ways in. I have to confess that I became quite a good climber and we found a way to carry on a social life despite tedious restrictions.

Charing Cross Hospital was a teaching hospital and there were always lots of good-looking medical students around to have fun with.

Another great bonus were the occasional cheap tickets we could get our hands on for shows at London's West End theatres.

I suppose one of my favourite memories of those heady days was coming off night duty at six in the morning and walking through Covent Garden amidst the hustle and bustle of the market that was always alive and buzzing with activity in the early hours. The smell of fresh fruit and vegetables, scents and odours from colourful and perfumed flowers permeated the air and helped dispel the antiseptic smell of hospital wards. Such welcome relief.

"There you go darlin'," a cheery Covent Garden worker would say to me as he thrust a mug of hot tea in my hand. Charing Cross nurses were very popular in those days and I like to think we brought some cheer into the lives of others with a sincere smile and brief exchange of pleasantries.

Situated in the vibrant West End district of Soho, the hospital also served the East End, a colourful district of London that had a well-earned reputation as a haven for gangsters. I recall how, at that time, a certain Jack Comer, a gangster better known as "Jack Spot" because of a mole on his cheek (though there were other claims made by the man himself that he was so-called because he was always on the spot when trouble needed "sorting out"), ruled the roost as one of London's underworld kingpins. The East End was his patch and, on numerous occasions, members of his gang would pitch up at the hospital's A&E department with quite serious slash and stab wounds needing attention. Gang members were instantly recognisable in those days by their razor-toed boots or "winkle-picker" shoes and their preferred side-arms of spiked metal balls on chains, more suited, I always thought, to jousting contests featuring mediaeval knights. The "tools of the trade" used by these gangsters inflicted horrendous injuries on others. Towards the end of Jack Spot's reign in the East End he deigned to put in one or two personal visits to the A&E department for emergency treatment.

Yet, as far as nurses' personal safety was concerned, we could walk through Soho at night unhindered so long as we were in uniform. Within the hospital we also had what was known as a "Stag Ward" a receiving area for tramps, vagrants, prostitutes and a sundry collection of what could only be classified as misfits and down-and-outs. Once a month we offered them a bath and de-lousing service, a good meal and a bed for the night. Next day they were sent on their way with a half-crown in hand.

We became familiar with regular visitors including intriguing characters like Gloria a long-serving prostitute who plied her trade in the bustling streets of Soho. A chronic alcoholic suffering from cirrhosis of the liver, she would arrive at the hospital in a pitiful state, often smashed out of her mind. She was in a constant state of anxiety and clearly in need of our help but she could never relax for worrying about who might be queering her pitch in Trafalgar Square whilst her back was turned. Gloria's vibrant make-up had to be seen to be believed.

I remember one occasion when she was very ill and had to be admitted as an inpatient. Fearing for her spiritual wellbeing, the Salvation Army often visited Gloria at which times she made sure her face was devoid of make-up and replaced by her ready-to-be-saved look. She would sit bolt upright, pale-faced and wide-eyed professing to have seen the light, even if it was only a red one. When the "Sally Army" left she would paint her face until she resembled Coco the clown and if we didn't watch her carefully she would hop out of bed and make a beeline for the men's ward hoping to bring a little sunshine and joy into their lives -- irredeemable to the end. With the likes of Gloria around to keep us entertained there was never a dull moment in Charing Cross Hospital.

As a brand new student nurse on the wards I lived in fear of ever putting a foot wrong. To incur the wrath of the ward Sister was the next worse thing to being sent to Matron's office. How well I remember being asked to clean out a cupboard containing various bottles, all glass in those days. It was just before the consultant's ward walk-a-round, a daily occurrence similar to a visit from royalty.

With the bedpan round over, beds neatly made with tight "hospital corners" and nary a crease in sight, nurses were aware it was a fate worse than death to sit on a patient's bed. I sometimes got the impression that it would be deemed a criminal offence for patients to move any part of their bodies before the esteemed consultant appeared bedside.

As I was cleaning out the cupboard a fellow student nurse was gathering in the bedpans and, because we were running a bit late, carried in her hands a large stack of them as she hurried towards the sluice room. Sister and staff nurse were standing stiffly by the door waiting to greet Matron, the consultant, and his stern-faced entourage.

Near at hand – too near in fact – I was standing on a small step-stool clutching a bottle of gentian violet. Used externally for a variety of conditions, gentian violet is a deep purple colour quite difficult to remove from skin or clothing. As luck would have it the top was not securely screwed onto the bottle. Add to this developing scenario that the ward's wooden floors were highly polished and we had the makings of a perfect storm. Predictably, I slipped on one of the steps and fell, bottle in hand, only to collide with my compatriot carrying the bedpans all of which went flying just as the doors opened and our VIP's entered. The contents of the gentian blue covered the ward Sister and staff nurse as did the contents of the bedpans. Luckily the consultant and Matron were spared a similar fate as they immediately turned heel and walked briskly away from the crime scene. From what I later heard from medical students in the entourage, the consultant and Matron were visibly amused. The ward sister was not. After that incident I had a hard ride on that ward and it came as some relief when I was redirected to Male Medical a month later. But that experience also had its moments.

In the formative days of my nursing career I was an innocent young thing open to pranks and disparaging remarks here and there. Take the case of the young man who summoned me to his bedside and asked me to get him a bottle so he could take a pee. I obliged the young man and, leaving him to his own devices, I went off to do something else.

"Nurse, nurse, please help me," he called out desperately as I walked away. I rushed back to his beside. Pulling back the bedsheets he revealed an enormously enlarged penis stuck fast in the bottle.

"What on earth happened," I asked, not sure that was the correct question, whilst totally unsure of where to direct my gaze.

"It's stuck and it's your fault nurse. You walk around with the top buttons of your tunic undone so it's hardly surprising I get a hard-on a cat can't climb, is it now?" I was mortified. I didn't know what to say or where to look.

Sister, a rotund woman with equally rounded experience, was duly summoned. Following her instructions I packed the bottle containing his pride-and-joy in a bowl of ice. I was left to shovel more ice into the bowl under the gaze of a host of grinning male patients all uttering witty obscenities. It's a wonder he didn't get frostbite.

I served for four invaluable years and experienced the many facets of life in the raw. I felt stronger, more capable and indeed very much more my own person. The strict disciplinarian methods of the hospital were a necessary part of the whole, and it taught me a great deal about myself. We are nothing if we don't have discipline in our lives or, as American businessman Jim Rohn put it, "Discipline is the bridge between goals and accomplishment". He got that right.

Looking back at how a hospital ward Sister ruled with a rod of iron, I came to realise that the lives of all the patients on a ward were her responsibility and training students to become good nurses was also her responsibility. There was no room for error; lives were

21

important and sometimes at stake. Every ward Sister had in mind at all times Florence Nightingale's edict that, "the very first requirement in a hospital is that it should do the sick no harm". And to meet that requirement required discipline at all times by all concerned. Yet, with all that nursing had to offer, I was still anxious to become an air hostess. I still had that mountain to climb though it could wait a while longer.

I can readily identify with Japanese author Haruki Murukami who said, "Memories warm you up from the inside. But they also tear you apart". I must confess there are so many heart-warming and tear-jerking memories engraved in my mind from my earlier years in a hospital environment and, indeed, after returning to nursing later in life.

Take for example the eccentric consultant surgeon Mr Shemault who always wore his pyjama bottoms in theatre. I could never decide if it was affectation or a fashion statement on his part. Anyway, he was quite adamant in the matter and no amount of peer pressure to observe theatre protocol could persuade him otherwise. He was a brilliant man and I suppose because of fellow colleagues' respect for his abilities he always got his own way. Sadly he committed suicide after the unexpected death of his wife. As a young woman I found that both upsetting and puzzling at the time.

Also, I remember clearly a very brave woman who, at a very young age, was diagnosed with terminal cancer. She was too ill to leave hospital and go home to her two very young children. With only months to live, she set about knitting jumpers and cardigans in increasing sizes for her kids so that they would have warm woollies to wear as they grew older -- all made by mummy. She told them that her love for them was knitted into every stitch so she would remain with them forever. She was a great inspiration and all the nurses and other patients set about knitting for the children. I was astonished to see how her great courage made others so strong.

Then there was the lady who had a lung surgically removed. I was on duty the night of her operation. She was a terminally ill patient and the operation was conducted with the hope of buying her some extra time. As I sat with her she made it clear that her only thought was for me to go and make myself a cup of tea. I was astounded at her display of concern for others despite the grim reality of her own situation. It was a moment in time that bolstered my faith in my fellow human beings.

I will never forget my first day on the wards after leaving training school. I had to assist the staff nurse with a very elderly lady who was in a diabetic coma and had severe gangrene in one leg. I was instructed to support the foot in my hand whilst Staff inserted a drainage tube into the patient's leg to drain off the gangrenous fluid. To my horror the patient's foot removed itself from the leg and I was left holding it with no leg attached. I was mortified.

It was a well-known fact that when one first went on wards, student nurses found themselves relating to every possible symptom experienced by the patients. I can recall a fellow student nurse doing her first stint of night duty and creating a real nightmare for herself. One of the final duties before "lights out" was to remove patients' false teeth and take them into the sluice for cleaning, each pair in a preassigned glass labelled with the patient's name. All dentures were thoroughly cleaned then returned to individual glasses to be reunited with each patient the following morning. This particular young girl, however, thought she would be clever. She filled a bowl with warm soapy water and poured in the contents of all the glasses. Her idea was to save time. The only problem, apparently unseen by her at the time, was she did not know whose teeth belonged to whom. Scenes in the ward the next morning bordered on hilarious as each patient tried in vain to fit someone else's teeth into their mouth. I was reminded of Cinderella's ugly sisters frantically trying on the glass slipper. Ward sister failed to find anything amusing in the incident nor did Matron when this young nurse was summoned to her office for a well-deserved dressing down.

There was never a dull moment on the wards. I remember a retired army Matron being admitted to hospital. She held the rank of colonel. Along with other medical ailments she was suffering from the onset of Alzheimer's. The colonel would regularly leave her bed to go on patrol. Invariably, we would find her in her nightdress doing a "ward inspection" of the men's wards. Of a ferocious disposition, the colonel had them all but standing to attention by their beds. Time and again we would collect her and attempt to explain where she was supposed to be but with very little effect.

Subsequently, on a visit home I told my parents about the Matron and because of her army background both became quite curious. When I revealed her name I got the greatest surprise of all. It transpired that she was the young army nurse who had delivered me into the world in 1938 at Woolwich Military Hospital. At the time I was very special to her because I was the first baby she delivered on her own. She called me her little rosebud and would not let me out of her sight. She and my parents had kept in touch until the war years. When she became a patient on my ward my parents began visiting her. Sadly she suffered a massive heart attack. I was with her when she died. Somehow it seemed that her life and mine had come full circle. She helped to give me life; I supported her in her last moments of life. In an odd kind of way I still feel her nearness to me and that I may still be her little rosebud. I like to think so.

During a more humorous moment, a fellow nurse described an entertaining incident that occurred in the operating theatre. A young girl was rushed into casualty in an emergency suffering from peritonitis and in need of immediate surgery to remove her appendix. She was taken promptly to theatre and prepared for the op. To the entire theatre staff's bewilderment and incomprehension, it was apparent that the young lady's pubic hairs had been died a bright green colour. Above the mass of colour there was a tattooed warning to "Keep off the grass!" She awoke from the operation to find that the surgeon, using black biro, had written above the tattoo, "Sorry, I had to cut the grass!" Those were days when people were not afraid to exhibit a sense of humour.

Then there's the case of the malaproprian American lady, a regular hospital visitor and a most hilarious woman who spent her time visiting elderly ladies who didn't have anyone in their lives. She just loved to be among the ladies, reading to them or simply holding their hands whilst she talked…and talked. I guess she was as lonely as they were but she managed to deal with her issues by making everyone else her family. What made her so funny to the staff was the fact that she was another Mrs Malaprop. She always managed to get the wrong words in the wrong context.

"I have been in hospital with Casanova of the uterus," she told me on one occasion. Another time she regaled us with the ugly details of her late departed husband's haemorrhoids. She said, "…his adenoids were hanging out of his bottom like bunches of grapes before he had the operation." I am beginning to wonder, dear readers, if these revelations are becoming almost too graphic for words. So, moving on…let's take a closer, if more misanthropic, look at my time nursing - - past and present.

When I returned to nursing for the second time I was in my fifties. Life had changed in the profession as I'd known it thus dismissing any thought of returning to hospital routines. Training had changed out of all recognition and in my opinion not for the better. Professional, all-round training that created a clearer understanding of one's interests and strengths was missing in all aspects of the job. Today, students nominate their areas of interest in nursing prior to training and that leads to and encourages specialisation. Also, training for three years in a classroom with occasional hands-on is not my idea of a good, all-round nurse. In my day I worked in the midst of a community that was most rewarding. We were constantly hands-on and we had to think on our feet.

I look back to one lady in particular, who had also been a nurse in her day. She lived alone and suffered periodic bouts of memory loss. We regularly visited her mainly to assess the situation and to make sure that she was coping adequately. She was aware of her medical problems and fiercely guarded her independence. One day I arrived at her house to find a whole load of banana skins pegged out on a clothes line. Chatting over a cup of tea I tactfully mentioned that it looked as though she had been very busy that morning. She agreed, quite enthusiastically, and told me she'd done a very large wash before my arrival. Without thinking I replied, "Yes, I can see that from the clothes line." I received a very odd look, then in a loud scathing voice she said, "Don't be so bloody stupid, the banana skins are pegged out on the line for the birds. The washing is drying in the tumble drier…are you quite mad?" I began to wonder myself.

For five years I worked with terminal cancer patients, by far the most rewarding and humbling experience of my life. I came across such marvellous people and witnessed immeasurable courage. I was deeply grateful for having the opportunity to play a small part in the scheme of things.

There were many courageous patients I can remember though three stand out more than others: The first was an American gentleman who lived alone. He had a passion for opera so we got on very well as we shared the same interest. The poor man was in the final stages of terminal cancer (as were all the patients I attended) thus most of the time I spent with him was at night time. Right out of the blue, just a few nights before he died, he turned to me and asked, "Do you believe

27

in guardian angels?" I replied that I hoped that there were such beings for all of us. He paused for a while then another question: "Do you think one could have more than one such being?" "I hope so," I answered truthfully. Another short pause then he posed this question: "When I die will you allow me to be one of your guardian angels?" I thanked him and accepted his kind offer.

"But how will I know when you are with me?" I wanted to know. After some thought he replied, "When I am there you will always see a big feather at your feet." That was the end of our conversation.

I was with him when he died in the early hours of the morning. He had become such a friend and I was extremely upset by his departure. After attending to all the necessary details I left his house and drove through the countryside. I was feeling dejected and reluctant to go straight home.

I drove around for a while and found myself outside a large garden nursery. I waited for it to open for business to buy a shrub for my garden in his memory. I was the only person there when the gates opened at 8.30 a.m. As I looked around, my eyes fell upon the most beautiful white hydrangea. No matter where I looked I kept coming back to this shrub and, after some consideration, I decided to buy it.

I struggled to carry this enormous plant to the car, carefully placing it on the roadside while I searched for my car keys. To my surprise, lying there at my feet was the biggest fawn-coloured feather I'd ever seen. In that instant I knew my mission was accomplished; my friend was safe and on his way "home". Chatting to his niece after the funeral, she told me of her uncle's great love for white hydrangeas.

Another very dear soul who comes to mind was an elderly lady who always called me "Petal". My routine was to drive to her home and check on her late in the evening. On arrival I was always greeted with, "…make yourself comfortable Petal and if you want anything just call me and I'll get it for you." She expressed her disappointment each time I told her I couldn't stay all night.

She'd led a very hard life and I always remember her saying to me when I had my arms around her waist to support her in a standing position, "Eee, Petal, give us a bit o' love. I 'aven't had a cuddle since me mother died when I was ten years old." This delightful lady was in her nineties. Before she died she asked me to promise her that if I should be there at her last moments I would put her false teeth in before the undertaker arrived. She said that she didn't want him to see her with her face inside out. Bless her heart, I was there when she died and her request was duly carried out.

Then there was a family I will never forget. The gentleman was my patient and had gone home to die. He and his wife were ordinary folk with limited financial means but with hearts of gold and a love between them that made one's heart sing. They were in their eighties and as much in love as the day they'd first met. They would lie together on the bed for a cuddle and he would sing, "If you were the only girl in the world…" and she would sing, "…and you were the only boy…"

They had a large family of sons, all married with children. The entire family would gather at the house day and night to support the old couple. I spent the entire time with them knowing as I did that my patient had very little time left. The sitting room looked like a public house, there were so many unopened bottles of whisky on the sideboard. Every time anyone came to the house they brought alcohol with them. My patient couldn't eat but for the last few days of his life he lived on whisky chasers. The attending doctor said nothing could save the poor man so he might as well enjoy what time he had left.

On one occasion I was regaled by his wife and her sisters recounting the life they had had together, in this case the wife's efforts to save money to buy what she described as a "Humphrey Bogart-style raincoat with belt". The first day she wore it, she said she felt "a right smasher" as she stood at the bus stop. Just before the bus arrived a large dog jumped over the garden gate and approached her from behind. I should explain the circumstances: She was about four foot eleven in height and the dog was a very big Alsatian. Acting on instinct the dog mounted her from behind, and with paws on shoulders proceeded to have his wicked way with her as the double-decker bus drew alongside the bus stop. From on board the bus all eyes were trained on the poor woman. It was the bus conductor who broke the suspense of the moment by asking the lady, "Are you going to get on the bus or not?" Without moving, she snapped back: "I can't move till Rover has had his way." She never again wore that raincoat.

The day came when my patient's health took a downward plunge. I gathered the family together and advised them that his condition had deteriorated, but I felt that it would level out and that nothing further would happen that night. Hearing this updated news, they all got up and trooped into the bedroom like the Von Trapp family singers in the Sound of Music. I stayed in the sitting room to give them some privacy.

Then someone summoned me to his bedside. "Eee, just come and 'ave a look at our lad. Doesn't he look lovely in his new paisley pyjamas which we bought to lay him out in?" They had obviously been saving up for the occasion. A little later on I informed them that their lad's condition had indeed levelled out and no further untoward occurrences were imminent. There was a mass stampede back into the bedroom and the lad's new paisley pyjamas were removed with indecent haste.

No matter when or where I worked, as a student nurse and in later years, life's daily occurrences constantly presented me with what later became wonderful memories. For this I will always be grateful. It always seemed that something interesting happened to me, or other people, wherever I worked. Also, I am lucky to have inherited my parents' wonderful sense of humour to see the funnier side of life, which has certainly buoyed me through all the years. Thinking about the lighter side of life brings to mind another incident when I was a student nurse and visiting my parents. It certainly tested my father's sense of humour…

Mother Teresa said we should *"…always meet each other with a smile, for the smile is the beginning of love,"* but I don't think she had in mind the situation I encountered one day when I went to visit

31

my mother and father. I was a trainee nurse at the time and took the opportunity to drop in on my parents when they were living in Aldershot the English town best known as the home of the British Army.

I arrived to learn that my father had had all his teeth removed. When informed of the need to have this done he elected to have new dentures made prior to the extractions so the new dentures could be put in immediately to prevent his gums from shrinking. Anyone who's undergone this surgical procedure is unlikely to forget just how painful it can be as raw gums remain sensitive for some time and the new dentures must be kept in place until the gums harden.

Though assured otherwise, mother was convinced my father had alternately removed and replaced his false teeth during the crucial period, but she couldn't prove it. Naturally she was careful not to reach any controversial conclusions she may not be able to support if challenged.

On the day I arrived home there was another tooth-related development. As usual, father had returned home for lunch and was taking a short nap prior to resuming his work. The peace and tranquillity of the moment shattered when mother burst into the study convulsed with laughter that quickly became infectious.

"Come with me into the hall Eunice," she insisted trying to resist the urge to laugh out loud. "I want you to see something." I looked to where she was pointing.

Sitting halfway up the sprawling staircase was Judy, our cocker spaniel, proudly wearing father's upper dentures. They fitted almost perfectly apart from the dog's soft jowl that was caught up in the denture giving her a gangster-like sneer. It was difficult to stop laughing but something had to be done to put matters right before father woke up.

Unaware of what was going on around him father snored loudly as the comedy played out on the staircase. But mother and I had to act.

We made vain attempts to catch Judy; attempts made doubly-difficult by our inability to stop laughing. After a frantic chase throughout the house we cornered our delinquent dog and swiftly relieved her of father's false teeth. Mother popped them into a saucepan of boiling water. The first part of our mission was a success. But there was no time to relax.

Treading carefully we entered the bedroom where father was sound asleep and, by sheer chance, stumbled upon dad's secret hiding place mother had suspected but never found. On the floor near his bed a large white handkerchief was draped over one of his shoes -- halfway in and halfway out. His shoe hiding place had been found.

I stifled the inclination to chuckle out loud as I watched mother carefully reunite the upper denture with its lower counterpart before wrapping both in the handkerchief and tucking them deep into the shoe. We crept out of the bedroom leaving father to his snoring and, at the same time, leaving his secret hiding place intact.

It would be three years before we could bring ourselves to tell father what had happened on that toothy day in Aldershot that had brought a smile to many faces including our erstwhile cocker spaniel. For months later, each time we looked at father, both mother and I would shake with laughter. It is fair to say that father was equally amused when we did get around to telling him though I don't think he would have seen the funny side if he'd seen Judy wearing a smile at his expense.

*

During his service with the British Army my father was posted to an army base in Wiltshire. As befitted his rank at the time, he was entitled to have two orderlies – either two batmen, or one batman and one bat woman. He chose the latter believing a home-help would be good for mother. Looking back I still find myself laughing out loud at the bizarre situation that unfolded after Rosie, our domestic helper, a.k.a "bat woman", entered our lives.

First some background: Rosie was a delightful but rather simple soul who had missed out on an education. She couldn't read or write but she was determined that Michael, her illegitimate son, would benefit from a proper education. And to that end, she worked day in and day out as a domestic helper.

One Christmastime I arrived at the house to find mother beside herself with laughter; highly amused at something Rosie had said and done. It concerned Rosie's sister Freda who, unlike Rosie, had obtained a reasonable education, got married and left for Australia to join her husband's family. Her sudden disappearance years before had left Rosie in bit of a pickle, which affected her mostly around Christmastime because Rosie and Freda had always collaborated in the production of traditional Christmas puddings using an old, family recipe handed down through generations. When Freda left for Australia the recipe went with her.

However, very much aware that Rosie would be stumped without the recipe, Freda dutifully prepared and sent parcels every year with all the necessary ingredients weighed and packed in little blue bags. When the parcels arrived all Rosie had to do was to empty out the contents and mix and steam three puddings in the time-honoured manner. One was eaten immediately, as a test run, the others reserved for Christmas Day and New Year's Day. The puddings-by-mail scheme worked without a hitch for numerous festive seasons then, suddenly, things changed. A parcel of ingredients arrived one Christmastime but without a letter from Freda. Undeterred, Rosie prepared and steamed the Christmas puddings as usual and, with Michael's help, ate one of them. A week later a letter arrived from Australia, written by Freda's husband, which Michael (now at university) read out: "Dear Rosie, Sorry to inform you that Freda passed away recently. We had her cremated and the ashes placed in one of the bags I sent over. Her last wish was to have her ashes sprinkled on the River Serpentine in London's Hyde Park…"

Rosie was aghast to learn that her sister Freda formed a component part of the Christmas puddings' ingredients that year and, even worse, she and Michael had tucked into one of the puddings.

Quite concerned, my mother asked Rosie why she looked so sullen and depressed. Impassive and straight-faced Rosie explained that "…when we found out what 'ad 'appened, me and Mike felt like a coupla greedy cannibals. But at least we have two puds left to throw into the Serpentine don't we?" This they did with due ceremony, though the unfortunate event not only marked the end of the puddings-by-mail scheme it placed an end-marker on Christmas puddings altogether because the recipe died with Freda.

It was time to move on from nursing. I felt ready to sample life in the fast lane and developed a sense of excitement as I anticipated a career change. From now on I would direct my efforts towards fulfilling my dream to become an air hostess – at full throttle!

PART 2

TIME TO FLY

Prayer wheel to max revs!

After leaving the nursing profession in 1960 I decided to apply to Pan American Airlines. The name "Pan Am" conjured up so much glamour in my mind as one of the world's most prestigious airlines at the time. I picked up an application form filled it in and returned it the same day. To my sheer delight I was called for an interview.

By this time mother seemed inclined to accept my determination to follow my dream, but she did insist on accompanying me to the London hotel where I was to present myself for the interview. I supposed she still was praying hard that I wouldn't be accepted. The big day arrived, and my excitement was conditioned only by my mother's obvious apprehension for what she thought lay ahead.

I lined up alongside what seemed to me hundreds of the most gorgeous looking girls in the world, all with legs reaching up to their armpits. I was cowed by an aura of superiority as uniformed officials scrutinised me from what seemed a great height. In that moment I knew how Little Orphan Annie must have felt when she was let out from the secure block for a day. Compared with the others my physical attributes were insignificant and, for one moment, I considered discretely excusing myself and running like hell.

Mother, detecting my thinly disguised mental anguish, did a complete turnaround from her longstanding and entrenched "no flying" position.

"Pull yourself together Eunice and get ready for the interview." I will never know what it cost her emotionally to abruptly respond in that way but, in that one moment I loved her more than ever if that were at all possible.

I stood up when my name was called out. I was accompanied to the interview room by a very senior male member of the cabin crew department. He ushered me to walk ahead of him. What beautiful manners, I thought judging him to be a perfect gentleman. Then I realised, with horror, that he was scrutinising my every move from behind with eyes fixed on my derriere. It made me feel like I was walking on cobble stones in a skirt that was either too long or too short. I pictured myself the size of a fully-grown elephant and prayed for the floor to open up and swallow me whole.

In the interview room I faced a panel of uniformed staff. To this day I can barely remember the actual questions fired at me. But I went through the motions as best I could and was relieved at the end to hear someone say, "Go and have lunch and be ready to attend a second interview this afternoon." I was jubilant -- walking on air. I had survived the initial ordeal. Then came the agony of wondering what sort of a trial the next round would present. Mother looked quite smug as we went off for lunch and, as we passed other candidates still waiting, there was an almost triumphant twinkle in her eye though I couldn't tell what she was thinking.

Round two involved questions on education and an in-depth probe into why I wanted to become an air hostess. "It was all I have ever wanted from as far back as I can remember," I answered truthfully. My own words rang hollow in my ears as hackneyed and unoriginal, but I couldn't take them back. No doubt many other interviewees would come up with fantastic reasons not nearly as trite.

I was given to realise during the course of the interview that a background in languages was considered important. Luckily, I aspired to schoolroom French and a smattering of self-taught German picked up whilst living in Germany with my parents. I detected an uptick in the panel's interest when I disclosed how I had spent most of my early life in foreign parts including being schooled in Singapore and latterly in Germany.

In that respect, I have to confess I enjoyed a privileged education being schooled in educational establishments that were different in every way from British schools. At the school I attended in Singapore I was one of six Caucasian girls studying in a convent where all other pupils were Chinese or Malay. The spoken language was English and as far as standards were concerned the bar was set very high. We attended school from 7a.m. till midday; afternoons were free because of the intensely hot and humid climate. Each evening we returned to school for heavy homework sessions. In terms of education it was very competitive and students either met the required standards or were shown the exit.

In Germany I went to school in Kiel a spot on the Baltic Coast. An island location, it was originally a German submarine base during the war so we were strategically isolated from the rest of the world. As with recreational pursuits on most islands, our summer sports included sailing. And because of the wonderful forests that surrounded us, horse-riding was a sheer joy. During the winter months we revelled in skiing and ice skating among other things. Those were happy days.

However, getting back to the interview with Pan Am, as soon as I committed to speaking a foreign language the panel then engaged me in conversational French which I found to be a bit of a shock to the system. Rather clumsily, I managed to stumble through that phase but would not characterise it as my finest hour.

I was questioned about my other educational accomplishments and noticed a lot of interest among panel members when I mentioned my background in catering and nursing. In those days such qualifications were a real bonus. My confidence was building. Next hurdle – the medical examination.

In considering physical attributes, height was very important. Not too tall, not too short; they liked girls to be over five foot three, but not taller than five eight. I was five foot five so fell right in between. Weight was also important. No-one over nine and a half stones [133lbs], depending on build and height, need apply. Luckily I met that criteria too. Teeth were closely scrutinised as was skin tone. Spots and pimples ruled you out of the running and any dental deficiencies drew close attention. We were looked over with care, a bit like getting a horse show-ready for an equestrian event.

Up next: a very rigorous medical examination. It seemed to me the medical examiner was focused on finding candidates who were as fit as a flea and as strong as an ox. It struck me as odd at the time but, in later years, I came to appreciate the wisdom of taking that approach. It was no good being of a delicate disposition. Certainly it helped to look attractive but, at the same time, an air hostess had to be capable of coping with heavy loads and physically demanding situations. Let's be honest, flying was hard work; exacting at all times and demanding a great deal of energy. On board an aircraft there was never any room for error.

Interviews over, I left exhausted but still had to suffer the anxiety of waiting for the results. Fortune smiled on me but it proved to be a bitter-sweet outcome. I was one of the successful candidates but would have to be based in America. That was too much for mother. I was an only-child about to disappear off the face of the earth as far as she was concerned. She tried very hard to conceal her grief. At the same time I felt very guilty inflicting so much sadness on my parents. By this time my father who had suffered for many years with emphysema was developing even worse health problems. With a very heavy heart I declined Pan Am's job offer. At least I had managed to scramble to the top of the mountain and walk down at my own volition. Undaunted, I decided to take a look at airlines based in Britain.

*

By this time my parents lived in the Channel coastal town of Folkestone very close to Dymchurch the location of the cross-Channel air ferry service "Silver City" at Lydd Airport. For me it turned out to be a fortuitous location.

The managing director of Silver City Airways was among my parent's circle of friends at that time. Helpfully he suggested I might consider doing a season with his company whilst waiting to join a long-haul British airline which was my preferred choice. Although Silver City would not fulfil my dream of flying to faraway places it was a very good way to get into the industry and I would finally get to fly in an aircraft. There was the added bonus of being able to live at home which would please my mother. And so, in November 1960, I started working for Silver City Airways not knowing I was embarking on a journey which, from the very first day, would have a profound effect on the rest of my life.

*

Silver City's flying operations started in 1945 with the formation of a company called British Aviation Services (BAS). Its managing director, Air Cdre Griffith J. Powell, better known as "Taffy", had alongside him former Royal Air Force (RAF) colleagues who had served with him during the war years in RAF Ferry Command and RAF Transport Command.

Initially, BAS was to act as advisers to Alberto Dodero, a shipping magnate who planned an air service between Buenos Aires and Montevideo using BAS aircraft. Among the many passengers using this service was a Mr John Govett, chairman of the Zinc Corporation, a large mining company with mines in Australia, and offices in London. John Govett elected to form a company that could provide them with air transport and charter services; BAS had a small shareholding and thus undertook to operate the services.

The new company was called Silver City Airways because Zinc Corp's principal mines were in New South Wales, Australia at a location called Silver City. At one time the mines were principally silver mines. Operations commenced in 1946 with a fleet of Avro Lancastrians (developed from the Avro Lancaster heavy bombers) and Dakotas (DC3's).

The first charter flight in October 1946, from London to Sydney, Australia, was flown by an Avro Lancastrian and the round trip took fourteen days. A far cry from the fast-lane flying we experience today.

Shortly afterwards, Taffy Powell introduced the Bristol 170 Freighter to his fleet of Dakotas during the 1947 South Asia pre-independence airlift of Hindus from Pakistan to India, and of Muslims from India to Pakistan. The freighter had large doors in the nose of the aircraft and a substantial cargo hold.

From this a new idea was born: the B170 freighter would be an ideal aircraft for ferrying cars across the Channel.

The first Silver City car ferry flight left from Lympne airfield in Kent on 15th June, 1948 bound for Le Touquet, France with just one car -- an Armstrong Siddeley owned by Taffy himself. The inaugural public flight was operated on the 14th July, 1948. Later, Silver City Car Ferry Services emerged with full flying colours, carrying two cars

43

at a time across the English Channel to Le Touquet. This was great progress indeed.

By 1952 the cross-Channel air ferry was hugely successful and Taffy Powell introduced the "Superfreighter" with capacity for up to three vehicles. With a fleet of six new Superfreighters a new airfield was urgently required because Lympne was a grass airfield unsuitable for hard-paved runway expansion. Subsequently, a new airport called Ferryfield was built at the northern end of the Dungeness point at a place called Lydd in England's picturesque county of Kent.

How well I recall the abundant wildlife around that part of the English countryside. Routinely, every morning during springtime, the airport fire engine would begin a slow patrol down the runway and taxiways out of concern for a pair of swans that returned to the same nest year after year. Once the cygnets hatched it was a common sight to see the cob and pen taking their brood for an early morning constitutional, waddling in a straight line down the centre of an active runway in the midst of rural southern England. A kindly fireman walked ahead of the fire engine gently shooing the swans along the runway. But is has to be said that man and aircraft had to wait for them to complete their routine. It only ever happened early in the morning, and it was all part of that more genteel scene that prevailed in those days. Life was so accepting of all things. And avoiding bird ingestion in aircraft engines was, and still is, of paramount importance particular in airports close to wildlife sanctuaries.

By 1954 business was booming: Ferryfield-based crews were flying six round Channel trips each day. In 1955 Silver City became the largest carrier of freight in the country, and by 1957 had clocked up 100,000 Channel crossings since its inception twelve years earlier.

Later on, six Handley Page Hermes aircraft were transferred to Silver City ownership, but because Ferryfield was unable to accommodate these larger aircraft they used Manston Airport, also in Kent, flying to Le Touquet on the London to Paris Silver Arrow/Flèches d'Argent service. This particular era for Silver City ended when Air Cdre Taffy Powell retired in 1957.

When I arrived on the scene in November 1960, Silver City was already a very busy and successful airline. The cross-Channel service was the ideal way to take one's car across the Channel on trips that took just twenty minutes from take-off to landing. Quite a contrast to sea crossings that took five times longer.

Families, famous people from stage and screen, politicians and even royalty used the cross-Channel air service and Silver City became a successful operator providing a unique service in every way. It has to be said that the airline boasted a happy, relaxed and efficient working "family" of employees and had an excellent safety record. It will always be regarded by those who used the facility, and those who were employed to provide the service, as perhaps a most special and privileged experience in days when working folk were not a service commodity, but were regarded as the heart and soul of an industry.

In the tumultuous and sometimes chaotic years that followed I was to discover the true meaning of the oft used expression "flying by the seat of your pants!"

*

My first day at Silver City was mostly taken up with uniform fittings: navy blue tailored straight skirt with a kick pleat at the back and jacket; two white blouses; hat and raincoat. I still remember what a thrill it was when I finally saw myself in the mirror. I thought I looked very much the part of something I had dreamed about for so long.

Training for the Bristol Freighters took a week with the focus on cabin protocol, emergency procedures, and forms-filling for Customs and Excise. Afterwards we had an oral and practical examination followed by the presentation of wings, the final validation that I was ready to take to the skies.

I should point out that the bulbous-nosed Bristol Freighter carried three cars and fourteen passengers with two pilots and one hostess assigned to each flight. And to access the cockpit, pilots clambered up a metal ladder located above the cars in the nose of the aircraft. Communication with the pilots throughout the flight was via an intercom system, although it had been known for hostesses to climb the ladder themselves in order to have a quick word with the crew. This was not the easiest of manoeuvres if there was turbulence which was often the case during the twenty minutes it took to cross the Channel wave-hopping at a height around one thousand feet. The passenger cabin was small, and the only on-board service offered was a duty-free bar and perfumery sales service.

My first solo flight as hostess is etched in my mind and still gives me goose bumps when I think of it. The weather was very stormy and the aircraft was buffeted by turbulence not entirely unknown for English Channel crossings. I had previously met the rest of the crew in the crew room, and noticed that the first officer was showing a fair bit of interest in me. I didn't mind in the least as he was very good looking and displayed a great deal of old-world charm which I found quite flattering.

That first day we flew six cross-Channel trips to and from Le Touquet during which time the weather never improved one iota. I was as sick as a dog from start to finish. Believe me, dear reader, it was no joke trying to look cool, calm and collected in front of the passengers while rushing off to heave my guts up in the cargo hold, then returning with a forced smile to serve the needs of the passengers. The final trip of the day required a longer stay at Le Touquet airport which didn't help. We returned without passengers but had cargo on board that took a long time to load.

Having spent the whole day throwing up, I just wanted to lie down and die. This was not what I imagined flying to be all about. Then my admirer, the first officer, appeared before me. "Hi pretty poppet," he said, "how about joining us for a bowl of moules marinière?" I responded by throwing up all over his uniform jacket. Oh God, I thought, this has to be the end of a beautiful friendship before it's even begun.

How wrong I was. Later, I married the man and became Mrs Bill Musgrave.

*

In those halcyon days at Ferryfield, flight hostesses went into the airport departure lounge to collect the passenger manifest from the traffic staff. With only fourteen passengers on each flight we called each one forward by name over the PA system, greeting them with a smile before accompanying them to the aircraft. This was the age when interpersonal skills were important, sadly less evident in modern-day flying circles.

On one particular harrowing occasion while scrutinising the passenger manifest I came across one couple called Mr and Mrs Assoles. From the corner of my eye I noticed a large number of traffic staff gathered in a huddle, sniggering in anticipation of my impending public announcement which they expected, even hoped, would be a massive gaffe on my part. After what seemed an age, and approaching a state of sheer panic, I broke into my best, if somewhat limited, Italian:

"Would Signor and Signora Ass...ee...olees please come forward."

To my utter amazement, and eternal relief, both came striding forward beaming with delight at my correct pronunciation of their name. I savoured a moment of sheer joy looking at the disappointed faces of the traffic staff. Like a mother hen, I triumphantly led my fourteen passengers to the aircraft not stopping to look behind.

We worked flights on a Dakota, (Douglas-DC3) on occasions to the Italian city of Pisa, with only one hostess assigned to look after thirty passengers. I used to refer to the Dak as the aircraft where we walked uphill all the way. It was particular noticeable prior to take-off as the aircraft had a nose-up angle of almost 12° in the parked position. And, as pilots were required to enter via the rear door, they prepared for a climb up to the cockpit that left some gasping for breath. This is how air hostesses identified pilots who were out of condition.

Apart from offering on-board bar sales, we served a cold meal which was plated-up and loaded onto the aircraft by the company's catering department. Imagine my dismay during one flight when I passed out all the meals to the passengers only to discover the trays had no cutlery. I was so embarrassed…all the more because there was absolutely nothing I could do to resolve the problem. We were already airborne. Happily for the crew, passengers saw the funny side of it, and with aside remarks like "…when in Rome…" and "…fingers were invented before knives and forks…", everyone tucked into their chicken salad with nary a cross word. There was a far more relaxed attitude in those days and we had fun in ways that would not be sanctioned or tolerated today.

Talking of fun, how well I remember one of our pilots on the Dakota fleet who loved to play jokes on passengers. On the trip I have in mind, everyone was comfortably seated when the first officer announced over the intercom, "Folks, there will be a five minute delay in our departure today; we are waiting for the captain to join us." Passengers exchanged worried glances with one another before going back to reading their newspapers.

Moments later the captain, swathed in bandages, entered the passenger door at the rear of the aircraft. He had one arm in a sling and a plaster cast on his leg. With rising concern, everyone looked on anxiously as he hobbled up the aisle on crutches, pausing to introduce himself to passengers before disappearing onto the flight deck only to emerge minutes later looking very chipper, minus bandages, sling and pot. A brief moment of silent disbelief was broken by a spontaneous outburst of laughter and appreciative applause throughout the cabin.

On another occasion the same pilot, a wag who couldn't resist teasing passengers, made an appearance in the cabin halfway through the flight. He slowly backed down the full length of the aircraft holding two pieces of string, his face a picture of unwavering concentration as he slowly let-out the ball of string.

Stopping at the last row of passengers, he turned to an elderly lady sitting in an aisle seat. Smiling sweetly at her, he asked, "Madam, would you kindly take these two ends of string in your hands and hold them tight while I use the toilet?" As soon as she had a firm grip on the two pieces of string he said, "Madam, you are now flying the aircraft but please don't worry everything will be fine."

Moments later the captain came out of the toilet to find the lady still sitting bolt upright in her seat like a slab of marble, concentrating intensely on the task in hand. Thanking her profusely for all her help, he took the strings from her and disappeared back onto the flight deck. Later, he returned to present the gallant lady with a set of wings fashioned out of silver paper. She saw the funny side of it and was very thrilled with her wings which she said she would pass on to her small grandson.

I recall yet another mischievous pilot who delighted in teasing passengers. During the summer months the airline often invited passengers to sit in the sunshine outside the terminal where they could watch shipside activities in full flow. As the company's fleet of Bristol Freighters were usually lined up outside the passenger terminal, passengers could watch as pilots went around the outside of the aircraft, conducting external, pre-flight checks.

This particular pilot's party-piece was to beckon to a lad on a bicycle to stop by the parked aircraft where they would undertake a rehearsed word or two in conversation – all in front of the passengers. On cue, the lad would hand the pilot his bicycle pump and the pilot would pretend to pump up the aircraft tyres to the consternation of passengers looking on. Everything was always taken in good part and I think it helped relax both passengers and crews alike.

*

Ferryfield was a small but very happy place to work. Everyone got on well together and there was a genuine rapport between all departments that in many ways proved the secret of its success. At Christmastime every member of the company received a Christmas hamper -- something unique to Ferryfield. There was a spirit of goodwill among all employees, and the pure joy of teamwork all the way down the line proved to be its strength. I was extremely happy during the time I worked for Silver City, and probably would have spent longer had it not been for rumours of a merger with Freddie Laker's Channel Air Bridge airline. Freddie Laker was appointed managing director of the newly formed British United Airways (BUA), the result of a merger between Airwork Services and Hunting Clan Air Transport.

Channel Air Bridge continued to operate as an independent organisation for two more years then in January 1963 merged with Silver City Airways. Earlier, in 1962, BUA merged with British Aviation Services, the holding company of British independent airlines Britavia and Silver City Airways making BUA the largest unsubscribed airline outside the USA. Silver City's pre-merger status as the main independent provider of air ferry services in the UK gave BUA a monopoly among UK-based air ferry operators. In Freddie Laker's time as managing director of BUA it became Britain's largest, wholly-owned private airline. It was also the UK's first independent airline to re-equip its entire fleet with brand new state-of-the-art jet aircraft. Great changes were taking place in British aviation.

But getting back to Silver City, my first airline, it could rightly be said that from little acorns mighty oaks do grow. As for all the crew members involved, there was a great deal of sadness about the changes which were seen as inevitable. A very small but precious jewel in the crown had provided a great nurturing process for all those privileged to work at Ferryfield. But now we were all on our way to London-Gatwick to join the big boys and I, at last, would be able to fulfil my ambition to travel the world in style.

Making a career move to London-Gatwick Airport demanded quite a change of lifestyle. Up till then, I had been able to live at home whilst flying out of Ferryfield. Now, new accommodation had to be sourced nearer to Gatwick.

To my utter delight, Bill, the pilot on my first flight and hubby-to-be, and who was also moving to Gatwick, had not been put off by the disastrous moules marinière incident. By now our relationship was serious and we were already spending all available time together. In step with airline mergers, I was making my own course adjustment with the future in mind.

Those magnificent men

The breed of pilots with whom I flew all those years ago truly lived up to their reputations as "magnificent men in their flying machines." And, at the risk of repetition, or being boring, the baptism of fire for all of these pilots occurred during wartime.

"If it has wings I'll fly it," was their boast. And they did fly "it", sometimes under unnerving circumstances. This unique breed of aviators lived each day as if it were their last. Overworked exhortations such as "on a wing and a prayer" and "prayer wheel to max revs" were coined with apparent ease by these intrepid airframe drivers and were often appropriate catchphrases for those nursing home a crippled aircraft after a bombing raid over Europe. They were truly magnificent men in so many ways.

COMING IN ON A WING AND A PRAYER

One of our planes was missing

Two hours overdue

One of our planes was missing

With all its gallant crew

The radio sets were humming

We waited for a word

Then a noise broke

Through the humming and this is what we heard

Comin' in on a wing and a prayer

Comin' in on a wing and a prayer

Though there's one motor gone

We can still carry on

Comin' in on a wing and a prayer

What a show, what a fight, boys

We really hit our target for tonight

How we sing as we limp through the air

Look below, there's our field over there

With just one motor gone

We can still carry on

Comin' in on a wing and a prayer

The phrase was taken up by songwriters Harold Adamson and Jimmie McHugh and their WWII patriotic song "Coming in on a Wing and a Prayer", 1943, tells of a damaged warplane, barely able to limp back to base

On the subject of magnificent men and their flying prowess, my neighbours who live in the same village as I in the Yorkshire Dales, talked to me about their good friend Arthur Morris. This gentleman, also a wartime pilot, gravitated to civil aircraft at the end of the war.

Back in 1967, Arthur, a citizen of South Africa, flew as a commercial pilot in the UK. This is his account of what occurred during a planned night-stop at an ultra-posh hotel in the beautiful city of Bristol. It lends support to the assertion that aviators from that era would fly just about anything and say just about anything.

The Condom Graf Zeppelin

"When my first-officer and I arrived, we were a little dis-chuffed to discover that virtually all the public rooms had been booked for a private function which turned out to be a dinner-dance organised and hosted by the Lord Mayor and Lady Mayoress of Bristol.

"It was a splendid affair as it turned out; black tie and evening gowns with a guest list that came straight out of Who's Who. *There were lackeys all over the place wearing powdered wigs, knee britches, brass-buckled shoes and livery that must have been in mothballs since Henry the Eighth's last shindig. It all looked very impressive.*

"Feeling a trifle conspicuous in our uniforms, Geoff and I decided to go upstairs and survey the proceedings down the spacious stairwell from the fourth floor on which our room was situated. The Mayor and Mayoress were immediately below us, shaking hands and generally partaking in light conversation with arriving guests.

"There were doddering old dukes and dithering old duchesses interspersed with members of the younger set all putting it on and being very hoity-toity. It was all very serious and very upper-class. As we surveyed the scene from the fourth floor my co-pilot suddenly came up with a fiendish plan.

"In those days condoms were things that were bought from under the counter at the pharmacy or by a low furtive request from the barbers shop. Nowadays of course, one buys them with the groceries from the supermarket. Anyway Geoff had one in his wallet and in a matter of seconds he had blown it up to the proportions of the Graf Zeppelin, and tied a knot in the open end.

"Before I could stop him he had launched the infernal thing into space and it floated gently down the stair well. There must have been a rising thermal of hot air for the missile seemed to take ages to arrive on the ground floor, and when it did it struck the Mayoress a gentle blow on the shoulder before settling on the carpet. There was a deathly hush as everyone went rigid (no pun intended). The Mayoress peered at the thing through her lorgnette, and went a deep crimson.

"The Mayor's eyes were standing out like organ stops. There was a total silence and a stop to the proceedings until a be-knickered liveried lackey sprang to life. His intention was to stamp on the damned thing and burst it, but instead it shot out from under his foot, leapt in the air and whizzed across the room towards a couple of dowager ladies who couldn't get out of the way quickly enough, and didn't know whether to laugh or cry.

"A second lackey had a go with a similar result. It's surprising how tough these things are when you don't want them to be! Finally however, it burst but in so doing shot up onto the shoulder of a very astonished middle-aged lady from where it drooped like a tattered windsock after rain in windless conditions.

"We didn't see what happened after that because every eye peered upwards and we scampered off to our room like a couple of naughty school kids. Once there I turned to Geoff and asked him why the hell he did that. He replied that he was damned if he knew....but wasn't it bloody good fun!"

Courtesy Mainsheet 1991

Sad to say that Arthur Morris, a former Durban city councillor, art-restorer and accomplished artist as well as a pilot, suffered an ignominious departure from life just shy of his 90th birthday. He fractured his skull when he fell from a ladder while trying to change a light bulb.

*

My husband Bill, a Second World War Lancaster bomber pilot, had the rotten luck to be shot down twice. On the second occasion he was badly injured from shrapnel wounds some of which he still carries inside him today. Bill managed to survive after being taken to a mountain cave in former Yugoslavia and nursed back to health by a girlfriend of Marshal Tito, Yugoslavia's charismatic revolutionary and statesman. With the help of Tito's battle-hardy partisans, backed, one supposes, by a positive response to his prayers, he made it back to England and re-joined RAF Bomber Command and the fight against the Nazis.

That's how it was in wartime Europe; these magnificent men had flying in their blood. It wasn't just a way of life; for them it was their whole life. They lived in the fast lane and fate was their hunter. And they liked it that way.

At the end of the war, many of these aviators who'd beaten the odds and lived to talk about it, found flying jobs with a growing number of civilian airlines. From personal experience, I can vouch for them being the best pilots I have ever known. To illustrate in practical terms how I felt about these "knights of the skies", I developed an inner sense of security whenever I flew with them. I knew they had faced the best and worst of flying and survived to tell the tale. I also knew that if anything untoward happened on my flight, I would be alright because they had seen it all before and dealt with it. And to press the point a little further, dealing with an emergency during an actual flight is quite different from sitting in a simulator. What is the main difference you may ask? Well, that's easy to answer: you can always walk away from a simulator.

During the latter days of my flying career I worked flights that saw experienced veterans of the air teamed up with flying school pilots. All I can say is that hard-earned experience showed through every time. I do not intend in any way to denigrate today's men and women pilots who provide an indispensable service piloting some of the world's most sophisticated aircraft across crowded skies and through congested airports. That said, the pilots I knew, flew with, and even married (one of them anyway) were a breed apart. They don't make them like that anymore.

As I pointed out, Bill was a very attractive man with great charisma. He was unlike anyone I had known before. A Canadian by birth, he came over to England and joined the RAF in 1938, the year I was born, and spent the war years flying Lancaster bombers with RAF Bomber Command.

At the end of the war he remained in the RAF and became a test pilot working with the Empire Test Pilots' School (ETPS) which, in those days, was located at Farnborough, England. Bill was born to fly and was never happier than when he was in control of an aircraft. He always said that an aircraft should be handled like a woman, and in all the years I can honestly say that he was a great flier instantly recognisable as one of the magnificent few. Bill lived for flying and, to avoid ending up in a non-flying position with the RAF, he retired and joined Silver City Airways. Afterwards, he continued working as a civil test pilot as well as flying as a line pilot.

I have to say that Bill's illustrious career as a test pilot before leaving the RAF did not sit well with some members of the pilot hierarchy when he joined British United Airways (BUA).

As a former test pilot of the ETPS, Bill was both qualified and authorised to conduct test flights on passenger aircraft for ANY airline when an airworthiness flight had to be carried out prior to certifying the aircraft as being fit to fly with passengers. Some of the senior management pilots were uncomfortable with the fact that Bill, just a first officer [co-pilot] with BUA could enjoy such status and be called upon at any time to offer his skills. I put it down to jealousy on their part.

I have said before that Bill just lived to fly and never turned down an opportunity to do so. I recall receiving a telephone call from him on one occasion when he was in Jersey in the Channel Islands. At very short notice he was sent over to test a Handley Page Herald aircraft that had undercarriage problems. Before the aircraft returned to full-time line flying it had to be flight tested.

"When you turn on the television to check the news," Bill said to me on the phone, "don't worry about what you see or hear because I'm alright."

Earlier, when Bill was landing the aircraft at Jersey Airport the undercarriage collapsed on touchdown and the airport was closed for the rest of the day.

As fate would have it hundreds of passenger waiting for their flights witnessed the entire incident. Even before the shower of sparks had dissipated, dozens of travellers had already dashed over to the sea ferry terminal at St. Helier to board boats heading to the UK mainland. It was a day when many folk lost their appetite to fly.

Over the years Bill flew with many famous names in the test flight community. We were all part of one team, he used to say. He did some work on the sound barrier speed tests with John Derry the first Brit to exceed the speed of sound. Derry was killed in 1952 flying at the Farnborough Air Show when his DH110 (later the de Havilland Sea Vixen) broke-up in flight due to a design fault. Thirty-one died including John Derry, his flight observer Tony Richards, and twenty-nine spectators. Bill was there that fateful day, also flying in the air show. He had previously worked with other test pilots on high altitude experimental flights flying single-seat fighter aircraft "...we were looking for the edge of space", as these pilots would say. These flights were precursors to the moon-shots that came later.

Test crews flew in triple formation; three test pilots each with his own aircraft. Back on terra firma they would open the hatch and slide down the side of their aircraft. Subsequently all three went down with radiation sickness caused by constant contact with the exterior of the airframe. That's when scientists discovered just how much radiation there was in the atmosphere. And that's why aircraft today are hosed down between flights. Two of the pilots flying with Bill had their gall bladders removed because of radiation contamination; there wasn't a cure for the problem in those days. Bill only knew what he'd been told: there was every likelihood they would all die because there was nothing that could be done to save them.

Removing gall bladders was an experimental operation, and I don't know why they did this. Whatever the reason, Bill knew that without a gall bladder he would never be allowed to fly again. For him, that prospect was a death sentence. So, he refused the operation. Around about that time somebody, quite fortuitously, suggested there was a drug in an experimental stage and to test its efficacy the manufacturers were seeking a guinea pig.

"Would you care to volunteer, Bill?" they asked.

"I will if you guarantee I will live to fly," Bill shot back without hesitation.

The drug was cortisone: it saved his life but destroyed his immune system. Nevertheless he lived to fly again and, apart from his work on the Comet and other aircraft already mentioned, spent his life flight testing aircraft to the limits always knowing his next flight could be his last. Many of our friends did die in the course of duty. Test pilots in those days were a dying breed from their very first test flight.

During his time with BUA Bill popped off to test-fly many hush-hush aircraft destined for service with the RAF including the Avro Vulcan bomber, the Harrier Jump Jet and more. This was another reason why some senior management pilots were jealous of Bill's broad and proven aviator skills. It was the worst kind of jealousy and quite uncalled for because Bill was never one to blow his own trumpet. It was difficult even to get him to talk about the things he'd accomplished. He was never a shy man but he was very modest about his own exploits.

*

"Eunice, the only thing that makes me airsick," Bill once said to me, "is having to listen to the bullshit flying around in the bar." There were those pilots who talked about it, mostly airline pilots, and those who simply got on with it. Test pilots fell into the latter group.

This brings to mind a great friend of Bill's, a fellow test pilot and graduate from the Empire Test Pilots' School. His first name was Jimmy.

Both men, on this particular occasion, were assigned test flight duties on the same day. To save on petrol, Bill volunteered to drive to Jimmy's home and give him a lift to the RAE at Farnborough. Arriving at the house, Bill was surprised to see Jimmy tearing out of the front door and slamming it behind him. It transpired he was in the midst of a blazing row with his wife.

"There were no goodbyes that day as I recall," Bill said, "and I could still hear loud shouting from outside the house as we drove away." For Jimmy there would never be another opportunity to say goodbye because the aircraft he flight-tested that day suffered a catastrophic failure. Jimmy didn't make it home.

As a close friend of the family it fell to Bill to break the tragic news to Pat, Jimmy's wife. He drove back to the house pulled alongside the kerb and stepped out from the car. He was still trying to marshal his thoughts when Pat burst out of the house: "OK Bill, you can tell the swine I forgive him; it's safe for him to come in," she yelled loud enough for the entire street to hear.

Concerned for the family, Bill took Pat and her five-year-old daughter under his wing. Each evening he read a bedtime story to the little girl and kissed her goodnight just as daddy had always done.

Test pilots and their families always came to the aid of wives who lost their husbands in the course of flying; it was like being in one large family. Ironically, Jimmy had replaced another test pilot on that fateful day.

One night, as Bill was getting ready to leave the house, the little girl turned to him and said: "Uncle Bill, do you see that big, bright star up there?"

Looking skywards Bill said, "Yes, little lady, I see it."

"That is my daddy. He is looking after us but he is going to be in a bloody mess with mummy."

The kind of camaraderie that existed between test pilots was quite different from anything outside the test flying community. There was an *esprit de corps* among these highly-skilled aviators that forged an alliance under which mutual support was an important component.

They never lost sight of the fact that what they were doing was essential but dangerous. It took a special kind of man to test new aircraft to their design limits day after day. Regularly, test pilots reached into the unknown, keen, eager and first in line to probe problems, real or imagined, in the performance of whatever flying machine they had strapped to their backsides. The lucky ones lived to report back to those on the ground and design flaws were remedied. Nothing was left to chance. Safety was paramount.

Unfortunately so many of our friends were killed while air testing new aircraft. All were former RAF pilots attached to the test flying wing. We were always drinking to absent friends and could not help but notice how fewer pilots turned up each year for Farnborough's annual test pilots' ball.

Yes, test pilots were a very special breed. Yet, in all the years I knew them I never heard a single one of them brag about what they did. It was different when they were in a closed group such as in the mess bar. In the privacy of their bar they would let their hair down, joke, laugh and let off steam – but only among themselves, never with outsiders.

*

Bill has always been an important part of my life, the best part in many ways though the source of great pain at times. He was a devil for the ladies; a womaniser of the first order. And that was part and parcel of his considerable charm. One can readily imagine how my world crumbled when my husband was spirited away by Pat (another Pat), someone I thought of as a friend.

Pat expected Bill to marry her but he never did. She was little more than his mistress. Unlike me, she failed to realise that his first love was flying; everything else, including his marriage to me, came second.

Looking back over the years and despite what happened, I never stopped loving the man I fell in love with and married. And I will always love him.

Over the years Bill inherited a legacy of poor health: he had a lot of shrapnel deeply-embedded in his thigh area too close to his spine for medics to remove. Periodically, the shrapnel shifts and puts pressure on his lower body and legs. Add to this the radiation sickness that left him with immune problems, plus years of flying with the RAF enduring a large amount of G force from aerobatic flying and flying-related manoeuvres that have all taken a toll. Somehow Bill managed to keep going and is now in his nineties. Nevertheless, his physical disabilities have consigned him to a private nursing home. Unable to walk, he needs a great deal of one-to-one care, though he is sound of mind. Sadly, the responsibility for his continued care proved to be too much for his lady friend.

In the early part of 2015 Bill asked me to visit him at the nursing home. He appeared to be very happy to see me. We talked a great deal.

"I have always loved you Eunice," he wanted me to know, "and I did not leave you because of anything you did." It was confession time. He told me he would always love me and only me and regretted what he had done. We made our peace. I was grateful to learn his true feelings. When I left him I could see he was struggling with his conscience.

He wanted me to continue visiting him but his partner blocked that idea. She was getting her own back at me because of what I told her when she prised him away from the marriage.

Many women wanted Bill but I was the one he truly wanted and got. I am positive Pat knows that he still loves me; a pleasure she will never enjoy. I am sad that so many years were wasted, but I do have peace of mind and, as far as Bill is able, I hope he finds peace too. He will always be my husband…till death do us part.

I know in my heart after my journey through life with this man that if he had been able to die as a result of his job he would have accepted it rather than live without the greatest love of his life – flying. In many ways that was why he couldn't settle to life outside of flying. He became insular and bitter and lost the spark of life that kept him going.

Maybe he had found me difficult to live with day in and day out because I was a constant reminder of the wonderful times we shared together over the years; a period of time never to be repeated. There are many maybes but one thing I know as a result of our brief meeting: I was able to forgive all the hurt done to me. And I know he loves me as he always did. What more could a woman ask for?

All of this, as I see it in the cold light of day, is part of one's journey through life confronting peaks and valleys. Love does conquer all; you just have to have faith in destiny. If I were given the same opportunities and the same choices again, knowing what I now know I wouldn't hesitate to choose the path of destiny.

Yes, these pioneering aviators were magnificent men but, in my experience, only when they were in their flying machines where destiny was not a point on their compass.

Bill has always said that when he dies all he wants is a single-seater aircraft and a flight plan to guide him to the stars -- what aviators call "high flight". This brings to mind the sonnet "High Flight" written by American pilot John Gillespie Magee who flew with the Royal Canadian Air Force in the Second World War. He started to compose this whilst test flying a Spitfire Mark V at high altitude. He was killed at the age of nineteen on December 11, 1941 during a training flight from the airfield in Scopwick in Lincolnshire.

High Flight

By John Gillespie Magee, Jr.

"Oh, I have slipped the surly bonds of earth,

And danced the skies on laughter-silvered wings;

Sunward I've climbed and joined the tumbling mirth of sun-split clouds -

and done a hundred things you have not dreamed of -

wheeled and soared and swung high in the sunlit silence.

Hovering there I've chased the shouting wind along

and flung my eager craft through footless halls of air.

"Up, up the long delirious burning blue

I've topped the wind-swept heights with easy grace,

where never lark, or even eagle, flew;

and, while with silent, lifting mind I've trod

the high untrespassed sanctity of space,

put out my hand and touched the face of God."

Though there was almost a seventeen-year difference in our ages it never mattered; Bill was wonderful company and certainly knew how to romance a woman. Gifts of bouquets of red roses became a very regular occurrence, and I confess to having been completely swept off my feet in the most romantic way. There was a great sense of déjà vu between us that we both recognised from day one. We both firmly believed we were soulmates and to this day I still believe that to be true. My parents were somewhat disconcerted by the age difference between us, but in spite of that they were easily won over by his old world charm.

We became engaged within months of our first encounter, although there were no plans for an early marriage. Company policy in those days required air hostesses to be single. Once married, you could no longer remain in the job. It was a very short-sighted policy. So many girls got married, kept quiet about it and continued to fly. They were taxed in their maiden names so the company was none the wiser. As the saying goes; "Where there's a will, there's a way", and living in sin meant something very different in our day. Oh, what fun it all was.

A change of course

Many of the girls relocating to Gatwick from Ferryfield elected to rent a house to share. Bill and I decided to share a flat and found one in Redhill, Surrey. We thought it advisable that my parents shouldn't know that we were co-habiting – not for a while anyway. My mother, in particular, was quite old-fashioned in her ideas concerning such matters. However my father had a very soft centre, and after some time had passed, he took us to one side and suggested, with a twinkle in his eye, that it would be much easier to be honest and open about our status. And it would save Bill from having to spend much of his time hiding in the wardrobe during his frequent visits. My father was a real diamond.

The many air hostesses who did relocate to Gatwick as a result of the multi-airline mergers were already trained, checked-out and had their wings. But all of us faced a complete change having to contend with different types and sizes of aircraft.

Increased seating capacity on larger aircraft meant more passengers to deal with – a total contrast to the short-haul Channel-hopping services we were accustomed to previously.

In preparation for the next phase of our careers, we all went through a multifaceted, six-week training course at Gatwick with the main focus on safety. The course covered emergency evacuation procedures, chutes and life-rafts deployment; in-flight fire-fighting drills; jungle, desert and sea survival techniques; first-aid, ditching and emergency landing procedures; decompression emergencies and security. Added to this was the implicit need to take care of on-board catering requirements bearing in mind that in those days all in-flight food was cooked from scratch. This included silver service for up to seven-course meals on some flights. We were trained to offer a bar service and duty free goods sales service with all the attendant paperwork that had to be completed before the end of a flight, as well as general passenger care and public relations. It was all go.

We even received instructions on how to deliver a baby in flight, deal with anyone taken seriously ill, and the dying or deceased. In this respect, I felt I had a head start thanks to my formal training in catering and nursing and, once again, I bless my mother for insisting I had a good, all-round grounding before flying.

And this wasn't everything: we received coaching in deportment and make-up at the Cherry Marshall School for Modelling. It was so important to not only look the part, we were also required to be airline icons – models of the skies.

Originally, air hostess uniforms were designed to be both practical and inspire confidence among passengers; simple designs with straight lines (almost military) probably reflecting the transition in air transportation not very long after the war. Later, Christian Dior designed our new BUA uniforms. They were very elegant in turquoise blue with A-line skirts and box jackets worn over a beige, roll-collared blouse, tailored overcoats and raincoats with chic trilby-style hats. It was the first sign of a break with tradition. Our wings were in gold as was the braiding on jacket sleeves to denote seniority. We looked good and we felt great. We were stars in the skies.

Ferryfield was fast becoming a thing of the past; we were embarking on a whole new world of flying. It was an exciting time in aviation.

In Britain, the 1960s decade was known as the Swinging Sixties. But, for me, the year 1960 brought together some of the greatest airline names in British civil aviation: Airwork, Hunting-Clan, Transair, Air Charter and Channel Air Bridge, Morton Air Services, Olley Air Services and Bristow Helicopters. Thirty-two years of aviation merged into one airline aptly named British United Airways. By 1962, BUA and Silver City had joined forces under the ownership of Air Holdings Limited and BUA became the country's largest independent - and unsubsidised - airline, eager to compete with Britain's heavily-subsidised and state-owned airlines British Overseas Airways Corporation (BOAC) and British European Airways (BEA).

Thirty-seven companies were forged together under the BUA umbrella with the high-energy Freddie Laker (later Sir Freddie Laker) as its managing director. I could not have hoped for more than to be a part of such a young and prestigious company. BUA was certainly going places and I was lucky enough to be on board.

By now BUA had a large, mixed fleet of aircraft having inherited pre-existent aircraft from the amalgamated airlines including the Bristol Britannia, fondly known by those of us who flew in them as "whispering giants"; Vickers Viscounts, Douglas DC3s, 4s and 6s; the Handley Page Hermes, Bristol Freighters and Bristow's Helicopters.

International flights to all corners of the globe were now in reach. I felt the world was my oyster and I was going to eat my fill, though cognisant of the need to plot a course well away from the moules marinière.

*

Training over, we were all anxious to get airborne.

I was assigned to fly on both short- and long-haul flights initially, which meant I could be somewhere in Europe one week and in the Far East the next. Variety was the spice of life, not only in terms of destinations but in terms of aircraft. I found myself flying on all aircraft types. In today's world that probably sounds a bit tame, even laughable. But these were the "golden years" when aircraft were less sophisticated though the lifestyle we followed surpassed that of today's high-speed world.

I even did a stint on de Havilland Comets during a short-term secondment to an Egyptian airline. This assignment turned out to be quite a coincidence. When the Comet developed serious structural problems, Bill was one of the test pilots involved trying to discover what was causing them to break up in mid-flight. Subsequently the cause was put down to catastrophic metal fatigue in the airframe, something not understood at the time. All aircraft were withdrawn from service for extensive testing and it was discovered the root cause was due to design flaws, including dangerous stresses at the corners of the square windows [and not weather-related as previously concluded]. As a result of these findings, the Comet was extensively redesigned with oval windows, plus structural reinforcement and other changes. Nowadays all aircraft have oval-shaped windows. Sometimes we have to learn the hard way.

In 1961, when I realised my dream, flying was approaching its teenage years. However, there were scheduled passenger flights to continental Europe as early as 1919 when Imperial Airways began services from Croydon aerodrome. And in the 1930s four-engine Handley-Page biplanes operated from Croydon. I was told they bumped and bounced over the grass airstrip so vigorously that is was as good as getting a workout in a gym. In those days an aircraft's take-off weight criteria was a critically important factor so passengers and their luggage were weighed for safety reasons. Flight crews did not have the luxury of radar to help them navigate, they navigated by picking out familiar landmarks along the way, which proved tricky in poor visibility. And smog was common in the greater London area in the late fifties and early sixties.

In the early days flying boat services left from Southampton and later Poole Harbour operating approximately four-hour flight segments over to the Far East and Australia. Lots of stopping-off points were built into flight schedules. During stopovers passengers stayed at the same hotels as the crew and even dined together before continuing their journey the following day. Flying may have been low and slow but the in-flight service was the height of luxury with white-gloved air hostesses serving freshly-cooked food on the best china with silver cutlery.

A friend of mine, whose husband was a long-haul captain based at Gatwick in the 1960's, related to me her introduction to flying. Mary, who was an accomplished British actress, shared a flat with a friend who flew as an air hostess on flying boats. On this particular morning Mary's girlfriend was feeling a bit delicate after a night of revelry and certainly wasn't in a fit state to fly. Without batting an eyelid, Mary donned her friend's uniform, grabbed her own passport, and coolly presented herself for her friend's flight. No-one suspected she wasn't employed by the company. She performed as if on stage at a London theatre enjoying the experience so much she gave up acting and joined the airline. That isn't where the story ends because, through this incident, she met and married her pilot husband. Clearly, security wasn't a priority in those days; you couldn't get away with that today.

Cabin crew, cabin attendants, air hostesses, air stewardesses, whichever tag you prefer were all airline personnel whose job was to serve and take care of passengers on aircraft.

We owe it all to the world's first air stewardess. American Ellen Church was born in 1904 on a small farm in Cresco, Iowa. She created a new and exciting profession for young women of the 20th century by organising the pioneer group "The Sky Girls" while she was working as a nurse in San Francisco. As aircraft capacities increased to carry passengers as well as mail, Boeing Air Transport hired Miss Church, a registered nurse, to assist passengers on flights performed by its airline company called United Air Lines. Miss Church had approached officials of Boeing Air Transport and proposed that stewardesses be added to flight crews. Her idea was adopted and she and seven other nurses began flying between Chicago and San Francisco on May 15, 1930, exactly eight years and one day before I was born.

That sparked the launch of an aviation career for women that today employs thousands around the world. Sadly, Ellen Church was thrown from her horse while out riding one morning and died from her injuries. The accident occurred thirty-five years after making aviation history as the world's first air stewardess. She was only sixty years old.

In my day the title "air hostess" was proudly carried by most females becoming synonymous with such remarks as "leader of refined etiquette", and "snappy and smart dresser". In the decades that followed, many other world professions adopted the etiquette demonstrated by air hostesses as the gold standard for customer service.

Back in the 1960s, the glamour and status commanded by air hostesses equalled that of movie stars of the day. Air hostesses were always the centre of attention. From the moment they stepped inside an airport all eyes were glued on their slim and slender figures, proportionate body shapes, and glamorous uniforms - including white gloves. They strutted their stuff with grace and style towards their waiting aircraft like models on a catwalk. Wherever they went they had a commanding presence and all eyes were on them. The "trolley dollies" and "flight attendants" of today bear no resemblance to yesteryear's fashion models of the skies.

Air crews and passengers: the unvarnished truth

In that same era, passengers were also a quite different breed than today. Many were businessmen some accompanied by their wives. Others included families travelling on exotic holidays. But very few women seemed to travel alone.

Then there were the famous celebrities of stage and screen. I remember actors David Niven, James Robinson Justice, Robert Morley, Robert Mitchum, Cary Grant and comedian Max Bygraves among others.

Robert Mitchum was a laconic individual, curt and terse and exhibiting an exceedingly dry sense of humour. On one trip I chatted with him about a film he was making; I believe it was a World War II drama. I asked him if he'd served during the war. He said he had.

"May I ask what service you performed?"

"I was an asshole inspector."

End of conversation.

In total contrast, we sometimes had the pleasure of royalty on board some of our flights. I remember HRH the Duchess of Kent flying on one flight I was working to Hong Kong. The Duchess, along with her first born child, was joining her husband on an overseas tour of duty. The baby's sky-cot that hung above the Duchess's seat in the Britannia aircraft had been thoughtfully decorated with red tassels in her baby's honour, which she found quite amusing.

It is fair to say we enjoyed the company of a rich tapestry of passengers back then, when everyone was courteous and respectful in every way. There was no in-flight entertainment, laptops, mobile phones and suchlike. Passengers seemed content to read, sleep or talk to the cabin staff.

Flying was hard work but satisfying in every way. We stayed at the best hotels in the world sometimes for several days and got to know places quite well. The world was ours to explore and we did. We shopped for shoes in Rome, bought perfume in Paris, sought pearls in Singapore, and got our clothes made in Hong Kong and India.

Bill was an expert at bargaining in the Orient. I remember on one occasion he went into a shop in Changi, Singapore and bought a dozen pairs of socks having bartered down the price considerably. Minutes later, he walked three shops down the road and sold the same socks for double the amount.

On another occasion I was on a trip with a captain who was carrying in his suitcase some bras for his sister-in-law. She lived in Bombay and had requested he buy the bras for her from Marks and

Spencer's. Aircrew were warned and discouraged from taking goods into India at the risk of being accused of trying to sell them illegally. With that in mind, the captain had taken the bras out of their cellophane wrappings and mixed them with other clothes in his suitcase. But his well-thought-out ruse flopped like a pregnant pole-vaulter when his suitcase was picked out for a random inspection. Slowly, and with more drama than a Punjab soap opera, the customs officer held up one bra and waved it at our assembled crew of ten, all of whom by now were sporting wide grins.

"My God captain, what is this we have here?" the officer asked, head jingling from side to side.

"Oh, that's an over-shoulder-boulder-holder officer," our straight-faced captain replied expecting the customs officer to appreciate the subtlety of his remark. But his little joke crashed and burned on the floor of the customs hall. Quick as a flash, and without much thought, our captain fired off another explanation: "Officer, it's like this… in my spare time I love to dress up in women's clothes."

He got away with it, but never lived it down with the rest of the crew. He hurried out of the customs hall tail between legs, leaving in his wake one very bemused customs officer.

Thinking about the Bombay-bra incident brings to mind another humorous occurrence involving the same captain - a man inclined to behave as though he were a law unto himself. He could be quite embarrassing at times. On some occasions he would spend the night before flights in his caravan in a field at the edge of Gatwick

Airport. But this didn't prevent him from reporting late. One cold and frosty morning, after oversleeping, he jumped out of bed and made a dash across the field to the ramp where he arrived breathless at the steps of a waiting DC6 aircraft. Smoking a large cigar, he wore only a long dressing gown over his underpants, plus uniform hat fixed at a crazy angle. The holdall he was carrying was stuffed with his uniform shirt, jacket and trousers. Those were the days! Aircraft might have been slow but aircrew lived in the fast lane, some moving a bit faster than others.

*

I worked my first flight from Gatwick Airport on a Vickers Viscount aircraft primed and ready for a round-trip to Rotterdam. An action-packed, one hour flight each way, these services were supported mainly by businesspeople. And, with one round-trip flight in the morning and another in the evening many passengers conducted their business in Holland in the space of a few hours cutting out an overnight stay. Hence, the same passengers who flew with us to Rotterdam in the morning often returned to Gatwick the same day.

With only two air hostesses looking after fifty passengers, we had to work our socks off to serve a hot breakfast (or dinner) and offer on-board drinks and a duty free bar service in less than an hour. We had to be thoroughly organised because time was never on our side.

Prior to take-off, we had to scurry down the cabin taking orders for bar sales and drinks. And, immediately after take-off, one of us would break open the bar bond seals and start dispensing duty free goods while the other poured out pre-ordered drinks. Time was of the essence, teamwork essential; we had to hustle.

For all early morning flights to near-European destinations, which were scheduled to leave Gatwick between 6.30 and 8 a.m., on-board ovens were pre-set to cook breakfast. We distributed meals as swiftly as possible, floating through the cabin, keeping cool and trying to show we were not in a great hurry. It was touch and go to retrieve the finished breakfast (or dinner) trays and glasses, give a pre-landing speech, conduct a cabin and seat-back check…and do all this with not a hair, or anything else, out of place. After bidding our passengers farewell we immediately prepared ourselves for the return trip. There was no time for anything else.

Having transitioned to the Viscount flights operating to continental Europe, I felt thankful for prior experience gained from flying on the Bristol Freighter car ferry services. Those flights had just fourteen passengers and we had only twenty minutes to deal with the bar sales before landing at our destination. It was all about time-management, teamwork plus plenty of luck for good measure.

The four-engine, turbo-prop Viscount carried fifty passengers in a single class (first-class throughout to all intents and purposes) in the days before inclusive tours became popular. Inclusive tours were altogether something different from a cabin staff's point of view, which I will get to later. As the aircraft was pressurised we could fly higher and faster and offer a great deal more comfort to passengers. Before pressurised cabins, 10,000 feet was the ceiling for passenger aircraft. But with pressurised cabins, equipped with heating and air-conditioning, flight crews could vie for higher altitudes to achieve smoother flights for passengers.

Although I was mainly assigned to long-haul flights, which I loved not only because I could get to fly with Bill on occasions, I preferred them because I could return frequently to Singapore and Hong Kong. Having attended school in Singapore, it was a bit like returning home every time I went there. The Far East was, and still remains, very close to my heart.

Pilots stuck to one aircraft type at a time, but air hostesses alternated with ease between long-haul and short-haul aircraft. When I started my flying career there wasn't any legislation governing the number of hours we could work. So, on short-haul routes, we might fly two flights a day. I remember doing three in one day by which time I was almost on my knees. The senior flight hostesses on the two trips that followed my first flight were unable to meet their assignments, and stand-by crews on that day were in short supply. So, after landing, I left one aircraft and was driven to an adjacent aircraft ready to depart. On return to base, the same routine was repeated, and off I went again. That day, poor Bill travelled to the airport three times to pick me up before I finally made it home. On that occasion, I recall I had the pleasure of visiting Palma twice and Rimini once in one day. I saw flying as a job in a million but, glamour apart, it was very hard work. This had much to with crews partying hard when they were off duty.

With ample opportunities to visit so many romantic places, often long enough to get to know them well, I really thought the sky was the limit. Keeping a personal life going, however, was a big challenge for many. I was lucky because Bill and I often found ourselves flying together, or in the same part of the world, enough to keep our relationship going. But not everyone was so fortunate. Looking back, Bill and I could say we had shared a bed in most of the best hotels in the world and certainly enjoyed some wonderful moments together.

In those days before emails, mobile phones, answer-phones and such, it was difficult for our friends outside of aviation to keep a track of us. And for the girls who were trying to cultivate a relationship outside of flying, only the most determined of men succeeded in winning the fair lady of their choice. I guess this is why so many air hostesses married pilots.

Although it was characterised as a short-haul aircraft, the Viscount operated long-distance flights including one from Gatwick to West Africa – in stages of course. I worked the inaugural flight to Bathurst (Banjul today) in The Gambia carrying men who worked for mining companies in the region. Every six months, some men were sent back to the UK for a break from working in the intense heat and high humidity. Once on board our Viscount they enjoyed a first-class service with a free bar all the way. This meant we had our share of drunks. I remember on one occasion one "gentleman" (I used a more colourful expression at the time) stripped off completely, apart from his tie. Jumping onto his seat, he started singing and gyrating his whole body. As senior hostess on that flight I drew the short straw to address this unsavoury character. Stepping into the fray, I picked out the burliest passenger who appeared reasonably sober and, with his assistance, got the drunk into his pants and string vest before he passed out. Immediately afterwards, I made sure he would not cause further problems for the remainder of the flight by fastening his seat belt across his lap and pinning down his nether regions with his hands jammed underneath. Then I tightened the seat belt to ensure there was no chance of a repeat performance from this particular individual. He was trussed up like an oven-ready turkey.

On another flight to the coast of West Africa, I found myself in the midst of in-flight drama. For the first time our crew was given nivaquine an antimalarial tablet as a substitute for quinine. Fortunately, I, and the other girls on the flight (and the first officer) had already taken our daily dose of quinine, so we didn't take the substitute drug. But our captain - let's call him Captain Q - took the nivaquine with disastrous results. Prior to our descent into Bathurst, his eyes became so swollen he couldn't see a thing. The co-pilot had to land the aircraft single-handedly. After landing, Captain Q was stretchered off to hospital and we had to wait for a couple of nights in Bathurst for a replacement captain to fly from Heathrow. None of us ever used nivaquine after that incident. Thankfully, Captain Q was able to resume flying duties after a short rest.

There was another instance, again on a Viscount aircraft, and again with "nether regions" connotations. After take-off, a lady popped into the toilet located at the front of the aircraft, just aft of the galley and forward of the first row of passengers. As I recall, we were destined for Amsterdam.

I was busily engaged in the galley when my attention was drawn to faint cries for help coming from the toilet. Gingerly, I knocked on the door. There was no response from within though the calls for assistance continued. By now the incident was generating secondary interest in the cabin; passengers' eyes were trained on the toilet and galley area.

Running down the centre of the toilet door was a hinge-pin which, if slid out, allowed the door to be removed. This I did only to reveal a pair of legs, inscribing a V-sign, with a head framed in between. The lower part of the rest of this poor woman had disappeared down the toilet. Little wonder she had not responded to knocks on the door.

I acted like it was an everyday occurrence; there was nothing to worry about. That was difficult as I found myself caught between bouts of hysterical laughter and a growing feeling of panic wondering how to extricate this unfortunate lady. She was stuck fast. Calmly, I told her there was nothing to worry about, "…and we'll soon have you back on your feet." She stared at me with a look of incredulity, her face now the colour of beetroot.

Making my apologies, I rushed off the to the flight deck to report the incident only to be greeted with jeers and looks of disbelief from the two gents flying the aircraft. "I'd better look into this," the captain said donning his cap and following me to the toilet.

"Good morning madam, I am your captain. What seems to be the problem?" I heard him say through my tears. Then, in a totally unrehearsed and somewhat clumsy move, he tried yanking her away from the bowl. It was no use. In that same instant, it dawned on him why she was stuck fast. He reasoned that on take-off from Gatwick, the retaining cap on the outside of the aircraft may not have been securely fastened after the ground crew emptied the toilets. Somehow, it must have worked loose during take-off and, as soon as the aircraft became pressurised, detached at the precise moment the poor passenger lowered herself onto the toilet.

She was sucked in with such force that her bottom became the retaining plug thus maintaining cabin pressure. With profuse apologies to the lady, who was incandescent by this time, the captain said "...don't worry madam, I will reduce height right away and depressurise the aircraft as quickly as possible." After which, he said with great confidence, she would be able to reclaim her derriere from the toilet.

We made the appropriate announcement to the other passengers and, without further ado, the problem was solved. The lady was so relieved to be free, and fortunately undamaged except for her pride. She was able to laugh at her own experience. An impromptu outburst of applause from the cabin was followed by free drinks all round. I believe our flight deck crew dined out on that experience for a long time afterwards. I know I did.

An uplifting and less dramatic event that still warms my heart concerns a little old lady who, for her ninetieth birthday, was taken to Pisa for a holiday by her doting family. As it was her birthday on the day of departure, she was accorded VIP treatment and the entire family was given priority boarding. That way we could get the lady nicely settled. She had never flown before, indeed was born before the age of flight so this was an important moment in her long life. I can see her now, a tiny soul wearing a navy blue basket hat decorated with red cherries. She looked just like a miniature Mary Poppins.

As was customary we piped soft music into the cabin during passenger embarkation, on this occasion a piano concerto by Semprini.

In the dear old lady's opinion, the flight was a huge success: "Oh, thank you dear; isn't this exciting," she kept saying over and over again.

All of our other passengers soon learnt she was ninety years old that day, and taking her very first flight, so there was a choral outburst of "happy birthday to you..." for the dear old soul.

When the captain popped into the cabin to introduce himself, she questioned if it would not be wiser if he went back to fly the aircraft instead of spending time with her. "How could you possibly know where we're going if you're not driving?" she asked?

Again I switched on the Semprini tape after landing at Pisa. She was first to embark at Gatwick but would be last to disembark in Pisa as a car and officials were waiting for her and her family to help them through the airport's arrival formalities. When she finally got up from her seat to leave, this dear lady threw her arms around me and hugged me tightly.

"Oh thank you dear," she whispered in my ear, "it has been so wonderful. But tell me, is that the captain playing the piano? I think he plays so beautifully."

To someone who was born before the age of flight, I suppose anything was possible. I will remember her always with great affection. Flying was never dull; we faced so many happy, funny, and indeed sad situations. But never, in the whole of my career, did I ever come across another hostess of my era who didn't feel as I did, and still feels privileged to have flown during the "golden years" when we had enough time to savour the entire experience.

Cockpit capers

Some of the more bizarre crew stories today circulating worldwide via the internet in private blogs or in books are not without foundation. Many have their origins in the sixties and seventies – even during wartime. Recorded conversations, sometimes deprecatory but always humorous, that take place between aircraft cockpits and air traffic controllers can bring welcome, on-board relief during a crew's more stressful moments on the flight deck. Here are just a few snippets:

Tower: "Have you got enough fuel or not?"

Pilot: "Yes."

Tower: "Yes what??"

Pilot: "Yes, SIR!"

A welcome to a new co-pilot from an old captain:

"Son, your wife's legs have more time in the air than you do."

Lady radar controller: "Can I turn you on at 7 miles?"

Airline captain: "Madam, you can try."

ARN851: "Halifax Terminal, Nova 851 with you out of 13,000 for 10,000, requesting runway 15."

Halifax Terminal (female): "Nova 851 Halifax, the last time I gave a pilot what he wanted I was on penicillin for three weeks. Expect runway 06."

LH741: "Tower, give me a rough time-check!"

Tower: "It's Tuesday, sir."

Equally humorous are the written exchanges between airline pilots and the company's mechanics patiently waiting at the airline's engineering base to scrutinise the aircraft's maintenance log. Crews were often left in stitches after reading these witticisms, I know I was.

Without doubt their teamwork ensures aircraft are safe to fly and, all other conditions being right, capable of withstanding Earth's gravitation pull which is the general idea once an aircraft gets airborne. After each flight, aircraft commanders fill out a check sheet listing known and suspected defects for ground mechanics to address and rectify before an aircraft makes its next flight. In my days the post-flight maintenance check list looked like this:

Technical problem or defect reported by pilot or crew. **Remedial action or answer reported by maintenance engineer**

*Something loose in cockpit. **Something tightened in cockpit.***

*Left-inside main tyre almost needs replacing. **Almost replaced left-inside main tyre.***

*Unfamiliar noise coming from No2 engine. **Engine run for three hours. Noise now familiar.***

Mouse in cockpit. **Cat installed.**

Target radar hums. **Reprogrammed target radar with lyrics.**

Number three engine missing [not firing properly presumably]. **Engine found on starboard [right] wing after brief search.**

Pilot's clock inoperative. **Wound clock.**

Aircraft handles funny. **Aircraft told to straighten up, fly right and be serious.**

Whining sound heard on engine shutdown. **Pilot removed from aircraft.**

Noise coming from under instrument panel - sounds like a midget pounding on something with a hammer. **Took hammer away from midget.**

Suspect crack in windshield. **Suspect you are right.**

Test flight okay except Auto-Land very rough. **Auto-Land is not installed on this aircraft.**

Dead bugs on windshield. **Live bugs on back order.**

Evidence of leak on right main landing gear. **Evidence removed.**

Three roaches in cabin. **One roach killed, one wounded, one got away.**

DME volume set unbelievably loud. [DME = Distance Measuring Equipment?] **DME volume set to more believable level.**

Friction locks causing throttle levers to stick. **That's what they are for.**

In those days aircraft checklists were still being tweaked to remove the possibility of misunderstandings, particularly pilot-to-pilot, to eliminate any potential mistakes. But mistakes did occur and checklists were adjusted accordingly.

On one occasion discussing this with my husband Bill, he brought to mind a potentially dangerous incident that occurred during his service with the RAF when he was flying with a very young co-pilot. The young fellow mistook Bill's cheerful aside comment "cheer up" during the take-off run for "gear up" and proceeded to raise the landing gear with predictable results. Fortunately both were able to walk away from the aircraft unscathed. The pre-flight checklist was adjusted.

On another occasion, when Bill was flight-testing a four-engine Lancaster bomber, he called "feather 4", meaning turn the propeller blades of the inoperative number 4 engine into wind to reduce drag. In this case, *all four* engines were "feathered", instantly turning the aircraft into a huge glider and forcing the crew rapidly to select "superfine" on all four props to regain altitude and avoid losing the aircraft altogether. After such instances check-list commands were specific: "Feather No.4 or No.3 or No.2 or No.1" for example. And that is why, today, aircraft pre-flight, in-flight and post-flight check lists are designed to make flying as safe as possible. To repeat: Some things were learnt the hard way.

I never came across a checklist for testing one's sexual preferences. And, in those heady days of macho men and their incredible flying machines, some fresh from fighting the Second World War and/or serving on the Berlin Airlift, it was wise to hide one's homosexuality from fellow crew members whenever possible. No one ever admitted to being openly gay in what was considered a "real" man's world. The term "gay" back then meant someone who was happy and didn't have a care in the world. But the world changed.

This is my story of one very accomplished, though "gay" pilot, let's call him Captain Eric R, who had difficulty camouflaging his sexual orientation and suffered the consequences.

Having lined up his aircraft for take-off, Eric requested permission from the tower to taxi-off the runway. "I am terribly sorry tower," he said to the controller, "but we have just developed a naughty problem."

"Please advise the nature of your problem captain."

"My silly throttles seem to be stuck," he said with a note of resignation in his voice, "what do you think I should do?"

"Try hitting them with your handbag Eric -- that should do the trick!"

I flew with Eric on one trip when the entire crew had to travel by train to pick up an aircraft from Luton Airport. As we all rushed down the platform to catch the train, which was primed to depart, Eric, in full uniform and sporting a rolled umbrella, clumsily dropped his brolly in his haste to board. A gruff voice behind him shouted, "'Ere, you bleedin' fairy, you've dropped yer bleedin' wand." Eric braked to a sudden halt, swung round on his heel, and looked daggers at the railway porter who was standing before him a huge grin on his face. Without further thought, and with grossly accentuated hip movements, Eric "minced" his way over to the porter where, with brolly in hand, tapped each shoulder of the porter and royally commanded him to "turn to shit my good fellow."

It's Security, Stupid

Once upon a time, when the world was different than today, catching a flight required little more than checking-in at an airport, collecting a boarding pass, jumping aboard the aircraft, and dropping into a seat pointed out by a smiling air hostess. Sadly those leisurely days of travel are long gone and never to return. The reason for this – and I do detect that hardened travellers are already way ahead of me --

is something called "airport security", which is now an industry within an industry.

Today, when we pitch up at an airport with luggage, we are greeted by a uniformed army of humourless, grim-faced, wand-waving security guards whose main purpose in life is to make sure our planned trip gets off to a miserable start. The meaner the sentinels the better, it seems. Burly men, and some even burlier women, compete for the coveted, annual airport security title of "Meaner than a Junkyard Dog". I jest, but only marginally.

My assessment of security personnel may seem a bit harsh, some would say, but to many travellers that's how it appears. Life as we know it stops at the first airport x-ray machine as we are drawn ever deeper into a confusing world of rising anguish, aggravated by body searches, endless queues, and miles of red tape. You can say goodbye to your last vestige of dignity at the kerbside as the hungry junkyard dogs take over. No-one is pardoned.

It is true we live in uncertain times with our thoughts and movements dictated by the every-present danger posed by terrorists domestic and foreign. And whilst no-one in their right mind would want anything left to chance, passengers are justified, in my humble opinion, in questioning the strict application of some security procedures.

What is missing is the application of common-sense in many borderline situations that manage to attract the attention of security personnel. Where some guards are concerned common sense has been replaced, it seems, by an unrelenting arrogance and the frightening realisation that many security officials are just "going-through-the-motions".

Take the case of one perplexed traveller who had in his possession one 100ml jar of marmite that was immediately confiscated by the gendarmes. Why? Because it was "gel-like" and therefore broke the rules.

"Not to worry," the security official announced seeing the look of dismay on the passenger's face, "it all goes to a local people's home." So, that's alright isn't it?

Another hapless traveller in his seventies and a beneficiary of a replacement hip got fed-up with being constantly body-searched. Each time he travelled by air he was asked to remove his trousers and expose his scar to satisfy security personnel and curious passers-by. The fact that he carried a note from his doctor, and was in possession of a card from the British Orthopaedic Association, made no impression at all on Heathrow's security machine. Common-sense had already left the building.

Today, security is the prime activity at world airports; so understand this: When you travel by air you are a potential terrorist *first* and a passenger *second*. Nowadays we are all subjected to "behavioural detection techniques" the application of which leaves one in no doubt we all sprang from primates. Alas, some of us didn't spring far enough. This is what I'm driving at:

- Have you ever yawned while standing in an airport security line? Well, depending upon how you yawn you could be suspect;
- And, if you tend to whistle to help pass the time, be careful which tune you choose; it may fall into the category of "suspicious";
- If you suffer from pre-fight nerves, perspire a bit, fidget, and appear generally restless, you could be suspect;
- If a man is perceived to have shaved recently (something to be admired in my flying days) he may draw attention to himself in a security queue as "formerly bearded with something to hide".

These are just a sampling of the 92-point checklist promulgated by the United States' Transportation Security Administration (TSA) to screen passengers for "suspicious behaviour". And based upon observations, which has to be subjective by definition, your behaviour may cause law enforcement officers to intervene. So, to all you unwitting yawners, casual whistlers, nervy fidgeters and travellers of a nervous disposition…you have been warned; big brother is watching you -- closely.

Today's procedures are a far cry from the golden years of flying I remember so well. My thoughts drift back to my friend, Mary Haddon, the British actress I introduced earlier. She was the lady who shared an apartment with an air hostess and stood in for her when her friend was suffering from a severe hangover the morning after the night before. Just to recap: Using her own passport, and her friend's uniform, Mary drew on her acting experience and filled in for her friend. (I think it's safe to say such breach of rules is highly unlikely today).

Mary found the experience so uplifting and fulfilling she gave up acting and, in the fifties, became an air hostess on flying boats. A while later she met and married a pilot and that's how I came to meet her. I flew with her husband, Gordon, on Britannia aircraft on many occasions whilst working for British United Airways.

While on the subject of security, I recall a security alert at Gatwick Airport when our Britannia aircraft was taxiing to the runway and cleared for take-off. The flight was destined for Entebbe Airport, Uganda. Right before we started our take-off run we received instructions from the control tower to taxi to the far corner of the airport and await traffic and security personnel to attend the aircraft. Apparently a bomb warning had been phoned-in regarding our flight.

Everyone disembarked in an orderly fashion and boarded a waiting bus parked nearby. All items of luggage were offloaded by baggage handlers and lined-up alongside the aircraft ready for identification by the passengers. Indications were the bomb was in a passenger's bag so the aircraft wasn't searched. One by one, passengers stepped forward to identify their personal luggage, which was searched, cleared and reloaded onto the aircraft.

Naturally, and as stipulated by Murphy's Law, one solitary item of luggage remained unclaimed and was picked up by a passing traffic officer. Without further ado, or thought, he waltzed through the cabin holding forth the suitcase, "Does anybody recognise this bag as theirs?" So much for security on that flight.

Whilst I fully appreciate security is now an essential part of flying, I also feel that common-sense must prevail if air travel is not to lose all its appeal.

It was a very sad day when we began locking flight deck doors on aircraft. Before that, passengers enjoyed visiting the flight deck to understand what was involved in flying an aircraft. Also, flight deck crews enjoyed their moments of glory when they had the undivided attention of curious passengers posing questions while they worked in their "office". Young children loved to pay a visit to the cockpit and talk to the captain. And that worked both ways.

I remember on one occasion during a flight to Tenerife in the Canary Islands the captain, who loved to show off in front of children, invited a young boy into the cockpit. I took the excited young lad to see the captain who was someone who revelled in being the hero. Plonking the child on his knee he put the lad's hands on the yoke. The aircraft was already flying on auto-pilot but the boy, in sheer delight and in his own little world, imagined he was flying the aircraft.

When the boy's father arrived on the flight deck to pick up his son, he let it slip that his little boy was still recovering from chickenpox and should not have been travelling.

A few weeks later, the captain went down with chickenpox, which he had managed to escape as a child. The poor captain became extremely ill and had to be hospitalised. His indisposition attracted a great deal of curiosity from fellow aircrew after reports that the captain's swollen testicles were tenderly arrayed on a soft, velvety pillow to ease the pain. I can't recall anyone having so many concerned visitors. This captain never lived it down. And I know he never again allowed anyone on the flight deck when he was in command of a flight.

Passengers – You either love 'em or hate 'em

Whenever I look back on the many treasured memories of my days as an air hostess, I tend to refer to them as the golden years because that's what they were. In the late fifties and throughout the sixties commercial flying was still in its infancy. Men and machines (and air hostesses who worked like machines) learnt something new each and every day. The belief that "experience comes from learning from your mistakes" was a truism in aviation circles in my days, and we had to be quick learners because a new experience was usually waiting on our next flight.

As for passengers, most were first-time flyers save for a small number of savvy travellers who knew and appreciated outstanding in-flight service when they experienced it.

Those years also saw the dawn of "inclusive tours", or IT's; those low-cost, prepaid holidays bound-up into a single package that purchased flights, hotels, meals and ground transportation at an all-inclusive price. IT's gave rise to more people flying overseas initially to European cities and Mediterranean sunspots. Without the advent of IT's, I believe these folk would still be spending their annual holidays at Britain's crowded coastal holiday camps as they had done for years. Prepaid holidays prevail because they offer consumers great value. Whether they offer great service is another, debatable matter.

However, getting back to the golden years...it was a magical period when passengers consisted of refined ladies and urbane gentlemen who showed respect and expressed appreciation for everything the cabin crew did for them throughout their journey. And some journeys could take many hours.

Those of us who flew during that era soon discovered it was also very hard work. The trick was to make everything appear seamless, effortless and pleasurable no matter what the circumstances. Instructions meted out when I was training still ring in my ears: "Look like a woman, but work like a dog," and "no matter what the problem is...always smile". We became self-disciplined and remained so at all times.

To this day I still find myself smiling in circumstances that would normally cause me to grit my teeth and cast care to the wind. Instead, my "cabin smile" will appear unbidden when I unconsciously slip into my "coffee, tea, or me" role in the company of friends. As strange as it may seem it still works. Maybe that's because people find it hard to argue with someone who won't play ball -- if that's what they're angling for. What many folk don't understand are the years of training undertaken to achieve a very high standard and more years putting that training into practice. Some may think it's their game, but they still haven't worked out that it's my ball.

I will always remember how important that smile was particularly when I recall an incident that I still find quite amusing. I was a member of the crew on a Britannia aircraft to Tenerife in the Canary Islands. Travelling with us in First-class that day, among other passengers, was a certain Max Bygraves. For those who haven't heard of him, Max Bygraves was an English comedian, singer, actor and variety performer who had his own TV shows. He made twenty Royal Variety Performance appearances before Britain's royal family and presented numerous programmes including *Family Fortunes*. It would not be an overstatement to say he was very well known throughout the United Kingdom especially for his catchphrase "I've arrived and to prove it, I'm here". And I have to say, on this particular flight, I'm pleased he was "here".

We were well into the flight when, without warning, an electrical fire broke out in the forward galley. Passengers became alarmed when dense smoke seeped into the cabin. Summoned to the scene, our valiant flight engineer tried to get the fire under control, beavering away in the galley in full view of everyone. Intuitively, and seemingly unperturbed, members of the cabin staff walked up and down the aisle serving coffee with silver service, all wearing their well-rehearsed "silver-plated smiles". Our intention was to make passengers believe there was nothing much to worry about. This was one of those occasions when we had to put on a brave face.

Appreciating the magnitude of the moment, Max Bygraves decided to make his presence known. Jumping up from his seat he took the coffee pot from me and began serving passengers while singing songs plucked from his repertoire as he strode down the aisle with great confidence. Within minutes the whole aircraft was alive with the sound of music as passengers joined in the singing – including our engineer who was still frantically trying to bring the galley fire under control.

Before too long we were on approach to Tenerife airport. Everyone settled down. The wheels touched down on the runway to loud cheers and grateful applause. On leaving the aircraft, Max Bygraves gave each air hostess a very handsome tip and thanked us all for an "interesting and enjoyable flight". After some reflection he said, "I felt reassured by your smiling faces that it couldn't be too serious." How mistaken he was. After my own period of reflection, and perhaps those of many passengers, I think we were fortunate that he didn't choose to sing *Smoke Gets in Your Eyes!* But at least he, and the rest of the passengers and crew, could honestly say, "I've arrived and to prove it, I'm here". Thanks Max.

*

Let me assure readers that it wasn't easy to appear cool, calm and collected at all times, especially at the tail-end of a very long flight, and we experienced plenty of those in the golden years. We worked very long duty days on Britannia aircraft flights to Freetown in Sierra Leone for example; flights that operated with a First-class and Economy-class layout. Patrons in First-class were offered a seven-course dinner (or lunch), afternoon tea as applicable, coffee for elevenses and a hot breakfast as applicable. The standard service for passengers in Economy-class was similar to First-class minus the seven course dinner/lunch. But they were offered four courses including a cheese board service. The entire service was an all-silver affair, and desserts and cheeses were always served from a dessert trolley and authentic cheeseboard…no plastic meal-trays.

The overall round trip time between Gatwick and Freetown, with a one-hour turnaround at Freetown, was just over twenty-three hours after which we were all suffering fatigue…yet the smiles stayed in place. In those days cabin staff were not constrained by flight time restrictions, unlike flight deck crews that flew under stricter limitations. However, anyone who thinks ours was an easy ride can think again.

I recall with dismay one particular trip to Freetown when we ran out of fresh milk. We had to source additional stocks from the catering department in Freetown. To my horror, a mangy-looking goat was brought shipside where an equally mangy-looking gent began milking it into a filthy bucket. No prizes for those who have guessed that the return trip was accomplished minus fresh milk. In those days Freetown did not have what is generally regarded as an "airport", just a rather a broken-down hut at one end of an airfield. It has since been brought into the 21st century.

*

I must confess that, at times, passengers could prove to be quite difficult. And I am certain that what we had to put up with during the golden years was less daunting than today. Before I retired from flying

I had worked on the above-mentioned inclusive tour charter flights and charter flights carrying wild, excited football supporters, all of which could be described as colourful for a variety of reasons.

I do not envy today's cabin staff. But I also have to say there is no comparison between the air hostesses of yesteryear and today's flight attendants. These days we even make a distinction between "hostesses", "stewards" or "stewardesses", and "attendants" which, to my mind, denigrates the cabin staff role even if unintentionally.

It seems that today's training standards are designed to meet a very different criteria: For example, uniforms, generally speaking, aren't particularly stylish, and not enough attention is paid to personal grooming and overall appearance. Elocution has fallen by the wayside and there is no sense of mystique which had prevailed since the advent of the first air hostesses. Gone is the *je ne sais quoi* among air hostesses that once turned heads and conjured up the image of taking-off for romantic faraway places.

I can appreciate that in today's high-tech, high-speed and highly-connected world, flying to one's destination is more a means to an end with a need to get there as quickly as possible. Because cabin attendants have so much to do in a relatively short space of time there is no particular interaction between cabin staff and passengers. The once omnipresent smile has all but disappeared…replaced, instead, by a steely glare.

Yes, there were awkward passengers in days gone by just as there are today. Let's face it: It is never easy maintaining an air of mystery whilst dealing with a planeload of airsick passengers faced with bouts of heavy turbulence. And that's something that won't change.

*

How well I remember a seventeen-hour-long trip to Bombay [now Mumbai] in the company of a full aircraft load of British military personnel and their families. In those days, Britain's Ministry of Defence "blocked-off" seats on civilian airliners at the time the UK kept military garrisons in Singapore, Hong Kong and other vestiges of the former British Empire.

On this particular trip we were flying over South Asia amid the worst of the southwest monsoon period. Turbulence was so bad the toilets forward of the cabin broke away from their fittings and the contents of two loos, probably visited by two hundred passengers for over fifteen hours, flooded the cabin treating all in the immediate vicinity to an Elson foot wash.

There were still two hours to go before we landed at Bombay and, I must say, the steadily deteriorating conditions had a measured effect on most of the passengers, particularly the officers who had lobbied for the front seats of the aircraft, upstaging NCO's and other ranks seated to the rear. Undoubtedly the rank-and-file found it quite amusing watching their senior officers suffer under such unfortunate circumstances whilst the squaddies remained…shall we say…squeaky clean.

*

On another occasion, again on a Britannia aircraft, we were transporting a full load of passengers from Tenerife to Gatwick. Moments before the seat belt signs were lit-up for landing, a gentleman came up to me and said, "Would you mind retrieving my dentures from inside the toilet?" Mindful that two hundred people had used the toilet over the course of a few hours, I declined -- much to his annoyance. I tried reassuring him that after we landed his dentures would be reclaimed by ground personnel and returned to him with as little delay as possible.

After landing at Gatwick, and whilst bidding farewell to passengers as they disembarked, I was again confronted by the same gentleman. "Good news," he beamed triumphantly, "I managed to find my dentures." My smile quickly faded when I realised that he was wearing them despite the conditions of the toilets. The flight deck crew offered a few effluvious comments when I related the story. I guess it takes all sorts to make the world go around.

*

It has always been a source of bewilderment to me the way passengers behave when a flight is delayed, either due to adverse weather conditions, such as thick fog or violent thunder storms, or a technical fault on the aircraft. Faced with setbacks some people seem to lose all sense of propriety. Do they really want to put their lives at risk when we are acting in the best interests of their personal safety? Or do they harbour thoughts that the inconvenience they are suffering is all part of some great conspiracy?

In unforeseen and unpredictable circumstances cabin crews are in the front line when frustrated, irate and, often times, irrational passengers are cleared to embark. Immediately, and in unison it seems, they begin their verbal attacks on the nearest air hostess as though it were all her fault. In my day, passengers stood by the gate until the aircraft was ready for them to embark. Then they were let loose to walk to the aircraft to be welcomed by the cabin crew who calmly, and in an orderly manner, showed them to their seats.

With the advent of low-cost charter flights, the calibre of passengers changed beyond all recognition. They became mob-like; something akin to a supermarket race where shoppers rush to cram into their trolleys as many goodies as they can before timeout is called. It was no longer possible for an air hostess to stand in the aircraft doorway and greet individual passengers. We just got out of the way, thus abandoning all that our training had taught us. One problem underpinning this, I believe, was a time when the pre-boarding seat selection procedure was discontinued, presumably to save time and therefore costs. As a result, passengers were apt to sprint from the departure lounge to the aircraft to be the first to grab a window seat. I was appalled by the level of aggression shown among passengers.

To illustrate how serious this could be, I recall one occasion when I was on the flight deck at the time the captain gave permission to release passengers who had been waiting impatiently to board. Along with the crew I watched as the crowd surged forward like a pack of hounds that had sight of a fox. In the rush an elderly woman was pushed to the ground and, unbelievably, stomped on by others determined to get to the aircraft first. Witnessing this, the captain dashed off the flight deck and fought his way through the melee to rescue her and bring her to the safety of the flight deck. She was shaken, but otherwise unhurt.

There is a postscript to this distasteful episode. It appeared funny at first sight to see the footprints the unruly mob had left imprinted on the front and back of the captain's shirt. He was stomped on while trying to rescue the woman and had rolled over to protect her so both the front and back of his white uniform shirt were soiled. When he returned to the flight deck he was not a happy Teddy. Patiently, the captain waited until all passengers had settled into their seats then he walked into the cabin. "Gather your belongings and disembark," he ordered, "I am not prepared to tolerate such behaviour as demonstrated by so-called human beings." It was a bold statement even in those days.

The flight was delayed citing the need to have a doctor check on the elderly lady before flying home. She was later allocated a seat of her choice where we could all keep an eye on her. The rest of the passengers were subjected to a long wait and were noticeably subdued on the homeward leg of the trip.

At Gatwick Airport a car was laid on to meet the lady and someone conducted her through customs to the baggage hall to link up with a family member. The other passengers were made to sit in their seats until the captain had personally walked the lady down the cabin and handed her over to a member of the ground staff. Meanwhile, our erstwhile skipper, having made his point, then stood at the aircraft doorway, still wearing his white uniform soiled with footprints, and glared pointedly at each disembarking passenger. They followed each other like sheep but in total silence, not daring to look the captain in the eye.

*

In all honesty I found difficult or unruly passengers to be in the minority. Most travellers were courteous and considerate. Maybe that's because in the old days we had a more socially interactive role with passengers with more time to strike up a relationship. Although there were some arrogant, insecure and domineering passengers, I believe, in the final analysis, they were all just seeking attention.

The more arrogant guys had designs on the air hostesses; all they had to do, so they thought, was to snap their fingers and one would come running.

Domineering types fell into two categories: those used to having servants at their beck and call, and female passengers who felt undermined, perhaps even maligned, by our image as air hostesses and what we stood for. It seemed necessary for these irritating women to try to outdo us by vilifying or maligning our image, probably to make themselves feel more comfortable and perhaps more relevant. I will let you decide, dear reader, from these examples:

A difficult lady who comes to mind had spent time in Singapore with her husband at the completion of his tour of duty with the British army. She was preceding him back to the UK with her fairly new babe-in-arms. It was obvious to the whole crew she hadn't put in

106

much time dealing with her child. Clearly she had enjoyed the services of a Malay *ayah* [nursemaid] to take care of baby. Now she had to do things for herself and found herself at the bottom of the learning curve of how to take care of babies.

I was in the crew that worked this lady's flight from Bombay to London-Stansted with a refuelling stop at Istanbul. As I passed by her seat a hand reached out and grabbed the hem of my skirt yanking me to a halt. Turning to face the owner of the hand, I politely asked, "how may I help you madam?" my smile sweetly and securely cemented in place.

Rudely, and without a please or thank you, she thrust her jacket into my hand insisting, "Take this away and sew a button on it." My first inclination was to stuff the jacket where the sun don't shine but, instead, I duly complied with her wishes – still smiling. Madam seemed to take this as a sign of how to show air hostesses who was boss and from that point onwards we were all subjected to a merry round of complaints or demands...this coffee is too hot, or too cold...the baby needs changing...the bottle needs warming. No please or thank you anywhere in sight.

When we arrived at Istanbul airport all passengers were disembarked while the aircraft was refuelled. Back on board again, and everyone settled in their seats, we carried out a headcount to ensure no one was missing. We counted and recounted yet we were still one short. It struck me as strange because all seats were occupied. Then the penny dropped: The rude woman's baby was missing; the poor mite had been left in the passenger lounge. The woman was visibly embarrassed and somewhat subdued for the remainder of the flight.

On another "trooping" flight, this time from London-Stansted transporting wives and families to Singapore to join their military husbands for a tour of duty, I encountered a most uncouth individual. She had three children possibly a year apart in age plus a new-born baby.

An important aspect of these flights was to instil into mothers the need to be wary of rapid temperature changes between the UK, Istanbul (a refuelling station) and Bombay onwards. At the start of each flight, particularly during UK winters, small babies arrived on-board wrapped in blankets and shawls. I repeatedly advised this particular mother to remove some of the swathing from the baby who had been placed in a sky cot above her seat. Several times I removed the unnecessary coverings myself only to find she rewrapped her baby as soon as my back was turned.

Despite getting the captain involved, who also had a word with her in transit at Istanbul, by the time she had re-embarked and the aircraft had taken-off, the baby had died from heat exhaustion. We had to return to Istanbul to allow a doctor to verify death, after which the baby's body was placed in a refrigerated container and carried to Singapore in the hold of the aircraft.

But this wasn't the end of it. On the leg from Istanbul to Bombay we found the same mother laughing and joking, even trying to raffle the baby's things. I spoke about her behaviour with the captain who thought she was perhaps grief-stricken and that could explain her rather odd behaviour. I approached her and quietly suggested she was perhaps suffering from grief and that it would be better to just sit quietly and get some rest. Her reply will resonate with me for ever: "Don't worry about me luv…easy come, easy go." I can still picture the vacuous expression on her face.

*

"*Ya Allah*, give us the chance to offer haj!"

Among the more bizarre trips I experienced were those to Mecca, Saudi Arabia, carrying hajis [Muslim pilgrims] making their once-in-a-lifetime trip to the birthplace of the prophet Mohammad as stipulated in the holy Koran. In those days, such passengers were rather primitive to say the least. And they seemed unable to understand a thing we said to them. As responsible air hostesses, our main role on these flights was to look after the crew and try to ensure the safety of the passengers, though I have to confess to not knowing how we would have coped with an on-board emergency.

Ground staff had to prepare the cabin for these unsophisticated devotees by removing comfortable seats for a more practical and serviceable type. Once on board the aircraft, no-one, save for the crew, used a toilet. The pilgrims urinated -- or worse -- just where they sat. Throughout the flight some hajis would start fires on the cabin floor of the aircraft to cook a meal or to boil water to wash their feet. Their food usually consisted of maggot-infested rats. I can honestly say that among hostesses I never encountered anyone anxious to crew a haj flight.

At embarkation time, staff had to wrestle large bundles from the pilgrims, an act that generated a great deal of fuss and noise at the foot of the aircraft steps. These sacks often contained ancestors' bones which the hajis had dug up to take to Mecca.

I well remember one new air hostess who flew with me on a haj operation. She had a "beehive" hairdo reminiscent of the sixties pop singer Dusty Springfield. Her hat was perched precariously on top of the beehive. At Jeddah, the terminal point for all haj aircraft feeding passengers to Mecca, she was checking the overhead storage bins when a large rat jumped out. Landing plumb in the middle of her beehive it got tangled up in her heavily back-combed coiffure. The poor girl became hysterical. It took three of us to hold her down while we conducted the tricky operation of removing one disease-ridden, but very lively and fat rat, from her hair. To repeat: These were not sought-after flights by air hostesses.

*

Another off-the-wall experience I recall involved a planeload of rowdy male students from Gothenburg. They were having the time of their lives fooling around and behaving in a fairly frisky manner. The main target was a very attractive air hostess who was being ogled as she served coffee. Caught off-guard, she accidently poured some of the contents of the coffee pot onto one young man's lap instead of his cup. Startled, he jumped to his feet and rushed to the galley. At that time I was conversing with the flight engineer, a lovely man whose diminutive stature was compensated by a great sense of humour. Unable to speak English the young man struggled with sign language to explain to us that he had suffered a traumatic experience in his nether regions. Hearing this, the flight engineer immediately broke into laughter. He turned to me and, in a broad West Country accent said. "I think he's scalded his todger!

By this time the young man had unbuttoned his flies and subjected his pride and joy to closer scrutiny. Quickly, I drew the galley curtain so the passengers couldn't see what was happening. Still laughing, but thinking on his feet, Des, the flight engineer, asked me for a bread roll and some butter. Within seconds he had wrapped the roll around the young man's penis and anchored it with an elastic band. Des steered the poor fellow back to his seat, "There you go lad, now you are the only man on this aircraft with a hot dog." Mustard was not applied.

I have no idea what the captain put in his voyage report about this incident.

*

From time to time I encountered a passenger who firmly believed rules were meant for everyone else. At every opportunity they took delight projecting their own importance. By deigning to mix with the hoi polloi they were somehow bringing a little sunshine into the lives of those less fortunate than themselves. Air hostesses indulged their vanity with some reluctance.

I chatted to one such lady on a very long flight who overwhelmed us with her loud demands and constant complaints. Her attention-seeking outbursts were designed to show everyone in the cabin the enormous sacrifice she was making by gracing us with her regal presence.

Obviously, she was more used to travelling First-class but, for reasons unknown, found herself on this one-class flight where all passengers were equal in everyone else's eyes except hers. A brief moment of welcome relief arrived when she took herself off to the toilet. However, she emerged moments later and walked back to her seat. I held my breath anticipating more aggravation ahead.

Then I noticed people were staring at her as she sashayed down the aisle. Some began to laugh out loud. Apart from a disapproving frown, she seemed to be otherwise unconcerned. After all, she was a class apart from everyone else.

"Madam, I regret to be the one to inform you that your skirt is hitched up at the back," a kind and helpful gentleman announced as she passed by his seat. "Furthermore," he continued, coolly and calmly, "you have dangling between your buttocks a very long piece of toilet paper. As a gentleman, I felt I had to tell you. But, as a member of the lower classes I don't believe it would be appropriate for me to help solve your problem."

Stunned, and stuck for words, madam remained silent for the remainder of the flight much to everyone's relief.

*

A few inconsiderate passengers came aboard prepared to fight for space for their carry-on baggage in the overhead containers. The more determined of these folk would even go so far as to remove fellow passengers' hand luggage to make room for their own.

Obviously such behaviour could result in unpleasant situations on board as I experienced on a packed flight from Rimini to Gatwick Airport. The passenger in question had shopped-till-he-dropped and had a great deal more carry-on luggage than he had on the outbound flight. Without a word to anyone, he removed a fellow passenger's luggage from the overhead bin and dumped it in the aisle. The owner of the displaced luggage, aware of what was happening, jumped up from his seat, and began to reverse the procedure. The confrontation morphed into a full-scale punch-up and the flight had to be delayed while the two protagonists were offloaded as instructed by the aircraft commander.

After their hand luggage had been stowed in the cargo hold, again at the behest of the captain, and an incident report raised, the two men were allowed to re-board. To ensure no further bad behaviour during the rest of the flight the men's passports were withheld until the aircraft touched down at Gatwick whereupon they were escorted off the aircraft by ground officials.

To a large extent these incidents had their origins during the onset of low-cost, prepaid, all-inclusive charter flights. The passengers attracted to these IT flights seemed to me to be a different breed of human beings, many losing all sense of propriety once they stepped on board an aircraft. Some of these antisocial acts, I am convinced, were a precursor to air rage we see today.

Many "packaged passengers" thought air hostesses were there solely to put their hand luggage in the overhead compartment for them. Not so. We always helped frail, elderly or disabled passengers of course, but for able-bodied men and women it was their own responsibility to stow their carry-on luggage and that hasn't changed.

*

Reclining seats were intended to increase passenger comfort and do so if used sensibly by everyone. But for those seated directly behind an insensitive passenger a journey can be anything but comfortable if the passenger in front suddenly presses the recline button. Back goes the seat and off goes the drinks, meal or laptop of the passenger seated behind.

It has to be said that restrictive seat pitches that accompany the aforesaid pre-paid, inclusive tour flights, requiring everyone to be packed in like sardines, offers the greatest danger particularly to long-legged individuals caught off-guard.

In my experience "serial recliners" never apologised for suddenly dropping their seat-back onto someone's meal tray. In fact they often feigned indignation making out it was the other poor fellow's fault his plastic chicken was killed for the second time in a day.

On one flight I worked on a long-legged man was pinned in his seat when an inconsiderate passenger violently reclined his seat-back as far as it would go with no thought for anyone save himself. When we went to the man's rescue the seat was firmly jammed under the poor man's chin totally disabling him. On the part of the violent recliner, there was no apology or any sign of remorse.

*

We will always have those folk who just love the sound of their own voice. Aboard aircraft, it is remarkable how these "talkaholics" always wind up sitting next to someone longing for a bit of peace and quiet. Faced with such situations there is little that cabin staff can do except offer alternative seating if available.

This brings to mind one long-haul flight and one lady who just wanted to chat, about nothing in particular, with the gentleman in the seat beside her. He, on the other hand, wished to be left in peace to work on his laptop or at least try to. Further along the cabin I had noticed a couple with a little girl who didn't want to sleep which offered me what I thought was a brilliant solution. I politely asked the little girl's father to swap seats with "Lady Chatterbox" for the remainder of the flight. Then I went to the talkaholic and asked her to help me solve a problem by sitting next to the mother with the little girl. I explained to her that the little girl's mother was pregnant and had to rest. Lady Chatterbox could help, I said, by keeping the little girl entertained.

She took the bait and my little scheme worked like a dream. Soon all were asleep save for the father and businessman who were both enjoying peace and quiet along with a few drinks from the bar.

This story had a happy outcome but it was not always so. I have known passengers to be trapped by talkaholics who prattle on incessantly even though their neighbour had fallen asleep hours before – or at least pretend to have done so.

*

Why is it, I often asked myself, that some parents are oblivious to their children's naughty behaviour like running up and down aircraft aisles to the annoyance of fellow passengers? At the same time, these kids obstruct hostesses trying to offer a cabin service.

Then there are the little imps who jump up and down on aircraft seats. Do they behave this way at home I wonder? And let's not forget the little darlings who lean over the back of their seat to confront and challenge the people in the row behind; or prod and poke the heads of passengers in the row in front all the while shrieking with laughter. Parents seem to ignore their little darlings' behaviour leaving fellow passengers to go home with an indelible memory of their hellish trip, and a bad impression of the airline, aircraft and crew.

Whilst it is true that children may need a lot of attention and flying can be quite boring for adults, let alone children, I feel parents should make some provision for entertaining their offspring and at least accept responsibility for their behaviour.

On numerous occasions I tried to tactfully intervene on behalf of a passenger who had reached the point of total surrender. I can't ever recall receiving a positive response from parents. However, such occasions brought to mind the words of the celebrated dog trainer, author, horse trainer and television personality Barbara Woodhouse who expertly trained some of the most difficult dogs and owners alike: "Clonk them and love them!" she would say. My sentiments exactly.

*

I can't recall the precise number of occasions I groaned inwardly when confronted by a passenger, obviously suffering from a heavy cold, who insisted on sharing his or her germs as he or she sneezed and spluttered all over me.

One disgusting man I can't forget, and God knows I've tried hard enough, had a continuous runny nose that constantly dripped onto his shirt and everywhere else. It was not a pleasant sight. Out of concern for other passengers I prayed he would not have cause to shake his head. I also noted, however, that passengers within range had tissues at hand ready to take evasive action in case someone hollered "incoming!"

Rushing away for two seconds from what could quickly turn into an on-board crime scene, I grabbed a box of tissues for our runny-nosed guest and delivered it along with a few words of sympathy. Pulling out a tissue, he proceeded to blow his exceedingly snotty nose and, with a misguided sense of duty, handed back to me one soggy, mucous-filled tissue. I cringed but remained calm as I plucked a sick bag from the seat pocket in front of him. "You might like to drop your used tissues in here," I suggested, with a smile, "for the sake of hygiene," I added with a further, more insistent, smile. He looked at me as though I'd just arrived from another planet. I judged it time to beat a retreat.

*

American singer Jill Scott once said, "I like a man who smells good. Puts on cologne; lotions his body. It keeps me wanting. I like feeling that way".

I don't think Ms Scott would have wished to change places with me on many of my flights sharing a confined space with people totally unaware of the need to observe personal hygiene. She most definitely would have been kept "wanting". Over time, I discovered that a surprisingly large number of travellers don't even use deodorants and some, I decided, were also allergic to soap and water.

In the course of a flight there's no escaping someone with bad body odour. Pressurisation and restricted space dictate we all have to share the same air and it can be unpleasant and embarrassing facing the pungent aroma of stale sweat, body odours of the most personal kind - and musty clothes.

I recall one passenger who said he always carried a car air-freshener disc with him. If the need arose he would hang it between his seat and the offender's seat. I thought it was a good idea that could be taken a step further by issuing every passenger with an air-freshener disc to hang around their neck.

Some time back when discussing this with hubby Bill, he recounted a number of occasions piloting cargo flights full of caged monkeys to Warsaw. Each flight had around two hundred monkeys travelling under the care of one male flight attendant who also had to cater for the crew's needs.

It is not difficult to imagine the appalling smell caused by two hundred urinating primates and the pungent river of urine swilling around the floor of the aircraft on protective plastic sheets. Bill reminded me how monkeys on one flight had collaborated by pooling their intelligence to break free from their cages. On arrival at Warsaw airport handlers spent four hours rounding them up; they were having a whale of a time swinging around in the rear of the aircraft. Of course the aircraft had to be cleaned and fumigated before it was fit for duty.

I had the same problem with Bill. Back home he had to strip off on the doormat. His uniform and everything else he was wearing had to be thoroughly cleaned and laundered. These kind of obnoxious, even toxic, smells stick to clothing in the same way that body odours cause offense to passengers and crews. The only people oblivious to their problem are the offenders.

Sorry to say, again, that the onset of low-price, all-inclusive charter flights hastened a rise in such instances along with the dreaded football fan who was often drunk and reeked of stale beer on top of everything else. Air hostesses hated working these flights but stayed the course for the sake of all the other passengers on board.

I have to say the dress code for modern-day travellers, which is euphemistically described as "casual", is at complete odds with the golden years of flying when passengers dressed up for the occasion. We saw an entirely different class of passenger. By this I do not mean to offend anyone but, to my mind, life has become more insouciant, more laid-back, and standards have dropped alarmingly. Nowadays, "casual" dress means anything goes from flip-flops to shorts or jeans with "designer holes" and ragged edges, paired with scruffy, message-laden T-shirts. Today, there is a complete absence of a delicate fragrance pervading the cabin milieu because of the overpowering presence of England's secret weapon: B.O!

To illustrate this using the experience of an unfortunate passenger I present as evidence this priceless letter written by a young lady called Mun Lee following a harrowing flight from Singapore to Australia. She suffered from being kicked in the back of her seat by an inconsiderate male who also insisted on presenting his smelly feet a bit too close for Mun Yee's comfort. She found herself dealing with the seatmate from hell.

Dear passenger 15A, you ruined my flight!

My nose was assaulted by a putrid smell of death and decay. You do not know me but I was seated in front of you during the flight from Singapore to Sydney on April 12th.

What I initially thought to be a routine flight turned out to be a once in a lifetime experience...and it was all because of you.

I am writing this letter to thank you personally.

Being the cheapskate that I am. I did not pay extra for a seat next to an emergency exit!

Though it offered more leg room I couldn't be bothered to read the special safety procedures. The last thing that I would want is to compromise the lives of all the innocent passengers because I do not know how to open the aircraft door.

Despite my common economy seat, you offered me a full back massage by repeatedly kicking the back of my chair. To date I have yet to regain full mobility of the lower half of my body. But being single I suppose I don't have much use for it anyway.

I didn't pay for the in-flight entertainment package and I was worried that I might get bored. But my concerns were unnecessary. You were talking so loudly, as if your friend was seated in the cargo hold, rather than right next to you. Perhaps she is hard of hearing? This might strike you as odd, but for the first time in my life, I wished that I had a hearing impairment too.

Also could you tell me where you bought those obnoxious snacks? I assume that they must have been delicious, because you ripped one open every 30 minutes.

Thanks for the loud rustling and ambient chewing sounds.

At this point I thought it can't get any better than this. But what I had meant as a rhetorical question, you took as a challenge.

For immediately, my nose was assaulted by a putrid smell of death and decay. The stench was so strong that I turned to check if the old lady seated next to me was still breathing.

It was so nice of you to take off your shoes and put your feet between my seat and the plane window. It must have taken considerable effort. It was a small space, but you stuck it as close to my face as you possibly could.

Your kindness moves me.

The sun is rising above the horizon, the sky is bleeding crimson and gold. But I cannot turn to gaze at this everyday miracle because every time I do I smell the anus of Satan.

I have half a mind to pull down the oxygen mask above me. But then I remembered that I was flying on a budget airline, so I probably would have to pay extra for that.

Did you know that you have made me a more religious person? I have said more prayers in that eight hour flight than I have in my entire life.

I was torn between asking God for strength to endure the rest of the journey, and SWEET GUAN YIN MA...TAKE ME HOME!

The experience has been so memorable that I am writing this from my therapist's office. I have also signed up for ten more sessions to talk about it.

Thank you once again.

Insincerely yours,

Passenger 14A

Please upgrade your flash plug-in.

My reaction to the letter, at the time and even now, was God bless Ms Mun Lee for succinctly putting into writing one of a number of grievances I hold about inconsiderate passengers.

*

Leaving aside bad smells for a moment, kindly permit me to introduce you to some passengers I have encountered and concluded to be suffering from "generalised oblivious disorder" or "GOD."

Cabin staff sometimes encountered passengers who thought cabin aisles were there solely for their convenience and no-one else's. Faced with such situations, I would try a soft approach: "Excuse me, would you please be kind enough to step out of the aisle to allow other passengers to pass?"

What I really wanted to say was, "Here's how it plays out pal: See that queue of people stretching from the door? They aren't admiring you; they can't get past you because you're hogging the aisle. Please take your seat and wait until you leave the aircraft before practising your *tai chi* or getting into the lotus position on the floor of the aircraft."

Then there are those who habitually ignore the captain's request to turn-off electronic devices that could interfere with navigation. Cabin staff know the commander's request is being ignored because we can see activity on mobile phones or iPods by passengers still wearing headphones. They don't even have the good manners to remove their headphones when you speak to them, which is particularly irritating because they tend to respond in a very loud voice that can be heard throughout the entire cabin.

Also annoying to cabin staff are those passengers who, prior to take-off, insist in talking loudly during the safety demonstration. I recall one hostess who, out of sheer frustration, tersely expressed her feelings by directly addressing one of these loud-mouthed travellers in a voice that could cut glass: "Thank you sir for keeping the entire cabin posted on the latest trends on how to pull a bird – undoubtedly that is more relevant to you than HOW THE HELL TO GET OUT OF HERE IF SOMETHING GOES WRONG!"

Another inappropriate form of "in-flight entertainment" is gratuitously offered to passengers by the occasional flasher. He normally positions himself in the toilets nearest to the galley. From there he can periodically reveal himself by dropping his trousers around his ankles hoping to be confronted by the hostess with the "mostess!" Equally annoying is the serial groper who, given half a chance, will pinch the girls' bottoms, and any other part of their anatomy that comes within nipping range. These bottom-pinchers are usual drunken football supporters so cabin staff are often pre-warned and able to prepare for any impending assault.

Sad to say that most travellers at one time or another have had the misfortune to sit beside an unruly or inconsiderate passenger and, consequently, can readily relate to what cabin crews endure on a daily basis.

At such times we looked to our training to handle all manner of situations in a fair and proper manner. We never forgot for one moment that we represented the company that employed us. We knew we were front-line staff and, irrespective of our personal feelings, were obliged to act professionally at all times.

I can illustrate this by relating an incident that took place on an American airline. This air hostess is a perfect example of how to handle a very tricky situation.

It all began when a passenger in her early fifties boarded the aircraft and walked down the aisle to her assigned seat. As she approached her seat row she noted, with unconcealed alarm, she would be seated next to a black man whom she assumed to be of African origin. Demonstratively unhappy with the prospect, and visibly furious at being placed in such an untenable position, she summoned the nearest hostess.

"Is everything alright madam?" the air hostess enquired politely.

"Can't you see?" the lady responded, pointing her finger, "I have been given a seat next to a black man. I can't sit there, next to him. You must change my seat." By now she had worked up a head of steam and was becoming quite emotional.

"Please calm down madam. Unfortunately all seats are occupied, but I will double-check and see what can be done."

Moments later the hostess returned: "Madam, as I said before there isn't an empty seat in Economy-class. This has also been confirmed by the captain. We have only one seat available on the aircraft and that's in First-class." Smiling, the hostess turned to the gentleman and said, "Sir, would you please be kind enough to retrieve your hand luggage from the overhead compartment and follow me. We are moving you to First-class."

Many of the passenger on board, especially those close to the action, were tuned into the entire conversation between the air hostess and the disgruntled passenger. As the hostess led the gentleman to the front of the aircraft everyone stood and applauded. Meanwhile, the poor man at the centre of the dispute had yet to utter a single word. I salute that hostess for displaying great tact and diplomacy in solving a potentially explosive situation.

It has to be said that passengers often have a point to make not necessarily against the cabin staff, though that happens, but against the airline for a number of reasons such as being seated next to someone who is obese, or next to a smelly toilet, or just taken for a ride.

Air transport today is all about cutting services to a bare minimum in the search for profitability, a fact reflected in every aspect of on-board service. Even aircraft seats are narrow of gauge and pitch in order to squeeze in another row or two.

Whenever I fly as a passenger I can't help but notice how cramped seating has become and, unlike many of today's travellers, I am not obese. Finding comfort today in a bulk-standard aircraft seat in a world of increasing obesity is a challenge both for the morbidly obese and anyone unfortunate enough to be seated alongside an overweight passenger. The unseemly struggle by both parties to protect their territory reflects a failure by airlines to address the root cause of the problem.

In some instances even seat belt extensions are insufficient to ensure overweight passengers are properly strapped-in for take-off and landing. Logic suggests such travellers purchase two seats, but that brings forth the argument that one passenger has to pay twice as much as another.

Thrown open for discussion on website Debate.org, some time back, respondents to the question "should obese people pay for two airline seats?" voted 83% in favour and 17% against. Here are a few comments for and against:

- Fat people should pay more: Obese people should lose weight or pay more. It's not fair if we have to sit there slouched over because they are too obese. It's not our fault that they are just that big, so why do they pay the same amount? Everybody should stand up and say they [obese people] need to pay more;
- Let's do the maths: What is heavier for the airplane to carry, A 400 pound man or a 170 pound man? Why must we pay absurd amounts for excess weight for luggage whereas everyone pays the same price independently from their own weight? It's an outrage to both other people's comfort and other people's pocket;

- Obesity is a choice plain and simple: Unless obese people can give a reasonable explanation to why they're fat (like a generic disorder) they don't really have an excuse. Maybe they should have thought about the expensive airline tickets when they were stuffing themselves with pies and cakes. The airline shouldn't be expected to hand out free seats to people and lose their own revenue;

- It is humiliating to make an obese person pay for two seats: I think it is so sad to make an obese person pay for two airline seats. They are most certainly already embarrassed and to make them take up two seats is inhumane. Airlines should make more of an effort to offer larger seats. It would provide comfort to smaller people and allow bigger people to easily fit;

- No, no, no, no, this is pure discrimination: It's embarrassing enough please don't do that to us. I would love to be skinny but can't I've tried every way possible. I think the airlines should do something like providing bigger seats they make enough money out of us. I am sick of thin people thinking they are better than us!

There is no doubt that many morbidly obese travellers seem oblivious to their own problem which is more than can be said about the unfortunate passengers dealing with an unwelcome "overflow" of body mass. In some cases it leads to extreme frustration and discomfort as illustrated in this letter written by a passenger of Jetstar Airways, an Australian low-cost airline headquartered in Melbourne:

Dear Jetstar,

Do you like riddles? I do and that is why I'm starting this letter with one. What weighs more than a Suzuki Swift, less than a Hummer and smells like the decaying anus of a deceased homeless man? No idea? How about what measures food portions in kg and has the personal hygiene of a French prostitute? Still nothing? Right, one more try. What is as fat as fuck, stinks like shit and should be forced to purchase two seats on a Jetstar flight? That is right! It's the man I sat next to on my flight from Perth to Sydney yesterday.

As I boarded the plane I mentally high-fived myself for paying the additional $25 for an emergency seat. I was imagining all that extra room, when I was suddenly distracted by what appeared to be an infant hippopotamus located halfway down the aisle. As I got closer I was relieved to see that it wasn't a dangerous semi-aquatic mammal, but a morbidly obese human being. However this relief was short lived when I realised that my seat was located somewhere underneath him.

Some time after I managed to burrow into my seat I caught what was to be the first fetid whiffs of body odour. His scent possessed hints of blue cheese and Mumbai slum, with nuances of sweaty flesh and human faeces sprayed with cologne. Considering I was visibly under duress I found it strange that none of the cabin crew offered me another seat. To be fair it is entirely possible that none of them actually saw me.

Pinned to my seat by a fleshy boulder I started preparing for a 127 Hours-like escape. Thankfully though the beast moved slightly to his left, which allowed me to stand up, walk to the back of the plane and politely ask the cabin crew to seat me somewhere else. I didn't catch the names of the three Flight Attendants, but for the purpose of this letter, I will call them……Chatty 1, Chatty 2 and Giggly. (I've given them all the same surname of "Couldn't-give-a-shit". After my request Chatty 1 and 2 continued their conversation, and Giggly…well she just giggled. I then asked if I could sit in one of the six vacant seats at the back of the aircraft, to which Giggly responded. "He…he…he…they are for the crew only, he…he…he…" I think Giggly may be suffering from some sort of mental impairment.

I tried to re-locate myself without the assistance of the "Couldn't-give-a-shit" triplets, but unfortunately everyone with a row to themselves had stretched out and was lying down. It was then that I realised that my fate was sealed. I made my way back to Jabba the Hutt and spent the remainder of the flight smothered in side-boob and cellulite, and taking shallow breaths to avoid noxious gas poisoning.

Just before landing I revisited the back of the plane to use the toilet. You can imagine my surprise when I saw both "crew only" rows occupied by non-crew members. I can only assume that Giggly let them sit there after she forgot who she was and why she's flying on a big shiny metal thing in the sky.

Imagine going out for dinner and a movie, only to have your night ruined by a fat mess who eats half your meal then blocks 50% of the movie screen. Isn't that exactly the same as having someone who can't control their calorie intake occupying half your seat on a flight? Of course it is, and so that's why I am demanding a full refund of my ticket including $25 for the emergency row seat.

I am also looking to be compensated for the physical pain and mental suffering caused by being enveloped in human blubber for four hours. My lower back is in agony, and I had to type this letter one-handed as I am yet to regain full use of my left side. If I don't recover completely I will have to say goodbye to my life-long dream of becoming Air Guitar World Champion. If that occurs then you will pay.

No regards.......Rich Wiskin

However dreadful this letter reads in relation to the finer feelings of the overweight passenger, it is indisputable that he caused undue distress to another passenger with his overbearing presence. It should not have been allowed to happen. Clearly every member of that cabin crew was useless...and totally insensitive which is another sad reflection on a lot of today's flight attendants who seem more inclined to talk among themselves than take care of passengers. I wonder what kind of training they received, if any.

And, in the context of aircraft safety, we have to ask what would have happened had the flight experienced an in-flight emergency. The overweight passenger was taking up half of the other passenger's seat. The occupant was pinned down and semi-crushed. And both passengers were occupying seats adjacent to an emergency exit.

This could and should have been handled differently. There were plenty of spare seats as passengers were able to stretch out in empty seats (thanks to Giggly). The semi-crushed passenger could have been relocated to one of those. A better solution, however, would be for the obese passenger to be relocated because he was seated in an emergency row and may have been unable to activate the emergency door if the need arose. Any flight attendant with even the tiniest amount of intelligence should have seen that. With a switch of seats, the obese passenger would not have offended his neighbour and would not have been the centre of a horrendous string of complaints. Surely it is time airlines took obesity seriously.

Difficult situations arise on many flights and cabin crew, as airline ambassadors and "first respondents", have a responsibility to deal tactfully with whatever arises on their watch. That's how it was in the golden days of flying so why not now?

This complaint letter sent to Continental Airlines illustrates a typical disconnect between airlines and fare-paying passengers flying today. Yet another case of an airline squeezing in more seats in its quest for greater profit and, in the process, downgrading the comfort and wellbeing of the poor punter who, in this case, drew seat 29E.

Dear Continental Airlines,

I am disgusted as I write this letter to you about the miserable experience I am having sitting in the seat 29E on one of your aircraft. As you may know this seat is situated directly across from the lavatory, so close in fact that I can reach out my left arm and touch the door.

All my senses are being tortured simultaneously. It's difficult to say what the worst part of sitting in seat 29E really is. Is it the stench of the sanitation fluid that is blown all over my body every 60 seconds when the door opens? Is it the whoosh of the constant flushing? Or is it the passengers' arses that seem to fit into my personal space like a pornographic jigsaw puzzle. I constructed a stink shield by shoving one end of a blanket into the overhead compartment – while effectively blocking at least some of the smell, and offering a small amount of privacy, the arse-on-my-body factor has increased, as without my evil glare passengers feel free to lean up against what they think is some sort of blanketed wall. The next arse that touches my shoulder will be the last!

Putting a seat here was a very bad idea. This sucks! Worse yet is I've paid over $400 for the honour of sitting in this seat.

I am picturing a boardroom full of executives, giving props to the young, promising engineer that figured out how to squeeze an additional row of seats onto this plane by putting them next to the lavatory.

I would like to flush his head in the toilet that I am close enough to touch, and taste, from my seat.

Does your company give refunds? I'd like to go back where I came from and start over. Seat 29E could only be worse if it was located in the bathroom.

I wonder if my clothing will retain the sanitizing odour ...what about my hair?

I feel like I'm bathing in a toilet bowl of blue liquid, and there is no man in a little boat to save me. I am filled with deep hatred for your plane designer, and a general dis-ease that will last for hours.

We are finally descending and soon I will be able to tear down the stink shelf, but the scars will remain.

I suggest that you initiate immediate removal of this seat from all of your aircraft. Just move it and leave the smouldering brown hole empty. A good place for sturdy, non-absorbing luggage maybe....but not human cargo.

Thanks Continental Airways!

Unfortunately that is the sorry state of modern-day flying. It seems that everything that once made flying a wonderful experience has gone down the pan.

One more example of disconnect or miscommunication between the airline and passengers was highlighted in a letter from a passenger who just wanted to go from A to B but found himself on a bit of a mystery tour. Again, not an unfamiliar experience in today's world of air transport. This highlights a lack of communication between crew and passengers. Unlike many letters filled with rage and woe, this one is amusing but, at the same time, presses all the right buttons. It was addressed to Leeward Islands Air Transport (LIAT) a small airline that serves some twenty or so destinations in the Caribbean. The complaint was found by another airline CEO to be so funny that he tweeted it to his three million followers.

Dear LIAT,

May I say how considerate it is of you to enable your passengers such an in-depth and thorough tour of the Caribbean.

Most other airlines I have travelled on would simply wish to take me from point A to B in rather a hurry. I was intrigued that we were allowed to stop at not a lowly one or two, but a magnificent six airports yesterday. And who wants to fly on the same airplane the entire time? We got to change and refuel every step of the way.

I particularly enjoyed sampling the security scanners at each and every airport. I find it preposterous that people imagine them to be all the same. And as for being patted down by a variety of islanders, well I feel as though I have been hugged by most of the Caribbean already. I also found it unique that this was all done on "island time", because I do like to have time to absorb the atmosphere of the various departure lounges. As for our arrival, well, who wants to have to take a ferry at the end of all that flying anyway? I'm glad the boat had long gone by the time we arrived into Tortola last night...and that all those noisy bars and restaurants were closed.

So thank you LIAT. I now truly understand why you are the Caribbean Airline.

PS You can keep the bag...I never liked it anyway!

So, dear reader, as far as in-flight obesity, "toilet" seats and mystery tours are concerned, we still have a long way to go in the air transport industry.

*

Today's airline passengers seem more prone to bad behaviour on board aircraft (and other forms of transport) than during what I unashamedly keep referring to as the golden years of flying. I stick to my view that the introduction of low-cost, all-inclusive package tours brought forth a different kind of traveller whose on-board "crimes" range from inappropriate comments or touching of cabin staff, to fighting for space in overhead containers, to full-on air rage.

By comparison Premium passengers, apart from the occasional drunken movie star or spaced-out rock idol, are a pretty docile bunch.

I well remember several incidents analogous to passengers and their ill-mannered behaviour. On one occasion aboard a Bristol

Britannia aircraft flight out of London-Stansted Airport bound for the Far East one of my colleagues was assaulted.

This particular flight, bound for Hong Kong, was a blocked-off charter for Britain's Ministry of Defence carrying service personnel and their families. As mentioned previously, we referred to these flights as "trooping flights".

I was walking down the cabin making sure seat belts were fastened before take-off. Across the aisle from me, my colleague Adrianne was doing the same thing. A soldier seated in a widow seat pretended to have difficulty with his seat belt and as Adrianne stretched across two seats to see what the problem was the squaddie grabbed her and tried to kiss her. Simultaneously, the soldier in the seat across the aisle slid his hand up her skirt. She was surrounded, outmanoeuvred and outgunned.

After wrestling free from the squaddie who'd tried to kiss her, Adrianne swung around and dealt the other soldier a hearty slap across the face.

She was disciplined for her actions. Regardless of the soldier's outrageous behaviour, Adrianne was punished because one must never behave that way with a passenger – even if he has a hand up one's skirt. I thought it was disgraceful on the company's part. It was reported because the senior military officer on board filed a report with the ministry. Both soldiers were reported and the incident caused a delay to the flight so the matter was brought to the company's attention.

On another occasion, a flight I would characterise as a "football supporters special", two passengers on the return flight began to argue about the football match they had just attended. The argument turned into a fist fight that was observed by a number of fellow passengers some of whom intervened to make sure it didn't get totally out of hand. We separated the warring factions to different ends of the "pitch" – one at the rear of the aircraft, the other at the front. We red-carded both of them by refusing to serve any alcohol and found a couple of strong men to sit by each one for the rest of the flight.

On another flight from Gatwick I noticed a young man who was particularly quiet. In fact he looked ill to me. As I made a final check of seat belts prior to take-off I paused to see if he was alright. Sweating profusely and shaking like a leaf he said, "I survived an air crash some time ago and this is the first time I've flown since the accident."

I persuaded the passenger next to him to move to another seat and I sat with the young man for take-off. Strictly speaking he should have forewarned the ground staff before boarding the aircraft because he could have reacted differently and caused serious problems on board. The captain was alerted to the incident and I found a kind and understanding passenger to sit next to the young man to keep him company and busy in conversation for the short flight to Jersey.

Sometimes schoolchildren behaved unpredictably often catching us by surprise. I was working a flight from Venice with schoolkids who'd been on an educational cruise with a few teachers. Two weeks previously, they had flown from Gatwick to Venice to board the cruise ship and were now returning home. On the flight back to Gatwick we noticed a great deal of fumbling – even worse -- going on beneath blankets making me think it was the cabin crew that were getting the education. Later, I understand someone conducted a survey and discovered there'd been a sudden spike in teen pregnancies – obviously not an intended part of the educational content of the tour.

I worked on a BAC 1-11 aircraft full of happy holidaymakers returning to Gatwick from Rimini. Every single one of them had picked up a bug at their hotel and were suffering from acute diarrhoea. Believe me when I say the toilets were in overdrive.

On checking one of the toilets I discovered someone had jettisoned a pair of what Cockney folk would call "cor blimey bloomers", the subject of an unfortunate, diarrhoea-linked accident. A vain attempt had been made to rinse them out in the wash basin. It became my dubious pleasure to walk the aisle from seat to seat to find the lucky owner. There were no takers as you may have already guessed. No-one had the courage to own up.

Then there's the story of Maureen one of my colleagues known for her bright ginger hair and vile temper to match. I recall she married one of our line captains and, during their civic wedding, they argued back and forth all the way down the aisle to everyone's astonishment. She was with me on a flight where we were unfortunate to have on board the passenger from hell. Nothing was right for this woman; she tried the patience of the entire crew and many of the passengers.

As she disembarked from the aircraft she turned to Maureen and, inches from her face, shouted, "All air hostesses are cows!" To her everlasting credit Maureen remained calm, venting her anger only after the woman had left the aircraft.

As luck would have it, or was it Sod's Law, two weeks later Maureen and I were on the same trip. While boarding passengers at Rimini who should we see but "the passenger from hell". My heart skipped a beat.

Maureen had also spotted the woman clambering up the aircraft steps. She rushed out to stand at the top of the steps to greet her. As they came face to face, Maureen, grinning, screamed at the top of her voice "Moooo!"

*

I remember a Mr and Mrs Churton an elderly couple travelling with a tour group. They were a delightful elderly pair who had spent years in India before retiring to Kent. As they came on board the aircraft, Mr Churton's braces broke and his trousers dropped around his ankles before anyone could help. I had to walk behind him holding up his trousers until we found seats for him and his wife. I then went to pick up some very large nappy pins from the first aid bag to see him through to his hotel with no further accidents.

His wife was such a pretty little lady with a lovely smile. It was obvious that life for them was not as it was in India where they had servants to fall back on. Mrs Churton was clutching a medium sized basket with a cover. I suggested she let me put it in the hand luggage compartment above her seat for the flight, but she absolutely refused. Instead she sat with the basket firmly on her lap, leaving little room for herself. I began to wonder what was in the basket as it was obviously important to Mrs Churton. I asked her outright. "You seem reluctant to part with your basket madam. May I ask why?" To my alarm she replied "Freddie will be upset if he can't sit on my knee."

I tried to explain that we could not allow livestock in the cabin of the aircraft. "Indeed madam it could prove difficult taking Freddie abroad with you without the proper documentation," I informed her. Still she insisted, in fact she mentioned that Freddie had been everywhere with them since returning from India many years ago. Apparently they were inseparable. I couldn't imagine what was in that basket. "Madam would you mind if I took a look at Freddie?" I asked gently. With delight she took off the lid of the basket to reveal Freddie to be her pet miniature Yorkshire terrier that had died years ago and been stuffed. Looking rather moth-eaten, Freddie glared at me with beady black eyes. I think he had an Al Capone leer on his chops.

Words for once failed me. I just smiled at Mrs Churton before consulting with the captain. Somehow we had to prise Freddie away from the lady so that she could do up her seat belt for take-off. The captain thought it all hilarious. Leaving his seat he donned his cap and came to have a word with the old couple.

"Do you think Freddie might like to sit on the flight deck for take-off and landing," the captain asked. "We don't ask everybody," he added. Mr and Mrs Churton were thrilled and said Freddie would be delighted to be the guest of the Captain. Freddie was stowed on the jump seat on the flight deck, and another day was saved.

Observations from inside the cabin

Here are a few excerpts from a book written by Elliot Hester flight attendant, magazine writer and former Salon.com travel columnist. He writes "Out of the Blue", a syndicated travel column carried by the San Francisco Chronicle, The Dallas Morning News, The Sun-Sentinel, New York Newsday and other daily newspapers. He lives in Miami Beach, Florida.

The write-up states...*Charm, youthfulness, and a fine sense of the absurd. In this day of air rage, nothing could be a more timely tonic than Elliot Hester's captivating observations from inside the cabin.*

MANCHESTER, ENGLAND. OCT 5th...COUPLE CHARGED AFTER IN-FLIGHT SEXCAPADE

Two British business class passengers were arrested after an alleged drunken sex session aboard a flight from the United States, press reports said yesterday.

A forty year old man and a thirty-seven year old woman were arrested at Manchester Airport on Saturday after the pilot of their American Airlines flight from Dallas radioed ahead to complain about their behaviour.

Witnesses said that the pair were strangers when they checked in for the ten hour flight but got friendly after making the most of the free drinks on board.

At first huddling under a blanket, the couple allegedly later threw caution to the wind and ignored pleas from the other passengers and cabin crew to halt their sex session.

The pair, both married, have been charged with outraging public decency, being drunk on board an aircraft and with an offence under the new "air-rage" laws for conduct causing harassment, alarm or distress. They are to appear in court in November.

Re-printed with permission of Agence France-Presse, 1999

I read another version of the same incident described in the book when the captain interrupted them by shouting "This is not a shag-house!"

BRANSON INVITES VIRGIN TRAVELLERS TO JOIN MILE HIGH CLUB

London June 8th (London Daily Telegraph.).....Paul Marston.

Air travellers are to be offered private double beds, along with legitimate membership of "The Mile-High Club" by Virgin Atlantic.

Virgin intends to install up to ten full-sized double beds in private "cabins" separated from other passengers by screens.

Steve Ridgway, the airline's managing director, said there would be no requirement to produce marriage certificates, and no bar on couples of the same sex.

Return fares between London and New York would be about £6,600 per twosome, the same as two individual business class tickets.

He did not think that the noise of love-making would be a nuisance for other passengers because there would be "quite a lot of ambient aircraft sound." Richard Branson the airline's chairman, who launched the facility at Behr, said...You can do it on the cruise ships. You can do it at home. Why not on planes? He said occupants would not be disturbed by prying cabin crew.

The more serious focus of £37 million revamp of Virgin's Premium Class is a new seat that becomes a single bed.

This will be introduced from September, three months before British Airways hopes to start a similar product.

Virgin also displayed a new aircraft livery with union flag wingtips and the legend "Britain's flag carrier" beneath a billowing standard on the fuselage side.

Richard Branson said that prior knowledge of his new design had "panicked" British Airways into its weekend announcement of the restoration of the flag to most of its fleet at the expense of its much criticised ethnic art tailfins.

The Telegraph Group Limited, 1999.

*

GROWLING WOMAN TIED TO SEAT

MISSISSAUGA, Ontario, Sept. 13th (Edmonton Sun)

A woman on a Paris-Toronto flight got down on all fours...growling like a dog...at fellow passengers before biting and punching three flight attendants, police say.

"She was crawling in the aisle, growling at passengers and kicking in the air," said Peel Regional Police Inspector, John Byrne.

Police arrested a woman when the Air Canada flight landed at Toronto's Pearson airport at 2pm Monday.

Staff on the flight noticed a woman drinking cognac from a bottle in her carry-on luggage, Byrne said.

About half-way through the eight hour flight the woman started yelling and annoying fellow passengers, then struck a 37 year old flight attendant on the arm, Byrne said.

She then returned to her seat and began an unprovoked attack on the male passenger seated next to her.

When flight staff tried to calm her down she threw newspapers and magazines around the cabin and crawled up the aisle, growling at passengers, he said.

She was tied to her seat, but not before she hit another flight attendant in the face, bit the finger of a 51-year-old male steward and grabbed another flight attendant by the throat.

Finally staff tied her arms and legs to her seat for the remaining two hours of the flight. Cops boarded the plane on arrival and arrested the woman.

Sylvaine Marie Martin-Kostajnsek, 44, a Canadian living in Paris, faces numerous charges including aggravated assault.

The police said the woman is a composer who was flying to Toronto as part of a month long residency at Gibraltar Point Centre for the Arts. Her flight was paid for through a $1,000 travel grant by the Canada Arts Council.

...reprinted with permission of Sun Media Corporation, Toronto, Ontario. 2000.

*

AIR HOSTESS ATTACKED BY WOMAN SMOKER

MANCHESTER, ENGLAND May 20th (London Sunday Times)....Russell Jenkins

A woman who was asked to stop smoking in a lavatory of an aircraft, allegedly head-butted a stewardess during a transatlantic holiday flight.

The woman, understood to have been travelling with her child, is said to have gone "berserk" on the Airtours flight from Florida to Manchester when the request was made. The pilot had to abort his landing and go into a holding pattern when the woman broke free from the cubicle where she was being restrained, and ran along the gangway. She was said to have been grappled to the ground by cabin crew with the help of two passengers.

The stewardess who was allegedly attacked, Vanessa Martinez, was taken to hospital for treatment to her injuries, which included a suspected broken nose.

The pilot made a radio call to alert the authorities at Manchester International Airport. A 26 year old woman was arrested after the aircraft landed.

Times Newspapers Limited. 20th May, 2000.

*

CONTROLLING AIR RAGE THE MEDIEVAL WAY

LONDON, June 2nd (Deutsche Presse-Agentur)

Airlines are testing a body restraint device much like the medieval torture instrument that would pin those succumbing to air rage to their seats, the Times has reported.

Former Police Sergeant, Roger Fuller, has developed a body restraint package which was being tested by a dozen airlines, including British Airways, the newspaper said on Wednesday.

It is designed to be thrown around the head and shoulders of air rage culprits and consists of an upper body restraint, handcuffs and a waist restraint belt and lower arm and leg restraints.

The upper body restraint...a large metal bar with a d-shaped strap, is swung over the back of the passenger's seat and looped just under the arms, and below the chest area.

Then it is pulled tight to prevent the offender from moving. The waist restraint, handcuffs and leg restraints can then be slipped on for full security.

At present, air crews are limited to handcuffs or make-shift rope and cargo straps, when dealing with disruptive passengers.

There has been a marked increase in air-rage incidents in recent months, with passengers on trans-Atlantic flights regularly succumbing to the effects of alcohol, jet lag and indifferent airline service.

Reprinted with permission of dpa, Deutsche Presse-Agentur GmbH, 2000

*

MAN TRIES TO OPEN AIRPLANE EXIT

AMSTERDAM, Netherlands, May 10th, Associated Press

A passenger on board a KLM flight from Amsterdam to Newark, spat on a flight attendant, threatened passengers with a cane and tried to open the emergency exit while in flight, an official said Thursday.

The 28 year old Dutchman, whom KLM spokesman Hugo Baas described as "clearly unstable," ignored orders from flight crew to turn off his mobile phone.

He ripped up his passport and threatened to hit passengers and flight attendants. He then took a seat in business class claiming to suffer from claustrophobia.

"At 37,000 feet he decided it was time to go, and tried to open the emergency exit." Baas said. However, due to the cabin pressure, it was impossible to open the aircraft's emergency door.

141

Eventually the man was handcuffed by the Captain, and guarded by two passengers for the rest of the flight, Baas said.

Upon arrival in the United States, the man was put on the next flight back to the Netherlands under the supervision of two security guards.

He was arrested at Amsterdam's Schiphol Airport, and will face charges of attempting to endanger the lives of passengers, the spokesman said.

Reprinted with permission of the Associated Press, 2001.

*

AIR STEWARD SAVES HEART ATTACK VICTIM, 83.

LONDON Dec. 6th (London Independent) ...Andrew Mullins

A tenacious senior air steward described yesterday how he saved the life of an 83 year old grandmother after two brain surgeons considered giving up the battle to save her.

British Airways purser Marc Harding refused to give up on Pittmanne Japal from Mauritius after she suffered a heart attack during a family trip to Florida on Friday.

Mr Harding rushed to the scene to find two neurosurgeons, heading for a convention, tending to the patient. "There was no breathing, there was no pulse," The purser said.

He began giving artificial respiration as the two doctors, one Irish, one Norwegian, massaged her heart. But after several minutes there was no response. "One of the doctors said...let's stop and evaluate this," then he said "I don't think there is much more that we can do," Mr Harding explained.

Using the cabin's defibrillator, which sends surges of electricity through the chest, he tried to re-start Mrs Japal's heart. Mr Harding said, "There was an amazing jolt though her body, and all of a sudden she groaned, and started breathing again, and her arms and legs twitched. I was in awe.

Reprinted with permission of Independent Newspapers (UK) 1999.

*

SEX AID GIVES FLIGHT A SHAKY START

LONDON, April 20th (London Evening Standard)

A pilot made an emergency landing when a suspect device was detected on a jet packed with holiday makers. But the threat turned out to be a sex aid vibrator.

The A-300 Monarch Airbus was two hours into the flight from Goa when the air crew became suspicious about a piece of hand luggage. The pilot, Captain Dave Johnson, radioed a bomb alert and was ordered to divert to Bombay.

The plane, carrying British based passengers and crew, was taken to an isolated handling bay where 369 people were evacuated.

142

Bomb disposal experts boarded the plane and examined the suspect baggage, and identified the device as a battery powered sex vibrator.

A Monarch-Air spokeswoman applauded Captain Johnson's actions. "We are looking into the incident to find out how it got on board," she said.

The passengers later continued to Gatwick.

Reprinted with permission of Atlantic Syndication Partners, London, 1999.

*

HIGHLY SEXED: A GUIDE TO THE MILE HIGH CLUB

LONDON, June 9th (London Guardian)...Felicity Lawrence

First Time. The first in flight sex is said to have taken place in 1916.The pilot was Lawrence Sperry, a designer of early aircraft, and he was flying a bi-plane over New York. He lost control and crashed, though he and his paramour survived.

Most famous exponents: Celebrities who have claimed to have joined the Mile High Club include, Pamela Anderson, and her husband, Tommy Lee, pop star Brian Harvey of East 17, and actor Oliver Reed. Barbara Streisand hired a private jet to fly over Los Angeles, so that she and her husband could become members.

Most powerful exponent (allegedly)...... Bill Clinton was accused of trying to run a personal Mile High Club aboard his jet during the 1992 election. The allegations of sexual harassment, uncovered by lawyers for Paula Jones, were dismissed as ridiculous by campaign advisors.

Most embarrassing coupling: On a BA flight from Nairobi a couple got stuck in the gap in the last row of cabin seats. Flight engineers had to be called to free them.

Most obvious coupling......... Passengers on an Air France flight from Nice to London clapped and shouted "Vivre la sport!" when a young woman emerged from the lavatory behind her boyfriend having forgotten to put her boob tube back on.

Worst consequences......... An air Stewardess took Air New Zealand to court for unfair dismissal when she was sacked for being caught (while off-duty) with a male passenger in the loo. She lost her case.

Reprinted with permission of Guardian News Service Ltd. London, 1999.

*

How to handle difficult passengers

For your continued interest and edification, dear reader, here are some of the golden rules cabin staff have in mind when dealing with difficult passengers:

- *Keep calm and remain in control at all times. Speak to the passenger using a reasonable and sympathetic tone regardless of the situation;*
- *Listen carefully to what the passenger has to say. In many cases complainants love to hear the sound of their own voice and invariably enjoy having an audience;*
- *If a passenger is sitting in a seat at the time of his or her complaint, go down on one knee to ensure eye-to-eye contact. It demonstrates a less-threatening stance than when standing and looking down on them;*
- *If all else fails, ask the captain to intervene.*

My own view was, and still is, that it is wise to always forgive your "enemies" because nothing annoys them more than that.

Memories to last a lifetime

Flying has always posed a raft of interesting challenges, but at least during the golden age there were many compensations for our hard work. Air hostesses were gutsy individuals and the world was their playground. Wings were earned, not given. There was an aura of mystery surrounding the "golden girls" that could be explained this way: Something that's difficult to obtain becomes more coveted.

An air of mystique accompanied the job which is not easy to put into words. What I will say, however, is that memories of those wonder years, when life was enjoyed in the slow lane, will remain with me for the rest of my life. For my feelings, in this respect, there is no cure, no antidote…and those who have never experienced life as it used to be in the early days of commercial flying will never comprehend just how powerful an experience it was…a dream encounter we all shared…unusual, daring and enterprising.

Air hostesses in the 1960's were the best dressed, best-groomed girls of their era. Uniformly young, slim, attractive and unashamedly female, they were also accomplished conversationalists, which was a pre-requisite for the job. They were hard workers yet able to make even the dreariest task seem like a walk in the park. Nothing fazed them; they were icons, stars of the skies.

Flying during the golden age invoked a lifestyle that can't be replicated in today's hectic world of travel. If passengers of that era formed an elite class so too did the air hostesses.

Sad to see, for me anyway, was the degeneration of air travel; to witness how something once luxurious and exclusive could devolve into something ordinary, mundane and barely tolerable.

Embarking upon a journey by air in the sixties was an experience to look forward to and savour. Passengers dressed for the occasion because it was something special. Meals were prepared from scratch offering a variety of steaks cooked to order, lobster thermidor and Chateaubriand carved in seat-side comfort and served on best china. I would describe the overall ambience as opulent with a touch of magic.

Flying today is a means to an end; a mode of transportation stripped down to the basics including the insalubrious dress code followed by some travellers. And what about in-flight service, where did it go? Like many services it fell victim to the overarching need to improve the bottom line by whatever means possible. The magic of in-flight service was sacrificed on the altar of profitability. I confess to feeling sorry for today's flight attendants. They never knew the joys of flying during the golden years so are unaware of what they missed. Today, as the saying goes, you get what you pay for.

Take this example: I worked an overnight charter flight from Gatwick to Malta years ago with a full load of tour passengers. One extremely large man in the group managed to get himself firmly fixed in his seat, a prisoner of his own flesh one might say. He claimed notoriety in other ways too: he was loud of mouth with clothes to match…vivid Bermuda shorts in glorious technicolour unaligned with an equally discordant shirt. All that was missing, I thought, was a knotted handkerchief on his bald head. It would have completed the picture and given him top-billing as the ship's in-flight entertainment. Even in those days of blasé holidaymakers his attire could be accused of being "loud and daring".

At the end of the flight the entire crew breathed a collective sigh of relief as our brightly-coloured amorphous blob shuffled his way down the aircraft steps. "Free at last," somebody muttered under their breath; but had they spoken too soon?

That evening the whole crew dined alfresco at the hotel. In good spirits and in anticipation of a good meal, we settled down at a veranda table to study the menu. To our collective dismay, plans for a quiet evening were shattered when Mr Loudmouth Blob and his wife appeared on the scene and, as luck would have it, plonked themselves down at a table close to ours. We cringed as the familiar sound of this ultra-loud voice established sovereignty over the entire veranda. A feeling of deep gloom enveloped the crew as appetites evaporated.

By now the restaurant was near-full with a mix of nationalities, what one might characterise as a UN of diners. Not wishing to draw attention to our table or let anyone know we were British lest we became associated with Mr L-B, all we could do was keep a low profile and watch, sheepishly, as the Blob scanned the menu. Seconds later he looked up, a smile on his face. He clicked his fingers at a passing waiter.

"What's this 'ere Lampuki eh?" he barked at the top of his voice, forcing the waiter to take a voluntary step backwards.

"It's a local fish delicacy sir," the waiter replied trembling before the UN of diners. "It's very popular in Malta."

"Right then," the amorphous blob declared decisively, "me and the missus will 'ave Lampuki and chips twice, so get a wiggle on!"

The days of wine and roses were a thing of the past. Fortunately my experience flying charter flights came at the tail-end of my career and I remain thankful that most of my life aloft was during the golden years of flying.

Airline food through the ages

It is important, I think, to review a number of key milestones marking the evolution of airline food over the years. To assess how airline food changed from the early part of the 20th century to the early part of the 21st century here are a few memory-joggers:

- The first in-flight meal was served between London and Paris in 1919 and cost three shillings, about 15 pence today;

- In 1936 United Air Lines installed the first on-board flight kitchens to provide passenger with hot meals. Other airlines soon followed;

- The 1950s, peak of the golden age of flying, saw the introduction of table cloths and silver service. In a promotional video in 1958 Pan Am claimed "Spacious cabins, air-conditioned but draught free. Roominess extends to the powder rooms. Near sonic speed but, inside, no movement at all. Delicious food adds to the enjoyment. It is prepared in four, simultaneously-operating galleys where the food is cooked. The travail has been taken out of travel";

- In 1969, Concorde entered service with British Airways and became renowned for its high-quality cuisine...Champagne, caviar, black truffles, foie gras and lobster with saffron at twice the speed of sound;

- By the 1970s, airline deregulation saw the cost of tickets fall and providing cheap fares become more important than offering the best food and service;

- Terrorist attacks associated with September 11, 2001 had an influence on in-flight dining. Real cutlery gave way to plastic. In some cases US carriers suffered so much financially that they dropped meals altogether for peanuts and soft drinks.

Some airlines continued to offer catering though maintaining acceptable standards proved elusive at times and that led to complaints from dissatisfied punters, even those who admired an airline as in the case of Virgin Atlantic. This amusing letter was sent to Sir Richard Branson and went viral in January 2009:

Dear Mr Branson,

Ref: Mumbai to Heathrow, 7th December, 2008

I love the virgin brand, I really do which is why I continue to use it despite a series of unfortunate incidents over the last few years. This latest incident takes the biscuit.

Ironically, by the end of the flight I would have gladly paid over a hundred rupees for a single biscuit following the culinary journey of hell I was subjected to at the hands of your corporation.

Look at this Richard...just look at this....

I imagine that the same questions are racing through your brilliant mind as were racing through mine on that fateful day. What is this? Why have I been given it? What have I done to deserve this? And which one is the starter....which one is the dessert?

You don't get to a position like yours Richard with anything less than a generous sprinkling of observational power, so I will KNOW that you have spotted the tomato next to the two yellow shafts of sponge on the left. Yes, it's next to the sponge shaft without the green paste. That's got to be the clue hasn't it. No sane person would serve a dessert with a tomato would they? Well answer me this Richard, what sort of an animal would serve a dessert with peas in it.

I know it looks like a baji but it's in custard Richard! It must be the pudding. Well you will be fascinated to hear that it wasn't custard. It was a sour gel with a clear oil on top. Its only redeeming feature was that it managed to be so alien to my palette that it took away the taste of the curry emanating from our miscellaneous central cuboid of beige matter. Perhaps the meal on the left might be the dessert after all?

Anyway, this is all irrelevant at the moment. I was raised strictly, but neatly by my parents and if they knew I had started dessert before the main course, a sponge shaft would be the least of my worries. So let's peel back the tin foil on the main dish and see what's on offer.

I'll try and explain how this felt. Imagine being a twelve year old boy Richard. Now imagine it's Christmas morning and you are sat there with your final present to open. It's a big one, and you know what it is. It's that Goodman's stereo you picked out of the catalogue and wrote to Santa about.

Only you open the present and it's not in there. It's your hamster Richard. It's your hamster in the box and it's not breathing. That's how I felt when I peeled back the foil and saw this...

Now I know what you're thinking Richard. You're thinking it's more of that Baji custard. I admit I thought the same too! But no. It's mustard Richard...MUSTARD. More mustard than any man could consume in a month. On the left we have a piece of broccoli and some peppers in a brown glue-like oil and on the right the chef has prepared some mashed potato. The potato masher had obviously been broken and so it was decided that the next best thing would be to pass the potatoes through the digestive tract of a bird.

Once it was regurgitated it was clearly then blended and mixed with a bit of mustard. Everybody likes a bit of mustard Richard.

By now I was starting to feel a little hypoglycaemic. I needed a sugar hit. Luckily there was a small cookie provided. It had caught my eye earlier due to its baffling presentation

It appears to be in an evidence bag from the scene of a crime. A CRIME AGAINST BLOODY COOKING. Either that or some sort of backstreet underground cookie, purchased off a gun-toting maniac high on his own supply of yeast. You certainly wouldn't want to be caught carrying one of these through customs. Imagine biting into a piece of brass Richard. That would be softer on the teeth than the specimen above.

I was exhausted. All I wanted to do was relax, but obviously I had to sit with this mess in front of me for half an hour. I swear the sponge shafts moved at one point.

Once cleared, I decided to relax with a bit of your world-famous entertainment. I switched it on.

I apologise for the quality of the photo, it's just that it was incredibly hard to capture Boris Johnson's face through the flickering white lines running up and down the screen. Perhaps it would be better on another channel.

Is that Ray Liotta? A question I found myself asking over and over again throughout the gruelling half hour that I attempted to watch the film like this. After this I switched off. I'd had enough. I was the hungriest I'd been in my adult life and I had a splitting headache from watching a crackling screen.

My only option was to sit and stare at the seat in front and wait for either food or sleep. Neither came for an incredibly long time. But when it did it surpassed my wildest expectations.

Yes, it's another crime scene cookie! Only this time you dunk it in the white stuff.

Richard...what is that white stuff? It looked like it was going to be yoghurt. It finally dawned on me what it was after staring at it. It was a mixture between the Baji custard and the mustard sauce. It reminded me of my first week at university. I had overheard that you could make a drink using vodka and refreshers. I lied to my new friends and told them I'd done it loads of times. When I attempted to make the drink in a big bowl it formed a cheese Richard...A CHEESE...That cheese looked a lot like your Baji-mustard!

So that was that Richard. I didn't eat a bloody thing. My only question is...How can you live like this? I can't imagine what dinner around your house is like! It must be like something out of a nature documentary.

As I said at the start, I love your brand. I really do. It's just a shame that such a simple thing could bring it crashing to its knees and begging for sustenance.

Yours sincerely...

Gone are the joyous days paired with high standards but memories of all the satisfaction we got from a job well done live on in those of us who experienced those wonderful times. As a pilot or a member of the cabin staff, flying gets into your bones and once a member of that elite group…always a member.

Service standards of yesteryear

I suppose the question we have to ask is whether or not any airline will manage to recreate the service standards of the golden years? Perhaps not, but it is encouraging to see that airlines still try from time to time. In recent years Eos Airlines, MAXjet Airways and Silverjet tried (and failed) to make a go of all-Business-class flights. Yet British Airways' BA001 is an all-business-class flight from London City Airport to New York with US pre-customs clearance at Shannon and is still going strong, one presumes, after five-six years.

In his informed article "High hopes for a high flyer's service", published in the Daily Telegraph on June 6, 2015, Matthew Bell wrote that British Airways' London City Airport service now has competition in the shape of La Compagnie, a new airline operating Business-class-only flights "…which aims to put the glamour back into flying at a fraction of the cost."

With two Boeing 757-200's leased from Icelandair, the airline operates from Paris to Newark offering an all-Business-class service with just seventy-four flat beds. In the latter part of 2015 La Compagnie planned to operate similar flights from the UK.

"If you are clever," writes Matthew Bell, "you can fly return to New York for as little as £1,100 which for Business-class is unheard of. So where is the catch? First thing to note is the route itself. La

Compagnie has chosen Luton to Newark, two airports with something of a marmite reputation."

While that may have pros and cons, Matthew Bell maintains that once on board "...the facilities and ambience are a gazillion times higher than any economy class or even premium economy seat."

The inflight entertainment, he says, is adequate and the menu, French, was very good on his outbound flight. "A lobster salad with lime was fresh and zingy and the roulade of Dover sole and salmon was very meaty and moist. It was surprising that they had run out of lamb, given that the plane was not full, and there seemed no contingency for those who don't like fish. But these are minor quibbles, and as the Champagne flowed and Sean Connery sparred with Pussy Galore, life seemed swell."

So, based on Matthew Bell's experience dare we hope for a return to the golden years of flying? I, for one, certainly hope so.

Looking back at the early years

I am now living in my own golden years, but I still love flying and everything about it. I guess it's in my blood. That said, with the many changes the industry has undergone over recent times I avoid flying wherever possible. It's just not the same. There was a time when we flew BOAC but, today, I prefer B-O-A-T and I know that may sound cynical.

Looking back in time, there is no getting away from the fact that the onset of the jet age has shortened flying hours by a considerable margin. That's precisely what aircraft manufacturers and airline companies set out to do in the belief that world travellers just want to get to their destinations as fast as possible. As I see it, today's flying is all about getting from A to B in the shortest possible time. It is a means to an end. However, for most travellers the destination is more important than the journey. Ralph Waldo Emerson said it best: "Life is a journey, not a destination," and that's exactly how I felt when I started flying and still feel today.

Once upon a time multiple stopovers were factored into our trips prior to reaching our desired destination. Those journeys could be jam-packed with new experiences often in the company of total strangers as we flew to some of the most incredible spots on the planet. On occasions we found ourselves in the midst of stark, sometimes romantic, surroundings enjoying some of the finest cuisine imaginable, accompanied by vintage wines and somehow hoping it would never end. At other times we found ourselves taking shelter from a tropical downpour as we patiently waited for our aircraft to be fitted with spare parts before we could get airborne again. Throughout these experiences air crews and passengers coexisted cheek to jowl for days, sometimes weeks, sharing the same hotels with everyone playing his or her unique role but as an integral part of the overall travel experience. The destination wasn't as important as the journey taken to get there.

The days of haute cuisine

Long journeys gave plenty of time for everyone to get to know each other both on board and at subsequent "watering holes" along the way. It was nothing less than a paid adventure with thrills galore.

Passengers enthusiastically participated in making the trip enjoyable for all concerned. They looked forward to their next meal because they knew it was going to be special. Why? Because their last meal, four hours earlier, was special; everything cooked from scratch by people who could present a gourmet meal in a pressurised cabin four miles high. It was a challenge but we succeeded time after time and still had time to chat to the passengers. These days, cabin staff spend more time chatting to one another.

First class menus from the 1960's were fantastic. To recap: Food was always cooked on board from scratch, and we prepared anywhere up to seven courses for passengers flying First-class with full silver service. Airlines competed to offer the best fine and wines available.

Swissair menu from 1966

HORS D'OEUVRE

- Imported Malossol Caviar, Melba toast, butter
- Slices of Foie Gras de Strasbourg, Pumpernickel bread.
- Fresh cold Lobster Bellevue, Chef's Sauce
- Glaced Asparagus spears, Air dried ham, sauce Mayonnaise
- Thin slices of Smoked Salmon, Fluffy Horseradish Sauce
- New Zealand Shrimp Cocktail, Cocktail Sauce

SOUPS

- Cream Soup, Real Turtle Soup or Cold Vichyssoise

MAIN COURSES

- Prime Filet Mignon with Truffles, Potato Balls, Artichoke bottoms, Grilled Tomato Salad.

- Chops and Côtelette of Spring Lamb with a thin layer of Swiss cheese, Noodles in Butter, Braised Lettuce with Chipolata Salad
- Roast Pheasant en Cocotte, Sauce Smitane, Mascotte Potatoes, Leaf Spinach Salad
- Swiss speciality of Minced Veal with Button Mushrooms in Cream Sauce, Spaetzlis in Butter, Salad
- Sauté of Fillet of English Sole with Truffles, Diced Artichokes, Olive Potatoes, Salad

In addition there would be a dessert trolley followed by a cheese board.

In those halcyon days of air travel, when travellers enjoyed something called "service-with-a-smile", on-board food and beverage catering was an all-important feature of the whole experience. Advertising slogans such as "linger over your luncheon or dinner with complimentary champagne and a choice of entrée," or "tenderloin steak to order", were some of the culinary war cries of American airlines of that era.

Miami-based National Airlines, I recall, rotated meals for variety's sake, even though their baked chicken and filet mignon were always popular. Pledges were made that no meals would be duplicated both eastbound and westbound, or northbound and southbound, and menus were changed monthly thus passengers enjoyed a greater variety of food.

In 1959, Northwest offered what was branded Regal Imperial Service: Scandinavian pastries and coffee after take-off; hors d'oeuvres including shrimp in curry sauce; frankfurters and meatballs in customised sauce; oil of wintergreen-scented hot and cold towels.

STARTER SERVICE: Lobster cocktail, salad and consommé; choice prime beef, or on Fridays choice of beef or lobster tail; duchesse potatoes. Choice of Italian white wine, French red wine or champagne.

DESSERT: French pastries or cheesecake, or cheese and crackers with coffee; after dinner mints.

I also recall UK airlines BOAC and BEA between them serving over ten thousand airborne meals a day, some consisting of seven courses. Again in 1959, BOAC offered four different classes of service on long haul routes: Deluxe, First-class, Tourist, and Economy-class. Flying was all about service.

With the introduction of high-class inflight services it was a case of "back to the drawing board" for air hostesses. Training had to be upgraded because on-board service had been totally transformed. Cabin staff had to be instructed on how to correctly set a table, bearing in mind in those days it was all silver-service. Food was brought to the passenger and served individually, one course at a time. Desserts were presented on a dessert trolley and the cheeseboard with a full selection of gourmet cheeses was offered to passengers on an individual basis. This was followed by a selection of fruit and tea or coffee – again on an individual basis. Dining on board an aircraft was an experience par excellence. Less so for air hostesses I might add; preparing and presenting haute cuisine on board an aircraft was more a case of hard work.

To prepare for some long-haul flights destined for far off places where we might expect a lower standard of hygiene we always carried in the aircraft hold large, green polar boxes to store food packed in dry ice for the return flight. Similar arrangements were made regarding cutlery for the return flight.

At the other end of the scale, in the days of the humble charter flight, for example, when catering bore little resemblance to cuisine, private UK-based airline Dan-Air produced something called seat-back catering. It was not one of Britain's finest hours in the air transport industry's culinary journey.

In his book *Food in the Air and Space*, author Richard Foss wrote, "This was one of the worst ideas in airline food history. It involved stocking a meal for every passenger inside the seat in front of them. And giving each flyer a key that could be used to unlock the storage compartment for use when they got hungry. Whilst this enabled a food service without stewardess time, it was a failure on multiple levels. The meals for both outbound and return flights had been locked in the adjacent compartment and passengers quickly worked out that the same key unlocked both. That meant that passengers on the second leg of the flight often found that the person previously in their seat had also eaten their lunch or dinner".

Reading this brought to mind the tale of Goldilocks and the Three Bears: "...and somebody's been eating my porridge and they ate it all up!"

Richard Foss went on to say: "Also, since Dan-Air flew many routes of several hours duration, whatever meal that had been locked in that compartment for the second leg of the trip, might have been unrefrigerated for six or seven hours. Even by the low standards of

English budget-class tourists of the 1960s and 70s, this was unacceptable".

Also from Richard Foss's book and in contrast: "On the older and less fashionable aircraft there was more time to produce a high standard service because there was more flying time in which to produce the service. Finnair on their DC8s produced various herring dishes, reindeer soup, and smoked lamb. British Caledonian maintained a Scottish-biased cuisine with smoked salmon to start with and Walkers shortbread to finish every meal. The airline often had a bag-piper escort a haggis on board a flight on the birthday of Robert Burns, Scotland's national poet".

It was always possible, given a bit of notice, for airlines to cater for passengers requesting special meals such as vegetarian, gluten-intolerant, diabetic, low calorie or to address some kind of allergy or even to conform to various religious beliefs such as Hindu, Muslim or Kosher.

How well I remember early on in my flying career working a flight to Israel full of people of the Jewish faith – around two hundred in all. After take-off the rabbi approached the galley and said to me, "May I please remind you Miss that before you serve Kosher food I have to bless it?"

In accordance with normal practice, the food was pre-prepared in the airline catering department's "special food kitchen" and brought to the aircraft. Each meal was individually wrapped in tin foil. My job was to place the meals in the oven to cook, and then peel off the foil and serve. However, before I was allowed to touch them, a blessing had to be given, especially as I was a gentile. After the ritual blessing I duly cooked the prepared food. Then came the awful moment of truth. Peeling off the foil covers I was mortified to look down on an array of juicy pork cutlets – every single meal was a pork chop.

I requested the rabbi to join me in the galley. "I am so sorry rabbi, there's been a terrible mix-up with the meals," I groaned apologetically, my voice trembling in harmony with my knees. Fortunately, he was a delightful man and immediately understood and accepted the situation. Without hesitating he addressed everyone on the intercom: "There has been an unavoidable technical problem affecting the meals," he announced solemnly, going on to outline the airline's unfortunate faux pas. A stunned silence followed when he mentioned pork chops; you could have heard a pin drop. After a few moments, which seemed like hours to me, raucous laughter broke out in the cabin. Above the din I heard a voice scream out: "Bring it on!"

I will never forget that day; everyone to a man tucked into pork chops a la Mexicana on their way to Tel Aviv. I am pretty sure a dessert of "post-event prayers" was next on the rabbi's menu.

I followed up on this embarrassing gaffe by requesting the captain to find out what had gone wrong. I felt we owed the rabbi an explanation. Word came back that two aircraft, parked on the ramp side-by-side, were loaded with catering at the same time and the meals were somehow loaded onto the wrong aircraft. I guess I'll never know what the passengers on the other aircraft got to eat that day.

I once did a "Burns Night" flight to Rome. For those unfamiliar with Burns Night it is an important occasion celebrated by Scots each year in Scotland (and elsewhere) on or around January 25 to commemorate the life of the Scottish bard Robert Burns who was born on January 25, 1759. It is also a celebration of Burns' contribution to Scottish culture including music: his best known work "Auld Lang Syne" being sung globally with great gusto at the beginning of each New Year.

On this particular flight all the passengers were Scots on a "jolly" and looking forward to bouts of unconstrained revelry. Indeed the aircraft had been chartered solely for the occasion. As is traditional, haggis was served but, on this occasion, one of the passengers got up and "addressed the haggis" before anyone could start eating. During and after the meal various people took turns singing or reciting poetry all the way from Gatwick to Rome. It was a fun night that sticks in my memory to this day.

Sad to say, many of today's economy flights only offer buy-on-board meals though I often wonder why it isn't possible to serve a light snack with coffee or tea offered as an option with a slight increase in the fare? That way, those who choose to opt out of the service could pay less.

Surely, it is all-important to give passengers a choice. Perhaps today's trolley dollies don't have the energy or inclination to offer such a service. But that can't be because they are worked off their feet. From what I have observed they spend more time chatting with one another than addressing the needs of passengers. These days it's all about promoting a bar service and pushing in-flight sales at exorbitant prices. When I travelled as a passenger to Spain all I was offered was a sandwich in an unattractive wrapper doled out to passengers who were stupid enough to pay over the odds for such unappetising food. It didn't even arrive in a presentable manner. What ever happened to quality control?

People travelling today seem to be preconditioned – almost brainwashed -- to expect very little and that's what they get. I guess they can't be too disappointed. But measured against other forms of "progress" in the air transport industry, flight catering has plenty of room for improvement. Nowadays, some people even bring their own food aboard flights; foul-smelling, fast-food snacks available at any airport at highly inflated prices. And thereby hangs another tale.

The food and culture magazine *Bon Appétit* ran a lengthy and very funny complaint written by Jason Kessler called "I'm sick of stinky food on airplanes."

"Have you ever been in this position? You're settling into a harrowing cross-country flight armed only with the in-flight magazine when someone sits down across the aisle from you holding a plastic take-out bag. It seems innocuous enough. Then, after you clear 10,000 feet, the stranger launches a full-on sensory attack. Turns out that the plastic bag is filled with hazardous material. Orange chicken from the Chinese place in the terminal. Within 30 seconds you are gagging on the sickly sweet smell of processed sodium-filled meat nuggets. After two minutes, you're thinking about an escape route, ten minutes in and you are taking out your cell phone, and are pretending to make calls just so the flight attendant will forcibly take you to the secret holding cell in the bottom of the airplane built expressively for people who attempt to make calls mid-flight. You didn't know that holding cell

existed, did you? Now you do! The scenario happened to me (sans prison) a few weeks ago...and it wasn't the first time. Bringing and eating stinky food on board a plane is one of the most inconsiderate things that you could possibly do to your fellow passengers. The air you breathe on the 747 is the same air that everyone else breathes because you are literally in a steel tube suspended in the sky (which, when you think about it, is disconcerting enough.) Those orange chicken molecules are being recycled over and over again until your brain makes a deal with your nose that it's just going to ignore the problem. An airplane is not a mall. At the mall you don't have to sit there and take it when somebody nearby digs into a foul-smelling lunch. You can move. On an airplane, you don't have that luxury. You are essentially trapped!"

I also think about how the lingering smells of some aromas tend to stick to clothing. Travel in some respects in this modern age may be a means to an end, but does the end justify the means? Thank goodness I can say I have been fortunate to have represented airlines when the whole experience of five-star, in-flight service was what travelling by air was all about.

Where have all the standards gone?

Regrettably, substandard service starts the moment you enter any airport terminal building. From that point onwards everything is a hassle as hordes of anxious people queue up to be processed like cattle. "Herd 'em up, and move 'em out!" Anxious travellers are tasked with negotiating endless queues -- even for restaurants and rest rooms.

The inconvenience we face today is a sign of the times and stems from heightened security at airports around the world to counter hijacking, bomb threats (real or concocted) and acts of terrorism. This has subjected everyone to body scanners and x-ray screening machines which many folk find intrusive particularly those unfortunate enough to carry in their bodies metal implants of one sort or another.

By the time passengers make it through the obstacle course to the relative comfort of their aircraft cabin, everyone's nerves are frayed, many are annoyed, frustrated or highly stressed by the whole experience. Not a great way to start a journey and not as it was during the golden years. Gone, alas, is the romance, excitement and sense of adventure that were such vital parts of yesteryear.

During the early years, flying was all about noisy piston-driven planes, later quieter turbo-props, both relatively slow types of aircraft. Sometimes, as a result of developing storms crews had to guide their aircraft around adverse weather. These days, modern jets fly at much higher altitudes and avoid the worst of most storms.

In my day we gritted our teeth and rode out the turbulence; bumpy rides were part of the job. We had to place our trust in the men in the cockpit as they manoeuvred planes through violent thunderstorms without the aid of radar. These magnificent men, as I mentioned previously, were seasoned veterans of the air – true airmen who had honed their aviator skills during wartime. They were men with years of experience to back up their judgement; brave men who flew by the seat of their pants and knew how to get the best out of the machine that was strapped to their backside.

My husband Bill was one such pilot. In his nineties now, he still carries in his body pieces of deeply embedded shrapnel from his RAF days. All were truly remarkable men who earned the right to be called airmen; skilled aviators who faced and dealt with daunting situations that many of today's flying-school protégés will most likely never experience. Back then flying was both an art and a skill. And aircraft were not the domain of computer-controlled, GPS-guided airframe drivers who had recently rolled off a flying school conveyor belt. In my view, modern-day flying has no soul. But that's just my humble opinion as someone who lived through the golden years of air travel.

I recall reading a report that most people who refer to the golden age of air travel had lived through those years but never got to fly. That's quite possible because flying was a privilege enjoyed by just a few. If today's flying experience is the only thing some people can relate to, then they have certainly missed out in terms of quality of service.

Today's travellers are spoon-fed with regular doses of high-powered advertising by airlines eulogising the attractiveness of their female flight attendants distastefully decked out in hot pants or miniskirts to reinforce the company's "fly me" campaign. When you get on board, however, you may be disappointed because this is nothing more than window dressing. I will always maintain that what you are unable to see makes a much more attractive statement about service than what you can see. How I wish we could bring back that aura of mystique.

WHEN LUXURY RULED THE SKIES. FLYING IN THE 50'S AND 60'S

Courtesy of the Sacramento Bee newspaper

Air travel today is more an ordeal than an adventure. It is little more than a chore one must endure to get from one place to another.

Once there was an era in the annals of air travel when passengers were pampered, not prodded like cattle in a chute. They were fed full meals, no extra charge, plied with liquor, and given a pillow on command.

This era, roughly from 1958 – 1978, saw airlines vying, almost begging, for your business, outfitting their planes with festive colours, and their stewardesses,(no "flight attendants" back then,) in provocative uniforms, promising an "experience," not just a trip. Passengers too, dressed up, unlike today's middle aged man in Khaki cargo shorts, his wife in skirt and flip flops, and his daughter in Daisy Duke cut-offs.

I'm talking about the Golden Age of Flying.

Passengers were treated better both on the ground and in the air, and didn't have to endure the indignity of paying separately for every single thing save the overhead air nozzle. "Even in economy the seats would be like the best premium – economy or business class today," said William Stadiem, author of a newly released book....Jet Set, The People, The Planes, the Glamour and The Romance in Aviation's Glorious Years........ "The seats were comfortable, the food was good. You had foie gras and smoked salmon along with caviar. Even in Tourist Class it was great. You felt special. That is why you dressed up to get on an airplane. It was a big deal."

Stadiem, a lawyer and journalist, who travels often for work and pleasure said he noticed the gaping maw of service between the one percent and the ninety-nine percent on a recent flight he took on BA from London to Los Angeles.

"First Class is nice...I looked at it," he said. "Huge and spacious. My business class is like a morgue. All the seats are in opposite directions...very unpleasant. Steerage (coach class) is horrible. It's on two decks, much more crowded, and the flight attendants tell me that they feel the turbulence more in the back of the plane. Not a pleasant experience."

He goes on to point out in his book that back in the 60's, and even through the 70's, and the advent of the mammoth 747's, the gulf between first class and tourist class was not so wide. The first 707's introduced in 1958 but not used widely until the1960's, was in every sense a futuristic spacecraft....Tomorrow land, today. *"The stewardesses were sexily stunning, pure Coffee, Tea or Me avian goddesses. Yet there was no haughtiness, just a crisp, omni-competent cheeriness befitting your favourite school teacher."*

How sad that quality has become a thing of the past.

Where have all the standards gone? Gone forever, every one.

Experiencing modern air travel makes it hard to imagine the way it used to be in the old days, glamorous and in every way personal. Having had the misfortune to travel with easyJet to Spain a few years ago I felt more like a battery hen than a passenger. It was two hours of sheer hell. Passengers were packed in like sardines with no leg room and it was obvious some of the passengers had not been made aware of the advent of antiperspirants. I didn't find anything "easy" about easyJet.

Even the in-flight entertainment amounted to nothing more than playing games on mobile phones coupled with seeing how much alcohol passengers could consume in two hours. I felt quite conspicuous wedged in my seat, reading a newspaper. In-flight meals were non-existent, and my blood ran cold when I heard the none-to-dulcet tones of a frosty-faced flight attendant announcing that if anyone wanted a sandwich they could pay the attendant as she passed down the cabin. Just before landing, two attendants appeared in the cabin holding a large black bin liner between them, into which passengers were instructed to throw their rubbish. Oh happy days.

The *coup de grace* came after we landed. The captain bade us farewell hoping we had enjoyed our flight. He thanked us for flying with easyJet as by doing so we were helping him to keep his job. I have to confess I haven't flown since though I hope he's still gainfully employed.

To say that flying is not what it used to be is an understatement. Gone is the glamour and the style, the service and the conversation. In today's airports it is all about queues, crowds, delays, bad tempers, mislaid luggage, security ad nauseam and a sense of complete disinterest in putting the needs of the passengers first. Of course as time goes by all things change but why does it always have to be for the worse. More people fly today than ever before but sadly it is just a means to an end. The real experience has gone for ever.

Romantic encounters

Universally, folk have always wanted to know if pilots and flight crews engage in romantic interludes away from base. Yes and no is my answer.

I felt lucky because Bill and I were able to remain romantically attached right from the start of my flying career. For much of the time we were able to fly together on long-haul flights and travelling the world in one another's company was great fun. Whenever I think back to when we first met in 1961 on my inaugural flight aboard a Bristol

Freighter, and the moules marinière incident when I threw-up all over his uniform jacket, I have to say that sharing that period of time together was a joyous experience – moules marinière apart.

Back then, air hostesses had to be of single status prepared to forego marriage. That was airline policy. However, by using a bit of tact and exercising a modicum of diplomacy, it was possible to marry (and many of us did) and get away with it. We continued to be taxed in our maiden names and never mentioned the "M" word to anyone. I must confess I found it somewhat incongruous and illogical that in 1961 it was considered perfectly acceptable for male and female aircrew to "live in sin" just so long as they were not bound in wedlock. My, how the world has changed since the sixties.

Though Bill and I lived together from 1961 we didn't get married until 1964. At that juncture our pattern of life was unsettled and that's putting it mildly. More often than not we slept by day and flew by night. When most of our neighbours were up and about, our bedroom curtains were still drawn. Our neighbours must have thought we were a couple of sex maniacs.

There has always been a great deal of curiosity, particularly among the travelling public, concerning the machinations and "goings-on" among aircrew thrown together for long periods of time. It's only natural for folk to be inquisitive considering that many of our trips abroad took us to some fabulous locations. And it's true we enjoyed protracted layovers in the best hotels with good per-diem allowances, all of which provided ample opportunities for romantic interludes. The opportunity to have romance in one's life was enhanced by some of those exotic locations, and of course in those days we had time to enjoy the entire experience.

While it was a case of life in the fast lane for some crews not everyone saw it that way. Generally, crews stuck together on long-haul trips some of which lasted up to two weeks allowing ample time for the entire crew to become well-acquainted.

Do they or don't they have sexual relationships at every opportunity? That is a question often asked about pilots and air hostesses. Many people I have met in my life seem to be convinced that all air hostesses and pilots enjoy long, steamy nights of debauchery at every given opportunity. They offer up an image of crews jumping in and out of bed with one another with gay abandon.

Allow me to present my view and perhaps a slightly different take on this subject born from personal experience. As in any other walks of life there are those who play and those who don't. Some pilots and hostesses embark upon long-term relationships; some prefer one-night stands. But this doesn't apply across the board.

Whilst it is true in the world of flying, particularly in my era, the emphasis has always been on glamour that does not always infer promiscuity. On long-haul flights during my era crews could be away from base for many days at a time. Coupled with the lure of romantic destinations, hot tropical nights and a wonderful social life, the scene was set for some crews to make certain one thing led to another. That wasn't everyone's choice of lifestyle however.

In my own case I had married a pilot and we worked more often together than apart. This meant we were fortunate enough to share a romantic life – on the job, so to speak. We shared beds all around the world and enjoyed every moment of it. For us, life was one long, romantic honeymoon.

Many air hostesses married pilots for a host of different reasons, none-the-least because leading a social life outside of flying circles was very challenging. Long-haul flights and unexpected delays en route made it extremely difficult to form a meaningful relationship with someone outside the world of flying, which really meant the airline for which you worked.

As I recall, a lot of girls struck up relationships with men they met in the course of their travels; you might say they had a guy in every port.

This brings to mind one hostess's romantic endeavour. She requested to be assigned to a Nairobi-bound flight so she could spend time with her boyfriend who was working in Kenya. He'd been unwell and she wanted to surprise him with a visit. The lady in question was a senior hostess. It was customary to assign one senior hostess to each flight but, on this occasion, we had two, a fact that had not escaped the attention of the captain.

After chatting to each one separately, and unbeknown to each other, the captain discovered that the other senior hostess was also going to see her boyfriend who hadn't been very well either. Needless to say the captain watched with some amusement as they both confronted the same man. I don't know how this ended.

Pilots and cabin staff around the globe all have similar tales to tell. When asked about his experience of romantic encounters a pilot for one of America's largest airlines said, "Maybe I'm jaded from all the years, but hook-ups...ha-ha...have you seen most crews walking around? It would make for the worst porn movie in the world. Here is what would happen: Old pilot tells tales of his flying stories or his high school football days – the glory days – and flight attendants show pictures of their cats, horses and dogs. At 7pm they fall asleep. I guess between our animal-loving grandmas in the back and the grumpy old farts up front, I don't think much will be happening. But hey, you never know."

A hostess had this to say, "Most cabin crew and pilots are too darn tired when they reach their destinations to do any major hooking-up. Even if they had the energy, few want to hook-up with the people they work with. They want sleep, not a roll in the hay."

So there you have it.

At least what went on in the sixties did so with discretion and behind closed doors. There has been promiscuity in all walks of life and workplaces since Pontius was a pilot. Sadly, in today's world of flying it's all about the so-called "Mile-High Club" and accompanying sexual innuendos. How sad life has become in the modern world of trolley dollies, compared with that wonderful world of elegance, dignity and *je ne sais quoi* I remember with great fondness.

Most of the pilots I flew with were married (or divorced) and some made no secret of the fact they were more than happy to play away from home. I worked a trip with Bill and another very handsome pilot who fancied himself almost as much as the hostesses did. Just prior to take-off I was present on the flight deck and overheard Bill greeting his ultra-posh co-pilot with a cheerful, "Hi, it's good to meet you Ted".

Ted didn't immediately return the greeting. Fixing Bill with a glassy stare, the co-pilot growled, "My name is Edward, not Ted, so please get that straight before we go any further." Turning in his seat, Bill fixed Ted with an icy glare that would freeze a corpse: "As far as I am concerned," he said slowly, "you are Ted…so let's get that straight before we go any further." Both knew they had an aircraft to fly and the conversation ended as abruptly as it had begun. But the encounter left an icy air hanging over the flight deck.

That wasn't the end of the Bill-Ted exchange. During a later incident, Ted, or Edward, had every reason to be grateful to Bill for his lightning-fast response that probably saved his marriage. It happened like this: Ted had already fallen hook, line and sinker for a stunningly beautiful air hostess. They flew together on long-haul flights as often as possible. Like Siamese twins Eng and Chang they were inseparable. On one particularly memorable day, I landed at Gatwick from a long-haul trip. Bill and Ted were on the same flight. This time, for some reason or another, Ted's air hostess girlfriend was not part of our crew.

As we all exited customs, walking line abreast, Bill and I spotted Ted's girlfriend hugging the barrier in the arrivals hall. She was eagerly waiting for him. Also eagerly waiting for him, and standing alongside Ted's girlfriend, was Ted's wife who had decided to drive to the airport to surprise him. Fortunately for all concerned the two ladies did not know each other.

Ted had eyes for no-one save his girlfriend and didn't even notice his smiling wife clinging to the barrier rail. On the other hand Bill, whose built-in radar was bleeping warnings of "stormy weather ahead", quickly summed up the situation and sprang into action. Anticipating a landside confrontation, he sprinted towards the barrier. Dropping his luggage, he threw his arms around Ted's girlfriend. "It's wonderful to see you darling," he said embracing her like a long-lost lover. Apart from Bill, no-one could see the surprise on her face. In the space of thirty seconds, Ted's hide, and marriage, were saved entirely due to my husband's quick thinking.

It was often the case that air hostesses married pilots because the element of romance was ever present in their day-to-day lives. To repeat: it was quite difficult cultivating a social life outside the airline. We were either flying overseas for long periods, or sleeping ahead of the next flight. Keeping a relationship going outside the airline was a major challenge. Look at it this way: A long-haul trip to the Far East, say Singapore or Hong Kong, could take anywhere up to two weeks including slip-over periods of three days in Bombay, two days in either Singapore or Hong Kong, and three more in Bombay on the way back to the UK. And this was the absolute minimum; bad weather delays and/or technical problems could prolong the journey time by several days. This didn't leave much time for home-based romantic interludes, but it didn't stop crews from trying.

*

It was on a similar routing to the Far East that I had the dubious pleasure of flying with a first officer who had a notorious reputation for sleeping around. This particular pilot was a very tall man, about six-feet-two. Working in unison, we hostesses decided to get back at him and teach him a lesson he wouldn't forget. We pressured our flight engineer to assist us with our scheme and he agreed. I should add that, by comparison, our comrade-in-arms flight engineer was only around five-feet-four in height. But that fitted perfectly into our plans.

Recalling previous phases of the flight, and the over-amorous first officer, we noted that one air hostess had been egging him on from the start of the trip. That night, after the first officer left his own room, and after the crew party ended in the captain's room, we checked and found the first officer made a return visit to his own room before going anywhere else. Minutes later, after donning a dressing gown, he darted into the hostess's room. It was time for us to act. Moving swiftly, and exhibiting great stealth, the flight engineer carried his spare uniform trousers to the first officer's room and swapped them for the first officer's uniform pants. The trap was set.

The next day we patiently waited in the crew bus for the first officer to put in an appearance. I could see from our captain's face that the first officer's apparent nonappearance was becoming a cause for concern. Keeping to schedule was very important.

Seconds later, our delinquent co-pilot showed up. He was in full uniform but his trousers barely covered his knees even though he tried hard to stretch them. His face was crimson but it wasn't sunburn. Not a word was spoken on the bus about the incident not even on the part of our captain who must have guessed what was going on. The first officer was forced to work the trip from Bombay to Singapore wearing his new-style, cut-down pants and we felt justice had been served.

It would be misleading to leave readers with the impression that romantic trysts during the golden age of flying were commonplace. That wasn't the case. Of course it went on but in my day ladies were trained to conduct themselves with a sense of decorum. Whatever occurred behind closed doors always stayed there; that was the golden rule. It was nobody else's business.

That isn't the case today: Unless you openly brag about your conquests, e.g. membership of the Mile High Club – considered so prestigious by modern trolley-dollies – you haven't lived. To my way of thinking that is a sad reflection on cabin staff and does nothing to enhance the image that should go with the job.

*

Aircrews flying with any airline should be aware from the first day they don their uniform that down-route gossip travels back to base on the jungle grapevine faster than their aircraft. For some, it was a hard-learned lesson and many suffered the consequences. Allow me to illustrate: An incident took place during a stopover in Athens involving a captain who had a keen eye for the girls. He considered himself to be charm personified, a regular "Don Juan" who could have any girl he wanted. He had his sights on this particular air hostess and persistently pestered her despite her impassioned pleas to be left alone.

She dreaded being part of his crew at any time but particularly on flights that overnighted away from base as in the case of this particular flight to Athens. Confident she would at some point succumb to his attentions, the captain kept knocking on the door of her hotel room which she refused to open. The flight engineer, watching developments closely, took pity on the girl and offered his help. "I have a plan," he told her. "What sort of plan?" she asked grateful for any intervention. "We'll swap rooms and we won't tell anyone"

True to form "Capitan Don Juan" arrived outside her room in the dead of night. It bolstered his confidence when he found the door was unlocked. He let himself in and slipped under the duvet.

"Surprise!" the captain shrieked at the top of his voice.

"Oh, captain," the flight engineer screamed, loud enough for everyone in the hotel to hear, "I didn't know you cared!" The jungle grapevine confirmed the plan was a resounding success and that this captain was cured. I am not certain of that, but it did stop him from coming onto her again, that much I can confirm. More than anything else, I believe his salvation had more to do with the fact everyone in the fleet, if not the entire airline, was aware of his shenanigans.

The African city of Entebbe in Uganda was another intriguing destination where we always enjoyed action-packed layovers. A full week at the Lake Victoria Hotel was something to look forward to: a beautiful location and even more amazing when you think this superb lifestyle was available to us as a result of our chosen occupation. We even had time to go on animal safaris.

But it wasn't always plain sailing and not always romantic. After landing at Entebbe Airport on one occasion I got into a blazing row with a Ugandan traffic manager. Short in stature, he was both awkward and clumsy beyond description. As I was leaving the aircraft with my clean shirt on a hanger over my arm I had cause to remonstrate with him about his unacceptable attitude during our arrival. Having said my piece in no uncertain terms, I turned and walked away. But he kept pace with me at the same time protesting and shouting at the top of this voice. What made matters worse for me was sight of the crew falling about laughing, seemingly at my expense. Then I realised why. The hook on my shirt hanger had caught in the man's flies which, in another moment of ineptness, he had left undone. I was dragging the poor man along with me. Later, we both saw the funny side of the situation and the incident did serve to take the sting out of our original disagreement.

*

Crews often returned from East Africa laden with sacks of pineapples, avocado pears and bananas. I can still smell the freshness of the fruit. This brings to mind another romantic incident. A former chief of police for Uganda, a British national, was returning to the UK after serving a long stint overseas. As was oft times the case, he had fallen in love with one of our air hostesses and the pair had decided it would be more sensible to marry and set up home in the UK rather than in Africa.

At a packed wedding reception, which Bill and I attended, the ex-chief of police presented the bride's father with a very large sack of avocado pears and an equally large sack of pineapples.

"I wish to buy your daughter," he announced, poker-faced, "and these are for her dowry." Although strictly not a UK tradition, it did generate a ripple of laughter among those attending the reception some of whom were from the African continent.

Not quite so funny, for me anyway, was another flight I was working from Entebbe when we ran into some very rough weather. Some metal canisters in the ship's galley came adrift from their fittings, rolled forward and pinned me to the cabin floor. I sustained two broken ribs which I didn't realise at the time so I kept on working. Worse still, one rib had pierced my lung which collapsed days later. I was off work for six weeks. It was a thoroughly unromantic end to that particular flight.

*

It wasn't until I began thinking and then writing this section on romantic encounters that I came to realise that among aircrew in general the pilots were the ones we had to be most wary of. I am sure flight engineers had their less-chivalrous moments but they could also be gallant in times of need. In fact, I recall many flight engineers offering to help some of the more quixotic, starry-eyed air hostesses to tackle their romantic dilemmas. To be perfectly honest, they did the same for some of the less-confident, head-in-the-clouds pilots caught up in webs of intrigue.

Many of the girls threw themselves at captains and first officers as if their medium term "flight plan" was solely to snare a husband. Some simply wouldn't take no for an answer. A few tried it on with Bill before we got married and one girl, who shall remain nameless, managed to get her claws into him. Granted, he played ball at first but not for long. I stepped in and nipped it in the bud. Others also tried it on but left with their tails between their legs after a few words from yours truly.

I detected a lot of jealousy on the part of fellow air hostesses who saw Bill and myself as an "item". It went on for many years. Lots of hostesses were envious of what we had because that was what they yearned for; for some it was their sole reason for working for an airline. Yet, Bill and I remained together despite various attempts from some of my more ambitious hostess colleagues to prise us apart.

*

One of our more amorous skippers and his inseparable sidekick flight engineer both of whom crewed DC-4 aircraft operating mostly to destinations in the Mediterranean, functioned as a double-act in their search for romantic trysts. Whatever the Lone Ranger was intent on doing away from base, Tonto was apt to follow. The dynamic duo were forever on the lookout for new conquests.

Just after he gave me my engagement ring, Bill told me that the Lone Ranger had bitterly complained to him, "…and now all the birds will want one." After we were married, again he complained, "…and now all the birds will want to get married." The latter was stated, Bill said, with more than a hint of sarcasm and deepening gloom.

His reaction turned out to be quite unfortunate because his "bird", who was living with him at the time, was cheated out of the prospect of marriage when her beloved captain flew his DC-4 into a mountainside en route to Perpignan. Even worse, she had had a blazing row with him before he left for the airport. She never got another opportunity to speak to him.

This is your captain speaking

Frequent fliers must have noticed how pilots flying for different airlines around the world have their own special techniques for making passengers feel at ease. We all know how flying can be a stressful experience at the best of times, especially navigating a way through the security checks and body searches that are conducted with wandering hands by some officials. On those occasions, and for the sake of expediency, we all try to appear nonchalant and ultra-cool to ride out the daunting experience. I often reflected on H. Jackson Brown Jr's assertion that "…good manners sometimes means simply putting up with other people's bad manners".

Safely on board, we can hope to relax knowing that the men and women on the flight deck and throughout the cabin are there to give us all the support needed notwithstanding the unavoidable and unexpected quirky behaviour of fellow passengers something we have already explored to a large extent.

When everyone has stowed their carry-on luggage in the overhead containers you might hear something like this as you settle into your seat:

"This is your captain speaking. Welcome aboard flight 007 to Malaga. We should have you on the ground at 5.30 local time depending upon headwinds and whether or not I still want to go there."

The announcement is meant to help passengers to relax and feel comfortable in the care of captain and crew. And it may even bring forth a wry smile. He may follow up with:

"Attention air hostesses this is your captain speaking. Two large whiskies to the flight deck right away please!"

In my experience flight deck crews are consummate professionals. They take seriously their flying duties, their own safety, and that of their passengers. They may appear flippant at times but it's only their way of trying to inject a bit of humour into pre-flight moments to take the edge off any anxiety passengers may be feeling after a stressful journey to and through the airport.

When assertive action is called for, however, pilots work assiduously to solve all manner of problems. This includes in-flight emergencies when they fall back on their years of training. Striking the right tone when communicating an emergency situation to passengers is vital to keep everyone on board as calm as possible. Consider the following incident and the manner in which the captain explained what was going on.

In 1982 a British Airways' Boeing 747 en route from London-Heathrow to Auckland, New Zealand flew into a cloud of volcanic ash thrown skywards by the eruption of Mount Galunggung, some 181 kilometres southeast of Jakarta, Indonesia. All four engines shutdown one by one rendering the aircraft a glider. The aircraft glided downwards some 25,000 feet as the crew made preparations to ditch in the Indian Ocean. But this story had a happy ending because the crew were able to "relight" all four engines by remembering their basic training, by focusing on the problem at hand and by getting lucky. Luck, many aviators will tell you, is a pilot's best friend.

Captain Eric Moody, whom I remember well, was later praised and received an award for his airmanship and his candid cabin announcement that was later described as a masterpiece of understatement. In forty short, direct, and simple words he conveyed the precise situation:

- What had happened;
- The urgency of the situation;
- The crew's intense focus on the problem without false assurances they could fix it;
- Concern for the wellbeing of the passengers without being patronising; and,

- A sense of perspective that probably did more to relax the passengers than a thousand words could ever do.

This was Captain Moody's succinct announcement:

> *"Good evening ladies and gentlemen. This is your captain speaking. We have a small problem. All four engines have stopped. We are all doing our damnedest to get them going again. I trust you are not in too much distress".*

The crew opted to head for Jakarta hoping to gain enough power to make a landing. After gliding out of the ash cloud the crew were able to restart all four engines and land safely at Halim Perdanakusuma Airport in Jakarta.

But it wasn't that straightforward. On approach to Jakarta, the crew had difficulty seeing through the windscreen. They made the approach almost entirely on instruments utilising the instrument landing system (ILS), but the vertical guidance system was inoperative. They were forced to fly with only lateral guidance with the first officer monitoring the airport's distance measuring equipment (DME). He called out how high they should be at each DME-step along the final approach to the runway, creating a virtual glide slope for them to follow. It was, in Captain Moody's words, "a bit like negotiating one's way up a badger's arse."

That wasn't luck dear readers; passengers were in the hands of skilled aviators, magnificent men who really knew their flying machine.

*

I remember working a Britannia flight to Pisa on which my husband Bill was one of the pilots. That day we had a full load of passengers all itching to get a sight of Pisa and its famous Leaning Tower.

During the descent into Pisa airport the undercarriage was lowered as usual but flight deck instrumentation indicated the nose-wheel was not locked in the down position. In truth, the flight deck crew couldn't ascertain whether it was up or down and there was no way of checking from inside the aircraft.

Air traffic control ordered us into a holding pattern. At that time we informed the passengers of the situation. Thirty minutes later, it was suggested we make a low-level run over the tower so controllers could see whether or not the nose-wheel was fully extended.

Bill took the left-hand seat (normally the captain's position) and prepared to carry out the landing. To keep passengers fully informed and to offset any concern from the low-level fly-past, Bill picked up the intercom and explained what we were about to do and why: "This is a rare opportunity for you to see Pisa close-up," he said, "and I hope you enjoy this unique experience not normally offered to everyone."

During the low-level manoeuvre passengers peered out of the aircraft windows anxious for a close view of the Leaning Tower but all they saw were fire engines and ambulances lined up on either side of the runway.

The crew decided to conduct a final approach and safely landed the aircraft to a spontaneous outburst of cheering and applause. On this occasion the nose-wheel was extended and locked down; the problem was a faulty instrument, which was often the case.

That wasn't the only nail-biting problem with aircraft undercarriages I came to experience. I had worked on a flight carrying pilgrims to Damascus, this time aboard a Douglas DC-6 aircraft. On landing, the undercarriage completely collapsed and the aircraft slithered to a halt partway down the runway. The underside of the aircraft was badly damaged.

During the approach and landing there was total silence in the cabin save for the muttering of prayers and the rustle of prayer beads. To everyone's relief, the subdued mood was broken by the captain: "Welcome to Damascus ladies and gentlemen. You will be pleased to learn that Saint Peter has no room at the inn today." His announcement was followed by laughter and enthusiastic applause from the relieved and happy, on-board "congregation".

We were all delighted to walk away from what could have been a much worse accident and very grateful to be repatriated on another aircraft that brought out spares and mechanics a week later.

*

I had a most frightening experience flying from Gatwick on a Viscount aircraft when, without any warning, everything went deathly quiet. I looked out of the cabin window and was mortified to see that all four props were idling. We had suffered a sudden loss of engine power -- but why?

I peeked into the flight deck in time to see two pairs of hands madly scrambling among the many switches and buttons. Quickly closing the door, I put in place my cabin smile and calmly walked down the centre aisle as if nothing was amiss. Almost immediately the engines were restarted and the captain came onto the intercom: "There was a small technical fault," he explained in a controlled tone of voice, "nothing to worry about but we are heading back to Gatwick to make sure everything is alright."

Later I learnt that when the crew switched to reserve fuel tanks the engines cut because the tanks contained sodium methylate causing fuel starvation. Fortunately, our magnificent pilots were able to quickly restore fuel flow before the Viscount turned into a 56,000 pound glider. Someone was definitely looking after us that day.

Quirky captains

- *A captain who flew on short-haul aircraft called in sick whenever he was rostered to fly on Fridays. He was taken to task and asked to provide an explanation. "I was persuaded by some unscrupulous colleagues to visit a fortune teller who told me to be careful of flying on Fridays." Later, after realising he was the subject of an elaborate hoax, he responded to every call to fly only to find he was always rostered to fly on Fridays;*
- *Another captain carried his guitar on every flight and played it at every opportunity until crew members were bored to death. He acquired the nickname "Captain Segovia" after John Segovia the famous guitarist. He took this as a compliment. His boring activities didn't end there: He made a point of never eating aircraft food instead preferring vinegar-steeped chip butties prepared by his wife. He would sit on the flight deck eating cold chip butties that reeked of vinegar;*
- *Another captain, considered by many of us to be an excellent pilot and delightful man refused to comply when asked to relinquish his passport during an overnight stop in Lisbon. He was the only member of the crew to refuse and the authorities responded by putting him in gaol delaying the flight until after court hearings. A relief flight deck crew had to be flown out from Gatwick to retrieve the passengers.*

Subsequently the captain was released and returned to Gatwick his pride, and passport, intact;

- *Stepping out from the flight deck of his VC10 aircraft the captain asked a passenger if he'd enjoyed a good night's sleep. "I didn't sleep a wink," he replied, "because the air hostesses chatted all night long." Apologising, the captain promised to have a word with the girls. "No, don't do that," he pleaded, "I learnt more about women in one night than I've learnt in my entire life!"*

Thanks for the memories

I have written much about the golden days of flying and the wonderful lifestyle that accompanied those days during which I enjoyed trips to magical places at a time when going abroad was an experience clouded by mystery and promises of romance. I never felt more alive than when I was travelling abroad and in the company of good friends. It was also a time when a woman was treated with tremendous respect.

I suspect by now readers may have gained the impression that I loved long-haul flights above all others. That's true. Jetting off to faraway places that offered a sense of mystery or a hint of romance, and time to enjoy both, was a truly wonderful experience.

For me, there were also opportunities to re-kindle the love of my childhood days with all the happy memories such reunions inspired, because I could again walk in my own footsteps in a manner of speaking and meet people who had impacted my childhood years. In effect, I always had the reassuring feeling I was going home.

Another important reason for enjoying long-haul flights was my love for the Bristol Britannia aircraft – a magnificent, kindly old giant of the air with the heart of a lion. Loved by all who flew in her, we always felt safe in her company for some inexplicable reason. I would describe this magnificent aircraft in the way I would speak of one of my favourite dogs: a noble golden retriever with a heart of gold; sure-footed in every way with a gentle nature and a unique personality. Odd, you may think, to describe an aircraft in such endearing terms, but that's how air crew felt about her. I have wonderful memories of flying the "Whispering Giant" to India, Africa and Singapore and would like to share one or two that still resonate with me so many years later.

*

Bombay

When I first flew to India there was still an air of the old Raj; ladies were referred to as *memsahibs* and old-world courtesies survived leaving one with a strong desire to go back again and again.

In Bombay (now Mumbai) city streets were always a hotbed of activity. A cacophony of sound radiated from roads and small lanes jammed with cars, trucks, buses, trishaws and heavily-laden, iron-wheeled wooden handcarts. The ubiquitous handcart, which comes in all manner of shapes and sizes, is still evident in today's sprawling metropolis of Mumbai carrying anything from motorcycles to blocks of ice.

When I first went there it struck me as a vast city of indescribable diversity and energy but with an air of complete mystery. The fine colonial architecture, hidden temples and street bazaars were all steeped in history providing a constant reminder of the days of the British Raj. To put Bombay into perspective, this sprawling city is the capital city of the State of Maharashtra and the most populous city in India with approximately eighteen million people in the urban area and growing.

We flew in the "Whispering Giant" Britannia aircraft from the UK to Singapore with stops at Istanbul and a crew change in Bombay, which could entail a three-day layover. There were plenty of opportunities to explore the city, go shopping and soak up the amazing atmosphere. Over the years Bill and I became quite familiar with Bombay and many of its people.

One great stopping-off place for crews was the Bombay Swimming Club, and if we went shopping we tended to go back to the same shops time and again where we had studiously built up a good rapport with stall vendors and shopkeepers. We spent hours bargaining – it was expected and gracefully accepted of course. We knew we were making headway when coffee or tea was substituted for something a little stronger.

When Bill was with me he always gave me the same lecture before we went shopping: "Never say how much you like something Eunice; act as if you're doing them a favour by taking it off their hands." It was sound advice of course and I have never forgotten it.

When it came to bartering I remember when we lived in Singapore how my mother, on one occasion, spent several days haggling over a roll of shantung. Her approach was different to the one

Bill advocated. Haggling got underway the minute the seller drew up at our house, his moped weighed down with all manner of goods. Straight off the bat my mother expressed an interest in the material and made the man an offer. Predictably, he asked for more. She refused. They bargained back and forth all morning until, red-faced, he departed with his roll of shantung across his moped. Mother wouldn't budge on the price

He was back the next day only for the bargaining session to arrive at the same outcome. He appeared again on the third day and agreed to lower the price – undercutting the one suggested by mother at their first meeting. Being the straightforward and honest person she was, mother insisted he accept her original offer. The deal was consummated and, as I recall, he never came to our door again. In mother, he must have met his match.

Whenever we were in Bombay crews always stayed at the West End Hotel, delightful accommodation in the city centre. I remember with great fondness the head waiter, a Mr de Souza, who was a perfect gentleman in every respect with a proud sense of honour. Formerly a regular in the Indian Army during the years of the British Raj he showed great respect for all things British. He loved to talk about those days, and we loved to listen to him as he related his experiences. Indeed Mr de Souza became a very special person in our lives showing interest in us as a couple. He was overjoyed when Bill and I told him we were getting married before our next trip to Bombay. We promised to bring him a photograph of our wedding and a piece of wedding cake, which we did. Imagine how devastated we were upon arrival at the West End Hotel to learn that he had died quite suddenly on our wedding day. I will never forget Mr de Souza.

Then there was little Alou. One of the receptionists at the hotel, Alou was a Parsi in Bombay's very large Parsi community. Centuries earlier, the Parsi people had migrated to India from what was Persia to avoid religious persecution by Muslims.

Petite and quite beautiful, Alou went the extra mile to make both Bill and me feel welcome. She would greet us like long-lost relatives, spoiling us as a result.

On one worrisome occasion when our entire crew, apart from Bill, were struck down by food poisoning, Alou took it upon herself to look after me. She would cook food at her home and bring it to the hotel. It was always wholesome and appetising fare and could not have been easy to prepare as she lived with a large family in cramped quarters.

In those days, and probably still today, Bombay had widespread poverty and unemployment. Citizens' health was generally poor and educational standards were below par for a large section of the population. Families often lived in incommodious and expensive accommodation with as many as three, four or more people sharing one room. Alou was the breadwinner for her family supporting her elderly parents and five other siblings. There were two rooms for sleeping and one communal room where all the cooking had to be done. I was both honoured and humbled by such acts of kindness, particularly as I was aware what it was costing her in time, effort and money. She was a wonderful friend.

I often recall the many conversations I held with her during which I learnt much about her family and their lifestyle. On one occasion, after the death of a relative, she described to me the traditional funeral procedure followed under Parsi culture. Within their religion it is customary for the deceased to be taken to the Tower of Silence in Bombay where the corpse is laid out to be quickly devoured by waiting vultures in the tower gardens.

The reason for this practice is that Earth, Fire, Air and Water are considered sacred elements that should not be defiled by the dead. As a result, burial and cremation have always been prohibited in Parsi culture.

The corpse is prepared by a priest who visits the house and says prayers to cleanse the sins and affirm the faith of the deceased. Formalities over, the body is wrapped in a piece of white cloth called a *sudreh* to denote purity of thought, word and deed. It is made of cotton as a reminder to respect the plant kingdom and is in one continuous piece symbolising one God. Finally, a *kusti*, made of lamb's wool to remind us to respect the animal kingdom, is tied three times around the deceased's waist to suggest good thoughts, good works and good deeds. It has four knots to act as a reminder that God created the human body from Earth, Fire, Air and Water. The *kusti* is made of seventy-two strands of wool and is hollow symbolising the physical and spiritual worlds. It is tied in the middle of the body at the waist to suggest a middle path of life. As the mourners make their way to the

Tower of Silence they walk in pairs all connected by a piece of white fabric. A dog is essentially a part of the funeral procession because it is believed that a dog can see death.

As interesting as all this may be, in today's world there is a major problem affecting Parsi funerals in Bombay. The population of vultures inhabiting the city has been drastically reduced through extensive urbanisation and the unintentional consequence of treating humans and animals with antibiotics and some anti-inflammatory drugs. As a result, disposing of a corpse according to Parsi tradition has become difficult to achieve in terms of the length of time it takes to dispose of it. Solar panels have been installed in the Tower of Silence to speed up the process of decomposition but this measure has only been partially successful. Ironically it could be that advances in today's modern world of science and medicine are creating fewer problems for the living, whilst at the same time creating greater problems for the dead.

I saw Bombay as a blend of traditional festivals, exotic food and evocative and expressive music. And because of the migration of the people from all over India since the era of the British Raj, the diverse range of religions, cultures and cuisine complements its overall charm.

At night the pavements are the domain of multitudes of homeless people seemingly born to live and die on the streets. Often, when walking back to our hotel after a late-night cinema show, we would see rats running over sleeping bodies.

On the plus side, shopping in Bombay was an absolute dream back then. You could buy just about anything you could name in the colourful bazaars that cluttered the lanes and which themselves were overrun by hordes of people bargaining for all manner of goods. Ornately carved Indian furniture, traditional Indian carpets and beautiful *numdah* rugs, linen, colourful towels, and jewellery -- everything you could imagine. Bill and I furnished our first home together with a lot of Bombay merchandise -- all bought for a song.

How well I remember the one hour drive from the airport to the hotel, truly the most dangerous part of the entire trip. Every taxi driver drove with his foot hard down on the accelerator, with no sense of danger as though there was no-one else on the road. It marked the only time I ever saw fear on the faces of the flight crew -- white as chalk and covered in perspiration. The journeys were not so much memorable as difficult to forget.

Bill and I once got into a taxi only to come across a foot, of the human variety, on the floor of the cab. We discovered that a passenger had reclined full stretch on the back seat with his bare feet dangling out of the cab window. Not too smart as an on-coming taxi, the one we were the next passengers to use, passed at high speed just inches from the other cab which was also going like a bat out of hell. One foot was sliced off and propelled through the window that was to be our cab. I don't know who was more shocked; the man who had lost his foot or the taxi driver who had to take it to the police station to report it as lost property. We changed our minds about the cab and took a low-velocity trishaw instead.

On the subject of taxis, I recall a pilot among our crew who was fanatical about personal hygiene. His fanaticism extended to washing his hands before using the toilet as well as afterwards. A super-sensitive kind of guy, he had a dread of catching anything. Imagine our amusement when he rushed into the hotel one day, covered in gentian violet after taking a cab back from town. Talk about having the blues.

The driver of the cab, we learnt later, was sleeping in the back of his cab before our pilot friend jumped in. When our friend got out of the cab he realised the state he was in and noticed that the back seat was covered in the lotion. The cab driver had impetigo and was using the prescribed lotion to treat his condition.

We never saw our alarmed crew member for the next twenty-four hours as he spent most of the time in the shower scrubbing himself with disinfectant. For the remainder of the trip he periodically examined himself for any sign of lesions. There were all sorts of casual comments such as, "is that a spot I can see on your back skipper?" As you can imagine he was a nervous wreck by the time we arrived back in the UK.

Bombay was a city of many faces but always presented an interesting and amusing profile to visitors so long as you kept your eyes and ears open. One of the funniest roadside advertisements I ever saw, for example, was in a village en route from the airport to the hotel. It was an ice-cream parlour resplendent in flashing neon signs which proudly and shamelessly advertised its name of "Shitty's Ice-Cream Parlour!" There's no accounting for some people's tastes.

I was on another drama-filled trip to the East. We took off from Stansted Airport in the late evening and, by the time we reached Bombay, half the cabin crew and flight deck crew had gone down with some kind of bug. Others fell sick later. Bill was the only one unaffected. To address this unacceptable situation, a fresh crew was despatched from Gatwick Airport to replace us for the next leg of our flight to Singapore.

Firmly stuck in Bombay we were reluctant to be split up as a crew and, as we were all being attended to by the same Indian doctor, we kept Bill busy ferrying drugs to us from a local pharmacy. Each one of us was asked to provide a urine sample and, to make sure the test results proved the same for the entire crew, Bill, our erstwhile go-between, kindly provided his own urine sample on behalf of everyone. The plan worked and, happily, we all stayed together.

For me, Bombay was an experience never to be forgotten.

I must confess I found the East to be a wonderful place both to visit and to live as I did for a number of years. It was so different; exotic in every way. How could I forget the wonderful smell of tropical fruits and flowers that greeted ones senses after opening the aircraft door? The pervasive fragrances conjured up a life-style so completely removed from anything experienced in today's world. It would be almost impossible to paint a picture of life as it used to be. I believe it was Rudyard Kipling who said the first condition of understanding a foreign country is to smell it.

As a child I lived in the Far East and went to school out there. When I returned years later, as an air hostess, things had already changed and my old Singapore was unrecognisable. The landscape was dominated by new skyscrapers evoking a certain exclusiveness and sophistication born from change. Old Changi was no longer recognisable as land was reclaimed from the sea for more high-rise buildings. The old order changed forever which of course is the order of life itself. Nothing is forever. There is no standing still which in many ways is good, but sadly something is ultimately lost through change.

For me, the gentle and beautiful way of life had gone. Now it seems to be all about making money against a pace of life that doesn't leave any time to enjoy the uniquely magical experience of savouring each and every moment. If I could fulfil one wish it would be to return once more to the very haven of all those memories, and to be at one with all the magic of those wonderful times that I was lucky enough to enjoy and touch the very heartbeat of the Far East for one last time.

*

Entebbe

When Rudyard Kipling wrote about the lure of Africa, I like to think he was referring to East Africa, somewhere I never tired of visiting during my flying days. Over time, land-locked Uganda soon became one of my favourite places to visit because of its rich culture, abundant wildlife and never-ending vistas of mountains, rivers and, of course, Lake Victoria the source of the great River Nile.

Director of the Hutchings Centre for African and African-American Research at Harvard University, Henry Louis Gates, got it right when he said, "For as long as I can remember, I have been passionately intrigued by 'Africa' the word itself, by its flora and fauna, topographical diversity and grandeur; but above all else, by the sheer variety of the colours of its people, from tan and sepia to jet and ebony".

Uganda gained independence from Britain in 1962 but has retained its membership of the Commonwealth of Nations ever since. However, it has had its ups and downs since becoming independent with forced changes in government on more than one occasion.

The airline I worked for, British United Airways (BUA) was a forerunner of British Caledonian Airways (BCAL) that played an important role in what was described in 1972 as the "Asian exodus". It was a time when one of Africa's most callous dictators, Idi Amin, forced almost 600,000 [British passport-holding] Asian Indians and Pakistanis to leave the country. BCAL was part of an intensive airlift organised by Britain. Idi Amin's ill-conceived programme of *Africanisation* left the country in economic ruin because it was the Asian community that constituted the country's entrepreneurial minority. The economy nosedived. A story repeated elsewhere in later years and still going on in various places around the world.

BUA's (later BCAL's) regular scheduled services operated from Gatwick to Nairobi in Kenya via Uganda's Entebbe International Airport about forty kilometres southwest of Kampala the country's capital. For us, Entebbe was a crew-change station where we enjoyed layovers that lasted up to a week at a time. We were accommodated at the prestigious Lake Victoria Hotel on the northern shores of the lake where crews had ample time to relax and take in the pristine environment. Some of my own favourite attractions included the snow-capped Rwenzori Mountains, Murchison Falls National Park, and the lake itself of course with abundant wildlife right on our doorstep.

Uganda was special because I could share time there with husband Bill. Together we explored much of the country sometimes taking safaris in the hope of getting a glimpse of elephants, hippos, mountain gorillas and some of the one thousand species of birds to be found in Uganda.

Although not necessarily recognised as a romantic destination some of my fellow air hostesses formed liaisons with young, white men based in Kampala. Hostesses referred to these young men, all of whom seemed to be suffering from very high levels of testosterone, as "Kampala cowboys". I can't say I recall any of them marrying one of these cowboys, but I wouldn't be surprised to learn that one or two had done so.

One thing Uganda does have is an abundance of tropical fruit. I was pleasantly surprised to learn the country grows more bananas than any other country, bar India. And, in my view, Uganda's pineapples are the best in the world. Avocado pears, another exquisite fruit that grows in abundance in Uganda, were always popular among visiting air crews. We used to take them back to the UK by the sack-load, stowing them in every available space on board the aircraft. I also saw passengers carrying boxes of the beautiful bird of paradise flowers on flights returning to the UK.

I remember one sad occasion after departing Entebbe airport for Gatwick when an elderly gentleman died on board our aircraft. I learnt that he and his wife had enjoyed the holiday of a lifetime, travelling independently, fulfilling a lifelong dream to visit Uganda. The gentleman's wife said her husband had only recently retired and had not shown any signs of ill-health. The poor man died from a massive cardiac arrest. Everything happened so quickly there wasn't time to do anything to help. I tried resuscitation but to no avail.

Our aircraft headed back to Entebbe to have the death confirmed. His wife, obviously very much in shock, insisted they make the trip home together; she did not wish to travel home alone at a later date. Nor did she want to leave behind the body of her deceased husband.

It took some organising but, after a lengthy delay, the body was loaded into the hold of the aircraft in a special container and we resumed our flight to Gatwick. To make sure the lady had someone to chat with on the way home, we took turns sitting with her so she was not left alone at any time. Even Bill sat with her for a short time.

After take-off we radioed ahead for the lady's daughter to meet the aircraft at Gatwick and I accompanied her off the plane and stayed with her until she was reunited with her family. A few weeks later, Bill and I received the most wonderful letter from the widow thanking us for everything we did to support her on that dreadful day that had turned her life upside down.

This brings to mind another awful incident that occurred in 1966 when Hazel Hester, the sister of one of our air hostesses, was strangled to death in Uganda after confronting two burglars intent on robbing her in her house in Entebbe. The perpetrators were sentenced to death by a court in Kampala. At the time, Hazel was an air hostess with the Belgian airline Sabena. I guess this serves to highlight the risks associated with flying and living in exotic parts of the world. It wasn't all glamour, there were troublesome times too. This incident reminds me of one of our airline captains who took his wife on holiday to Entebbe. She had her arm sliced off by a machete-wielding thief intent on stealing her handbag that she carried slung over her shoulder.

Yet another unpleasant incident occurred in Entebbe when some of our hostesses contracted a disease called *schistosomiasis*, or *bilharzia*, after sailing on Lake Victoria. Bilharzia is caused by parasites that live in freshwater in tropical climes. Virtually invisible to the naked eye, they burrow under the skin and lay eggs in the abdomen. Treated promptly it is curable but sometimes it isn't recognised by those inflicted until the situation becomes much more serious.

It always amazed me that such potentially serious diseases were never mentioned to air crews in a precautionary manner. Similarly, although we were always warned not to drink the local water down route, nothing was ever mentioned about cleaning teeth. So, to be on the safe side, we always used bottled water.

Despite these unfortunate incidents I personally found Uganda one of the friendliest places I've ever visited. The country may be small but, as the saying goes, small is beautiful.

Uganda's recent history is quite interesting: Back in 1907 a thirty-three year old adventurous MP called Winston Churchill made an arduous journey from the UK to Uganda sailing by ship to Mombasa; train from Mombasa to Kisumu; steam boat from Kisumu to Entebbe, then horse-drawn carriage to Kampala. Undoubtedly this was the best way to see the many interesting aspects of Uganda and almost certainly persuaded Mr Churchill to describe the country as "the pearl of Africa". How right he was.

Nairobi

As mentioned, BUA flights to East Africa flew from Gatwick to Entebbe in Uganda then on to Nairobi the capital and largest city in Kenya. In 1905 Nairobi replaced Mombasa as capital of the British protectorate and expanded through administration and tourism initially in the guise of big-game hunting. British settlers began exploring the region with Nairobi as their first port of call prompting the colonial government to build a number of spectacularly grand hotels in the city. The main occupants were British game hunters. Not surprisingly, Nairobi acquired the nicknames of "safari capital of the world" and "city under the sun" with many five-star hotels catering for safari-bound tourists.

During my time flying to Nairobi, BUA crews stayed at the prestigious Norfolk Hotel centrally located for Nairobi's many attractions in addition to being a jumping-off point for wildlife safaris. I also found the Norfolk Hotel very convenient for shopping trips to the many artisan crafts shops in the city. The woodcarvings were outstanding and, over time, I accumulated a selection of intricately carved giraffes and elephants along with salad bowls and servers. I felt we were spoiled for choice; my frequent trips to Nairobi made me appreciate how fortunate air crews were to be able to travel the world buying all kinds of artefacts while exploring the history and culture of different countries. At times I had to pinch myself to make sure it was all really happening to me.

On my first trip to Nairobi I remember being surprised and amused to come across a F.W. Woolworths shop, the retail phenomenon of the 20th century. I could hardly believe my eyes.

In terms of tourism, the Norfolk Hotel was an excellent location for visiting some of the city's many attractions including Sheldrick's Elephant Orphanage, established by David Leslie William Sheldrick MBE. Sheldrick, a famous naturalist and founding warden of Tsaro East National Park, died in 1977 of a massive heart attack. Afterwards, his widow, Daphne (later Dame Daphne Sheldrick) created the David Sheldrick Wildlife Trust (DSWT) to honour his memory and his outstanding contribution to wildlife conservation in Kenya. The DSWT still has, at its heart, the Orphans' Project which has gained worldwide recognition for its successful elephant and rhino rescue and rehabilitation programme. This project offers hope for protecting Kenya's elephant and rhino populations from poachers in search of ivory and horns. A problem then and still a problem today.

Fittingly, the Trust releases hand-raised infant elephants into the wild in the Tsaro East National Park where David Sheldrick was the founding warden as far back as 1948.

As a part of the many enjoyable occasions I visited Nairobi I would have dearly loved to have spent time in Aberdare National Park, the location of the famous Treetops Hotel. Back in 1932 the hotel was literally built into the tops of trees as a treehouse and in its original state had just two rooms. The concept was for guests to enjoy a splendid view of wildlife in their natural surroundings and in total safety.

Sir Horace Hearne, at the time Chief Justice of Kenya -- it was still a British colony -- escorted Britain's young Princess Elizabeth to a state dinner at Treetops where she and her husband Prince Philip stayed overnight coincidentally at the time the princess's father, King George VI's, passed away in 1952.

Naturally, the princess and her husband cut short their holiday and returned home in haste after which the princess was crowned Queen Elizabeth II at Westminster Abbey the following year.

As British hunter and conservationist Jim Corbett, who accompanied the royal couple, fittingly said when referring to Treetops, "...she went up a tree in Africa a princess and came down a queen. God bless her."

The original Treetops was burned down by African guerrillas during the 1954 Mau Mau Uprising a couple of years after the royal couple's visit. Later, it was rebuilt near the same watering hole and ever since has been a fashionable place to visit. Treetops has observation lounges and ground-level photographic hides from where guests can observe local wildlife at the nearby waterholes. Today it's a fifty-bedroomed hotel but will always be best remembered for the visit of Britain's Princess Elizabeth and her sudden and unexpected accession to the throne whilst staying there in 1952.

*

Singapore

Of all the places I've visited, Singapore remains one of the more prominent locations lodged in my mind because I spent an early part of my educational years in this wonderful island state. For me it marked the beginning of a never-ending fascination with the Far East. During the post-war period, when I attended school there, Singapore was still picking up the pieces after three and a half years of Japanese occupation. It went on to stage a remarkable recovery and today is not only a key member of ASEAN but also a world-class commercial and financial centre.

In later years when I returned to Singapore as an air hostess and saw the remarkable transition for myself I was overwhelmed by the charm and vibrancy of the city and the industriousness of its residents. But my fondest memories of Singapore stem from my days there as a child.

While serving in the British Army my father was posted to Singapore towards the end of 1946 soon after the war ended. My mother and I followed in early 1947 sailing aboard the *MV Empire*

Windrush formerly a German naval troopship but later acquired by the UK as a prize-of-war. My mother referred to this vessel as a "...slow boat to China..." as it took six weeks to sail to Singapore calling at many ports en route. When mother arrived in Singapore it was her intention to sing with Radio Malaya and play the violin in the Singapore Symphony Orchestra. For me, these were memorable years; I thought there was nowhere in the world quite as special as Singapore.

However, the island was still very colonial and prone to great risk from civil unrest that followed Japan's occupation. There were incidents of random shootings including one occasion on a bus I took to school. After that my parents decided to switch my school so that I wouldn't have to journey by bus. My first school was the Convent of the Good Shepherd; my new school became the Holy Infant Jesus in central Singapore just off Orchard Road.

Attending my new school was still not without difficulties. To get there I had to cross the road at the traffic lights at the junction of Orchard Road and Bras Basah Road. One day, to my astonishment, a policeman was shot right in front of me. After that I was always escorted to school.

I was educated in convents though I wasn't a Roman Catholic. My mother believed my education would be well-rounded with the influence of nuns. I wasn't so sure about that. However, I do remember that the second convent only agreed to accept me on the understanding I received extra tuition to bring me up to the same standard of the other children who were a year younger than I.

Nuns were in overall charge but the majority of teachers were lay teachers. Some of the nuns who did teach in the convent concentrated on music and religious studies. My principal teacher was a beautiful Malay woman called Miss Domingo. In those days, one teacher taught most subjects as opposed to today's practise of having teachers specialise in one subject only.

The standard of education was much higher than in England and there was a hunger among students to learn. Competition for an education was keen to say the least, so much so that children went to school in shifts.

At my school there were six white girls two of whom were English (including myself) and four Dutch girls. The other fifteen hundred pupils were Malay, Chinese and Indian. English was the predominant language then and still is today.

I found school life strict in every way, governed by stringent rules with no exceptions. School hours were 7am until 1pm with a break in the afternoons as it was considered too hot to study. From 6 to 8pm each evening I undertook supervised homework. A lot of Malay, Chinese and Indian children went to school in the afternoons, evenings and at weekends. There was a huge appetite among Singapore's children to learn with a longing to make something of their lives. For me, these were very happy days indeed.

When I returned to England years later, and attended boarding school, I was assigned to a class of girls almost two years ahead of my age group. This made life very difficult as I fell between two stools:

my own age group on the one hand, and as a younger person with older girls on the other. My preference was to finish my education in Singapore during my last three years. Alas, it was not to be.

On the social scene, Singapore offered a very enjoyable lifestyle. There were many parties; tiffin at the Officers' Club in Tanglin; the wonderful Singapore Swimming Club; Singapore Cricket Club and polo. And there were many memorable trips to Raffles Island for parties. There was something for everyone and I feel lucky and privileged to have been a part of that lifestyle as a child.

On the downside, however, I can recall the riots that broke out because of a thirteen-year-old girl called Maria Hertogh. A year older than I, she was born in 1937 to Dutch-Catholic parents. Her father, a sergeant in the Royal Dutch Army, was captured when Japan invaded Singapore and sent to a POW camp in Japan and remained incarcerated until 1945.

Maria was the third child in a family of six children. When the sixth child, a son, was born, Maria went to stay with a Malay women who was a close friend of Maria's mother. She was meant to be there for only three or four days, presumably to give Maria's mother time to recover from the birth of her son.

When Maria failed to return home as expected, her mother borrowed a bicycle and went to retrieve her daughter only to be arrested by a Japanese sentry on the outskirts of Bandung. As she had no permit she was interned. At the end of her internment Maria's mother lost touch with her friend and her daughter Maria. She could not find them anywhere.

As a consequence, Maria was raised as a Malay and could only speak Bahasa Malay. She wore the *kebaya* and worshipped Islam devoutly though she had been baptised Catholic by her biological parents.

As soon as Maria's father was released from internment in 1945, he and his wife set about searching for their daughter. In 1949, Maria's adoptive family were traced to the *kampong* where they were living. Just thirteen years old, Maria had been married off to a Muslim schoolteacher though the marriage was never consummated. Maria left her husband and returned to live with her adoptive mother. They became inseparable.

But that wasn't the end of the story. Maria's true parents refused requests to allow Maria's adoptive parent to have her. She, in turn, refused to give up her claim for custody. After lengthy court proceedings Maria's biological parents were awarded custody.

It was a decision that led to riots that began on December 11, 1950 and lasted for three days. During this time mobs attacked Europeans on sight. Cars were overturned and set on fire as were buildings. It seemed many officers in the local police force were sympathetic towards the adoptive parents and had insufficient numbers in their ranks to quell the rioting. The military intervened imposing a two-week curfew after which rioting was brought under control, but it was a long time before law and order was restored.

On the day the riots broke out, my mother was in Tanglin. She had taken a taxi to Singapore to collect me from school but was unable to get through because of the mobs on the streets. To get to me she had to disembark from the cab and fight her way through the mob to where I was waiting. It was an extremely brave thing for her to do. She could easily have lost her life were it not for a sympathetic Malay shopkeeper who knew my mother. She helped by dressing my mother in a *baju kurung* (enclosed Malay costume) afterwards accompanying her to the convent.

Thereafter I travelled to school each day by armoured car with a military escort for nearly a month. During this same period friends of my parents were married in Singapore Cathedral and the bride also had to travel by armoured car with an armed escort – rather indelicately described by some guests as a shotgun wedding.

Years later, when I returned to Singapore as an air hostess, I felt I was going home. I made regular visits to the convent and was welcomed with open arms and had many joyous moments. I introduced my husband to my former teachers who were thrilled at all of us being reunited.

Naturally, Singapore has changed almost beyond recognition from the fifties. Today it is a thriving island state and one of the world's most important commercial centres – quite different from the "Lion City" of my childhood. Yet it still holds a place in my heart. The famous Orchard Road, once lined with nutmeg and pepper plantations, is today the domain of high-end shopping centres, nightclubs, world-class restaurants, bars and lounges. However,

Emerald Hill Street still has some of Singapore's oldest and finest terraced houses and the streets are lined with sweetly perfumed frangipani trees. I remember how my mother would pick frangipani flowers to decorate a table for dinner parties. She would place the flowers in the refrigerator for a few hours beforehand where they would turn from white with yellow-tinged petals to blood-red making a colourful attraction on the dining table.

Singapore Botanical Gardens, established way back in 1860, always had an aura of Victorian gentility in my eyes and became a favourite place to visit. In those days I remember a snake charmer who possessed a warped sense of humour. Knowing of my mother's total dislike of snakes he would lay in wait for her then chase her through the gardens holding forth his basket of slithering reptiles.

One night I woke up with a strange feeling in one leg where a snake had wrapped itself around my leg. Luckily it was nonvenomous but, to this day, I can still feel that snake wrapped tightly around my leg. Perhaps that's why I have an inbuilt dislike of reptiles.

Then there was Singapore's famous Change Alley, much like an open market but full of colour and with a vibrant atmosphere. I well remember the smell of camphor cubes sold for use in wardrobes to keep the moths at bay; incense intermingled with pineapples; wonderful flower stalls in a blaze of colour all exuding the sweet smell of tropical perfumes. The hustle and bustle of the market no longer prevails having been replaced by a more sophisticated design.

Raffles Hotel, perhaps reassuringly, has not changed beyond recognition at least from the outside. It is immaculate in every way exhibiting an air of luxury throughout. I recall spending many happy occasions there as a child with my family enjoying Sunday lunch or for a more formal occasion such as the Christmas Ball at Raffles. Though it may have changed its face since my childhood years, fond memories endure as strong as ever, as does the love I have for the wonderful island of Singapore.

PART 3

LIFE AFTER FLYING

In between goals is a thing called life that has to be lived and enjoyed – Sid Caesar

For many wonderful and memorable years flying was my life during which I saw many changes in respect of in-flight services and the types of travellers we served. Over time, I came to the conclusion that the best years, once mine to enjoy, were now part of the past. I still loved flying with a passion but I felt it was time to bow out from what was more of a rat race, steadily eclipsing the world of glamour and adventure that had previously been my realm. I saw looming ahead of me a monotonous daily grind as semi-robotic trolley dollies replaced archetypal air hostesses, bringing an end to on-board gourmet dining and the use of interpersonal skills that had formed an integral part of my flying experience. It was time to seek pastures new. The thought saddened me.

Similarly, Bill was sad that he and I would no longer share travel experiences even though he was approaching retirement age himself. In fact, he had not enjoyed the best of health for some time; the unfortunate but inevitable legacy of radiation sickness that ravaged his immune system was taking its toll. If Bill picked up a common cold, for example, it often turned to pneumonia and, on one occasion, he suffered a pulmonary embolism that fortuitously occurred whilst he was in hospital recovering from pneumonia. Happily he made a full recovery and returned to flying. For Bill, that's what life was all about; he couldn't exist without being airborne and his determination to succeed always saw him prepared to fly another day. I had the same passion but was not similarly obsessed.

During our years living in the East Sussex county town of Lewes we made many friends and I now had time to enjoy a change in lifestyle that precluded the constant packing and unpacking of suitcases. I delighted at being able to enjoy my home and garden while ruminating about what the future may hold. I had always enjoyed entertaining friends, it gave release to my catering skills, so I began holding dinner parties again. It was a newfound luxury to have more time and enough energy to make use of it.

Life for me became one, huge social round of activity. It was quite a novelty to immerse myself in a changed lifestyle. Without doubt everything I learnt during my Cordon Blue course gave me all the confidence I needed at that moment in time. Life was such fun. Bill and I also had time to travel as passengers -- not crew -- and that introduced a big change in our lifestyle.

*

However, before we quit flying, Bill and I found ourselves on a trip to Germany and experienced an event that became the source of an amusing story.

We were walking around the streets of Limburg when I spied a cheese shop selling Limburger cheese. Remembering how partial my father was to it, I decided to take some back to the UK as a special treat. I was hesitant at first as I also recalled mother saying she could not abide the smell of it and would not have it in her house under any circumstances. But, as a special treat for father I was prepared to take the risk on this occasion.

Never having tasted it before, or even experienced being in the company of anyone who had, I had no idea of what I was about to impose on mother. I should say that the official assessment of this cheese, which originated in the Duchy of Limburg, is that its acerbity can be compared with bad foot odour. Before going further I should give readers unfamiliar with Limburger cheese some insight into the product – candid views from people who may be described as aficionados.

One man commented, "I understood it is supposed to smell like it had ripened between the toes but surely not the toes of a soldier with trench foot!" Another customer wrote to the manufacturer with equal mordancy, "…welcome to hell. The lunch menu today is durian fruit cup cocktail and Limburger cheese sandwiches."

Although I took these scornful and sniffy assessments in the spirit intended, father loved it so much I couldn't resist buying a fairly large piece for him. When we returned from Germany it was several days before we were able to visit my parents so I popped the cheese into the fridge.

The next day when I ventured into the kitchen my sense of smell was assailed by the most horrendous stench emanating from the fridge. I decided that leaving the Limburger in the fridge for one minute longer was not an option. So, holding the cheese at arm's length as though it was about to explode, I tied it up with string and hung it out of the kitchen window, which happened to be directly over the conservatory of our landlady. I should add that it was a hot summer that year.

The next morning the landlady knocked on our door and asked if we were suffering as a result of bad drains. "I have called out the plumber," she announced reassuringly.

"We haven't noticed anything out of the ordinary," I replied honestly.

Then it dawned on me: the Limburger cheese was the malodorous culprit, not the drains. Acting quickly I retrieved the offending cheese, packed it in a cool bag full of ice and dropped it into the car boot as we planned to visit my parents on the following day.

Father was delighted to receive the cheese. Predictably mother was furious and banished dad to the shed at the bottom of the garden never to return to the house until he'd eaten it all. I never pulled that trick again, but at least my dear father enjoyed his cheese.

*

Finding time to enjoy animals, once again, was another bonus in my new life that gave rise to a whole new canine family. Tragically, we had lost Bruce our Corgi and didn't seek to replace him while I was still flying. Now, we had Brucita, another Corgi, who was an absolute delight. We also acquired a miniature white poodle called Minnie Mouse, and a miniature Yorkshire terrier called Lulu.

I always remember Bill declaring with repugnance, "You can think again if you imagine I would be seen walking a poodle in public."

A short time later, after he'd become utterly devoted to her and she to him, I reminded him of his solemn pledge. Being a typical man he denied ever saying such a thing.

Later, two cats named Billy and Doodybugs also joined the family; the latter's name a compromise: Bill wanted to call her Doody and I wanted Bugsy. The important thing is we became one very large and happy family.

Our involvement with animals meant that the local vet, David, inevitably became one of our closest friends and we were to spend many happy hours with him and his wife Judith. In fact he came to my assistance when I fell ill with gastroenteritis and was unable to take the Yorkie for her annual booster. Bill substituted for me and when he returned home presented me with a bottle of medicine prepared by David. One tablespoonful of whatever it was, I was assured, had all I needed to feel better. Within two hours I was on my feet feeling much better and ready to declare the medicine a miracle cure.

The next time I bumped into him I thanked David and asked about the magic potion. "Well, it's something I always give to cows for colic and it certainly seems to work for them," he told me. Clearly he swore by it and I had to confess so too did I, although I was not enamoured at being likened to a cow. It transpired David was a man of many talents: not only a brilliant vet but also an author of books on rare species of orchids found in the British Isles.

On another occasion a good friend of mine was quite distressed because her horses were unable to stand properly and needed constant support from the attendant grooms. In trying to understand what had happened, all she was able to contribute at the time was that she'd put two horses into a field where, previously, there had been cows. David was summoned.

As soon as he arrived on the scene he could tell the horses were in a bad way: one was staring blankly at the gate in the field quite unsure where it was. It transpired the horses had chanced upon a manger containing cow fodder at the bottom of the field. Recent rains had accelerated the process of fermentation and the horses had tucked into the fodder and polished it off. As David indelicately put it, "they were as pissed as newts!"

On another "fetch the vet" occasion David received a telephone call at three in the morning. The woman at the other end asked him to make a home visit to attend to Rosie who had a very high temperature coupled with nausea. She sincerely felt a home visit was warranted.

Unaware of having on his books a patient called Rosie, David asked the woman if she was referring to a dog or a cat. "She's not an animal," the woman replied indignantly, "she's my five-year-old daughter."

"In which case," David informed her as gently as possible, "you need to consult a doctor. Why did you call me, a vet, for assistance?"

"Well," she said, with great sincerity, "I couldn't possible disturb the doctor at such an unearthly hour in the morning could I? That's why I rang you."

*

I had never before been to an obedience class for dogs and I will probably never go again after spending a couple of days in the company of Miss Peabody. Standing five feet high and looking conventionally "doggy" in her baggy jumper, tweed skirt and brogues, she was more than a match for all the dogs and owners attending her class. Her technique was fairly singular: "Clonk 'em, and love 'em, m'dear!" I later discovered this to be her rousing battle cry.

She was said to have tamed horses by blowing gently up their nostrils and laid claim to fame for increasing the milk yield of a local farmer's prize dairy herd by engaging them in conversation.

Anyway, twelve of us enrolled for what promised to be a coveted two-day training course in Yorkshire. The course attracted dog owners from far and wide who brought with them hounds of all shapes and sizes: large and small, smooth-haired and shaggy, but all with pedigrees as long as your arm. That is except for one: Mine!

Possum, a delightful "unknown quantity" was the size of a donkey. Not much of a brain to boast about but he exhibited more than his fair share of animal cunning and had a massive personality. A victim of horrendous cruelty, he had just three legs but, mercifully, no psychological hang-ups. He had a great big loving heart and a giant-sized sense of fun. His tragic start in life meant he was spoilt, but because of his size I felt that it was in the interest of both of us for him to learn which one of us was in charge. Somehow I knew that Possum was special.

When he was only twelve weeks old the poor animal had been held down by one man while another sliced off one of his front legs in a calculated and callous act of cruelty. I was asked to take him in because Possum needed a safe environment and lots of love and kindness. And he got this from just about everyone who came to know him.

I was a nurse at the time and recall going out on night duty on one occasion leaving Possum alone at home in the kitchen. Later I was to learn that my wine rack on the kitchen counter was not inaccessible to a three-legged animal. I returned home to discover old Possy laid out on the floor of the kitchen. At first glance I took him to be dead. Then I saw the wine bottle, broken off at the neck, its contents presumably swimming around in the stomach of one very drunk canine. He was plastered. Then it dawned on me that I faced a tricky problem ahead: How could I get into an upright position a drunken, three-legged, donkey-sized dog that was a total deadweight?

Luckily a friend dropped by as I was struggling to get Possum onto three legs and into the garden for some fresh air. With my friend's help I got the dog onto his hind legs and, with our arms encircling the dog's midriff, frogmarched him into the garden to walk some life into him. Perhaps you can picture the scene in our quiet, picturesque village in the Yorkshire Dales as we steered the dog around the garden. We were subjected to some very strange looks from people passing by in vehicles; even worse reactions when we shouted the occasional, "It's alright, don't worry, the dog's just pissed!" as they drove on by.

As Possum's shaky frame regained a modicum of normalcy, I noticed he had all the tell-tale signs of a huge hangover. It didn't last long but he did retain a predilection for alcohol thereafter. But to me, this dog was a gentle giant with the heart of a lion.

In later years, after Possum had gone to the great kennel in the sky, and I had acquired another dog called Simba, I found it quite uncanny to see in Simba enough of Possum's characteristics to believe he was still with me to this day.

But back to the canine training session and the erstwhile Miss Peabody.

We all felt a bit chary as our experienced instructor, who looked to be in her seventies, made a grand entrance into the training yard. Her face had a no-nonsense look about it that commanded silence from the assembled throng…a silence immediately broken by Possum passing wind. I cringed as it was sufficiently audible to stop Miss Peabody in her tracks. Looking sternly through her heavy horn-rimmed specs she barked, "Who made that noise?" Nervously, one by one, we shuffled our feet. It was then I spied other owners eyeing me up and down in an act of silent betrayal. At the appropriate time I would exact my revenge. For now I elected to bide my time. I stared at my feet and bit my lip.

Miss Peabody had her own secret way to identify owners by their dogs and, as I felt the blood rush to my face, I was acutely aware she was finding it difficult matching dog-with-owner in my case. It was an unnerving moment. For what seemed like an eternity she stared at both of us as though we were from outer space. Then her eyes lit up in a moment of elation, "Mrs Tripod, control yourself!" she yelled in my face at the same time making a disparaging remark about my three-legged Possum. I was incensed by her insensitive outburst but bit my lip...again. A ripple of laughter ran through the rest of the class making me wish for a safe haven of a kennel a million miles from where I was standing wherein to slink and lick my wounds.

"Sit," Miss Peabody shouted, indicating a row of chairs. Everyone, including the dogs, assumed she was addressing the owners. And that's when mayhem broke out among the assembled canines. Within seconds, snapping, barking and biting animals took centre stage. They also engaged in other unmentionable forms of conduct of the kind that got most canines into the class in the first case. With three dogs muzzled, and a safe distance between a very randy Alsatian and all the bitches, Miss Peabody began instructing us on the most effective way to talk to our dogs.

"Remember, that at all times," she announced, "great emphasis should be placed on sibilants: One should say Sss-i-tt and Sssttayyy. Be forceful!"

As commanded we began to practice our sibilants interspersed with timely and helpful contributions from Miss Peabody, "You are not producing enough spit. Spit is the secret of success. Now, once again everyone…and lots of spit this time," she commanded dabbing her wet mouth with a handkerchief. With renewed vigour we doubled-down on our sibilants until the yard was covered with a film of fine spray.

As you may already have gathered, none of the dogs took one iota of notice of our well-aimed sibilants. The three muzzled offenders continued to chew their way out of confinement and several others looked as though World War Three was about to commence.

The next most important word, we were told, intended to impress our canines, was "what" as in "What a good dog!" "And whilst praising the animal," Miss Peabody stressed, "one should embrace one's pet and tickle its chest."

As instructed, we obediently followed Miss Peabody's advice.

"What a good dog!" everyone uttered as we all rolled around the floor desperately trying to get a firm grip on our animal to embrace each panic stricken dog and tickle its chest.

By this time the canine contingent, to a dog, sniffed a free-for-all and, once more, chaos took centre stage. In due course order was restored after Miss Peabody singled out a delinquent Yorkshire terrier upon which she began demonstrating her tried and tested method of discipline. I don't know who felt worse, dogs or owners.

After several attempts, with scant success, Miss Peabody beat a hasty retreat to get a band aid from the first aid box after being bitten by one totally unimpressed four-footed midget. By the time she re-appeared, bloodstained but unbowed, most of us were beginning to feel the wear and tear of battle. Not so Miss Peabody; she was just getting into her stride.

Re-joining the battle, she unceremoniously pushed all the dogs into the sitting position then hauled them bodily to heel, and rewarded them with loud and enthusiastic shouts of "What a good dog!" followed by lots of tickling of hairy chests. At least right up to the moment when the Yorkshire terrier bit her again. A strategic withdrawal was in order. "I think the dogs need a play break," she declared with no loss of enthusiasm, or face, or sign of pain.

The unscheduled play break became a defining moment, a cause célèbre. Dogs' leads were withdrawn, owners readily collapsed onto chairs in a state of nervous exhaustion, and the dogs reverted to being their normal, despicable selves. The Yorkshire terrier deemed it his mission in life to pick a fight with anything that moved. The Alsatian made a beeline for the bitches and frenzied sexual activity broke out redefining the term "play break".

Pandemonium took over the yard. Miss Peabody was horrified: "Shocking, I shall have to fetch my clonking stick!" she shrieked yet clearly determined to win the day. Without further ado she strode off only to reappear seconds later with a stout, leather lead. Striding towards the unruly dogs she began dishing out punishment to the sex maniacs. Once again the term "play break" was redefined as a measure of order was restored. Everyone's breathing returned to normal. It would be short-lived.

Again the booming voice of a triumphant military commander: "That's it in a nutshell you know m'dears," she declared with supreme confidence. "Clonk 'em and love 'em, it never fails!" Her technique was put to the test and prevailed. And as the two days progressed a metamorphosis overtook both dogs and owners. Even the oversexed Alsatian and the stroppy little Yorkie fell in line and obeyed commands. It seemed like pure madness at times but nobody could say she didn't have a way with animals after her remarkable efforts to gain control.

The moment arrived for all of us to take our leave. But first the mandatory group photograph to prove our attendance and written confirmation that these fine canines had successfully completed a commando course for delinquent dogs. Dutifully, and for the final time, we all lined up alongside Miss Peabody. From the corner of my eye I noticed the Yorkshire terrier was in his owner's arms with his incisors dangerously close to Miss Peabody's jugular vein. An unspeakable thought crossed my mind but I remained tight-lipped not wishing to draw the wrath of our commanding officer.

At the precise moment the camera clicked to record for posterity this incongruous group of scoundrels, an adventurous, but not particularly smart cat, strode into the yard. Cue the Charge of the Light Brigade. All dogs set off in hot pursuit of a fleet-footed moggy, closely followed by their weary owners. Once more the air was filled with a fine drizzle of spittle as sibilants were dispensed with a pronounced measure of desperation.

Only my three-legged "Possy" remained blissfully immune to events unfolding around him, though he did decide it was time to go home. As we made for the car, Miss Peabody's voice rang out above the cacophony of sound, "Clonk 'em and love 'me m'dears! Don't forget!"

I glanced down at Possum and could swear he winked at me. I bit my lip…again.

*

Animals, by which I mean domestic pets, have always been an important part of my life. From my early childhood a steady stream of indignant dogs and cats had to put up with being dressed in dolls clothes and wheeled around in a pram. I steadfastly refused to allow any of their quizzical looks get to me. Yet I sensed, even at an early age, the animals may have considered I was behaving rather foolishly.

"The greatest pleasure of a dog," English author Samuel Butler asserted, "is that you may make a fool of yourself with him, and not only will he not scold you, but he will make a fool of himself, too." I would agree with that but, looking back as an only child, I would say I still preferred the companionship of animals to that of some of my peers.

Take Gyp for example, a small, white Pomeranian that on many occasions became a go-between and ultimate peacemaker whenever I was sent to bed in disgrace. I tied messages to his tail seeking clemency; Gyp transported them downstairs to my waiting mother who was always one step ahead in this game.

And how could I ever forget Sooty, our black Labrador bitch that gave birth to nineteen puppies – a record I believe. Each pup bore a striking resemblance to next door's smug-faced Boxer, which we found puzzling. How could an essential act of nature have taken place when we were always so vigilant? Sooty had never been out alone other than in the garden and that was securely fenced-off from the house next door. But the fence turned out to be the key to the puzzle. All was revealed months later when Sooty was seen in the garden her derriere backed up against the fence made from wooden stakes and large squares of wire that proved to be no impediment to our neighbour's randy and resourceful Boxer. Proof, if there was any doubt, that love will always find a way.

We decided to hang on to one of Sooty's puppies, a beautiful sable-coloured-cross we named Simba. He had quite a personality and a reputation as a very fine singer with an extensive repertoire. His soulful rendering of *My Heart is like a Red Red Rose* was delivered with heartfelt feeling. Mother, instantly recognising the dog's innate talent, was more than happy to provide piano accompaniment as Simba yapped and bayed with deep feeling.

Simba may have been a star but he also had a wicked sense of humour. He took playful delight in nipping people's bottoms particularly those of the dustmen who always approached our house with fear and trepidation. We were living on an army estate at the time and Simba had a habit of nudging his snout under everyone's door knocker then letting each one crash back against the door before beating a hasty retreat. I am fairly certain our neighbours never discovered the perpetrator of these childish pranks and I am pretty sure many of the local kids got the blame.

Another of our dogs with an endearing character was Bruce our Corgi. A dearly loved addition to our family he had a temperament that did not match the unpredictable traits of the average Corgi. To begin with, he had formed a unique affinity with my father; man and dog were regulars at the local public house. Bruce, popular among locals, even had his own special water bowl. On many evenings father and Bruce could be found socialising at the inn; master with his wee dram, and man's best friend with his bowl of water and packet of crisps.

Bruce's star billing was challenged one evening when another dog appeared on the scene. And, much to Bruce's annoyance, the newcomer received a lot of attention from customers. He spent most of that evening sulking and glaring at the intruder. Bruce was no longer the centre of attention in the pub, his pride was severely damaged; he ignored every friendly attempt at reconciliation.

After what father judged later to be a moment of deep-thinking, Bruce rose to his feet and with great dignity sauntered nonchalantly over to the communal doggy bowl. Fixing the other dog with a contemptuous glare, Bruce cocked his leg and emptied his innermost feelings into the bowl in an unmistakeable expression of his low opinion of the stranger. Personal honour was restored and Bruce's canine supremacy at the hostelry regained.

Looking back on life I can honestly say that many animals that played a part in my childhood, and many more fur-footed friends that have been part of my adult life, forever left their paw-prints in my heart when they passed away.

Loyalty is a quality fittingly attributed to animals. It is an unfortunate truth, however, that there are some human beings far less honourable than the animals they are meant to care for. Many are casual owners; folk who acquire a pet without understanding what is required to take proper care of an animal.

Sadly, we also have unscrupulous breeders who use bitches as puppy-making machines in their quest for financial gain. Puppy lovers, who can't resist holding their small bundle of loveable mischief, seldom realise how large their pet will be when fully grown. That becomes the moment of truth and results in many of these poor creatures being rejected. The luckier ones end up in dogs' homes, hopefully re-homed at a later date.

Less fortunate pets roam the streets, starved and in a state of utter neglect. Regrettably, many become the victims of extreme cruelty. I think Mahatma Gandhi was correct in his observation that "...the greatness of a nation and its moral progress can be judged by the way its animals are treated." Gandhi's assertion casts a wide net.

In recent years my life has been dedicated to the needs of badly-treated animals. I don't do this by running a commercial kennel business; I prefer to keep my association with them on a personal level. Having said that, I'm not sure if the animals live with me or I live with them. Suffice to say if ever a rescue case finds its way to my door, the home I offer is for life.

The West Wing

Looming large among our friends in England's beautiful county of East Sussex were a most delightful elderly couple – a viscount and his wife who, from time to time, would invite Bill and me to have drinks with them. I got on well with the viscountess, a begrudging invalid with a reputation for being difficult to handle. At one time very active, her ladyship hadn't taken kindly to her immobility and, to his lordship's constant concern, proved to be quite stubborn and a force to be reckoned with.

Regardless of the duo's eccentricities, each seemed to enjoy spending time with Bill and me. I can say we shared a mutual enjoyment of each other's company though I never expected it to lead to the next phase in my life. Strange, I thought at the time, how fate sometimes intervenes when you least expect it. Did destiny call?

Not for a single moment did I ever imagine myself living in one of England's historic stately homes deep in the heart of East Sussex, a colourful county of forests and rolling hills that extend to the chalk-white cliffs bordering Britain's side of the English Channel. But that's precisely what happened.

Our relationship with his lordship and her ladyship began to grow after Bill retired from commercial flying and when I accepted a position as private nurse to her ladyship. In her late sixties at the time, she had come to know me quite well and expressed confidence in my ability to care for her.

Over time, his lordship made me his personal assistant so I could handle the staff and help him with household tasks. In effect, I did all the catering for the family and their guests some of whom, to my pleasant surprise, included several fascinating celebrities such as actor David Niven, ballerina Beryl Grey, and Billy Graham the American evangelist.

At times, Bill was invited to go out on a partridge or pheasant shoot with "Lordy". I have to confess that living in the west wing of their huge house became a thoroughly enjoyable experience for both of us.

Thinking back to our first encounter, I judged them to be a charming, elderly couple. It was plain to see that her ladyship was a strong-willed woman who had led an active life with a passion for gardening as well as being a keen horsewoman and tennis player. Later, beset by breathing problems as a result of emphysema of the lungs, she was unable to pursue any further forms of physical activity. As an invalid she became frustrated with everything and everyone. She began drinking heavily and that created an incongruous situation in the home.

Conversely, her husband was an utterly delightful man. He worshipped the ground his wife walked on even though his constant concern for her wellbeing prevented him from taking his seat in the

House of Lords or attending other official functions. In his judgement she could not be left unattended.

Regrettably she was apt to get into needless arguments with the domestic staff causing widespread mayhem in the stately home. It was my assessment, at the time, that people simply failed to understand that it was her frustrations that led her to conduct verbal jousts with everyone just to see them squirm with discomfort. She expected household staff to give back as good as they got; something they wouldn't dare to do of course. In that respect she held an unfair advantage over them. And though she and I got on well socially, any advantage I had from that relationship was as her friend – not as an employee.

One day, Bill and I received an invitation to join them for lunch. Whilst in the great hall having drinks, the cook suddenly appeared and stood before us. She was dressed entirely in black and from her demeanour obviously quite upset. Tightly gripping two large suitcases in her hands, cook proceeded to strongly vent her feelings in her native Italian, creating a scene reminiscent of an Italian sitcom. Clearly, she was not happy and had decided to leave in haste.

Judging from the incredulous expressions on the faces of our hosts, lunch, that day, was deemed an unlikely prospect. Pushing back my chair I made a beeline for the kitchen to see what I could do to help save the situation, at the same time coming face-to-face with kitchen staff tittering about the goings-on in the house. Ignoring them, and everything else going on in the background, I managed to make something out of the chaos thanks to my Cordon Bleu culinary skills.

If I rightly recall, I was able to cobble together a fish roulade with a green salad, followed by a cheese board to salvage lunch for the elderly couple and ourselves as their guests.

A week later I received a telephone call from his lordship asking if Bill and I could call round to see him. This we did and during that visit I was asked to consider becoming his wife's private nurse and companion.

"She likes you," he said, "and I feel you will be able to handle her during her more idiosyncratic moments." It turned out she had already informed her husband of her desire for me to fill the role.

As Bill had recently retired from flying we were in a position to consider the proposal though it meant closing up our house before moving into the west wing of their lovely home where, as friends, we would be invited to attend all social functions and family occasions. I have to say we loved the idea of having 360 acres of parkland in which to exercise our three dogs.

After giving the proposal some thought, I decided I had to make one stipulation if I took the job: her ladyship had to "dry out", and I had to be allowed to do what I regarded as necessary to meet that goal. He readily agreed but, recalling his own unsuccessful attempts at controlling his wife, he was sincere in saying he didn't rate my chances very highly. I would prove him wrong, I thought, once I decided to buckle up and knuckle down.

The first thing I discovered was that Milady didn't eat breakfast -- she "drank" it. Neat gin in the morning, whisky in the afternoon, and brandy at night. Liver-wise she must have had the constitution of an ox matched, I suspected, with the temper of a raging bull; all in all an explosive mix. Under my stewardship, however, things were about to change.

My first executive decision was to half-empty every bottle of alcohol I could lay my hands on and top them up with water, thus diluting the alcoholic content by half. Every morning I gave her ladyship one shot of neat gin; after that her taste buds couldn't tell the difference between neat alcohol and an alcohol/water mix. For the remainder of the day she received diluted alcohol poured over a glassful of ice cubes. She was not only getting a reduced dose of alcohol, melted ice cubes diluted her drinks even more. I insisted she start the day with a slice or two of toast in order to line her stomach. Fierce temper tantrums became commonplace, but I only had to threaten to walk out on her and she buckled under. Before long she was drinking all day long as she always did but with a difference -- she ended the day sober without ever understanding why. Her husband was able to resume active duties as befitted his highborn status. By this time, he had made me his personal assistant. Thereafter I handled the domestic staff on his behalf and cooked all the household meals.

Ours was a wonderful life packed with many great social events. We even managed to get both of them to go on a world cruise which was something above and beyond the expectations of everyone who knew them.

In the fullness of time, her ladyship succumbed to ill health and passed away with me at her side. Her husband also asked that I stay with him until his death which I did.

At her ladyship's funeral, which she had planned herself right down to the last detail, the hymn she had chosen and which created a bout of stifled laughter in the church, was *Fight the Good Fight!* At the wake, one of her ladyship's best drinking buddies fulfilled a pre-lodged request and sang *Drink to me Only with Thine Eyes.* The latter offering was particular poignant given the first stanza:

Drink to me only with thine eyes,

And I will pledge with mine;

Or leave a kiss but in the cup

And I'll not ask for wine.

Even at the end of her life Milady was never very far from a tipple.

I should mention at this juncture that her ladyship's drinking partner – I will call her Mrs T -- was a frequent visitor to the stately home. She often stayed at the house for several days at a time and was quite a character in her own right but could also be an unmitigated embarrassment at times. On one occasion, cows broke out of their field and trampled her ladyship's dahlia beds at the front of the house. Mrs T ran downstairs and out of the house in full panic. My attention was alerted when she shouted, "Eunice, the bloody cows are loose and there's goddamned cow shit all over the porch!"

Her ladyship had her own indelicate moments, sometimes the focus of unwanted attention. On one occasion she attended a local funeral and, as she stood at the graveside supported on both sides by her husband and Bill, with me behind her, she suddenly screamed out in a loud voice, "My blasted knickers are falling down!" I made a hasty grab beneath her clothes for what I hoped would be her knickers and deftly removed them in front of the assembled congregation. If nothing else, it brightened up an otherwise solemn occasion.

Again, this time during her ladyship's final illness by which time she was bedridden, the local doctor came to examine her. She eyeballed him as he carefully put his hand under her nightdress. Curious as to his motives and wishing to question his integrity she shocked him by asking, "Just what do you think you are doing? Get your hands off my private parts at once!"

Another interesting interlude I remember, this time it concerned "Lordy" at Christmas time. He felt it was his duty to make sure we had the largest turkey he could find. Candidly eccentric at times, he showed himself to be quite mean on some occasions. I would put it this way: He was the only man I ever knew who could carve a pigeon and afterwards have enough left for seconds.

Following an enjoyable, traditional Christmas lunch, and before the remainder of the turkey was placed in the larder, I watched with amusement as his lordship took out a tape measure and measured the bird from front to back. He also weighed the remains recording all in a little black book he kept in his inside pocket. His intention was to prevent staff from helping themselves to the bird. On this particular occasion, he performed the measuring and weighing ceremony inside the larder and unfortunately left open the larder door as he departed. Later on, when I popped into the larder, I discovered to my horror that our little ginger cat was fast asleep inside the bird. Nursing a huge stomach, his head resting on the enormous parson's nose, the cat had a very smug expression on his face. The turkey hadn't been stuffed because of the bird's great size and the risk of the stuffing going off before the turkey was eaten. On this occasion it was the cat that was stuffed.

I recall another weird occasion when his lordship developed inflammation of the middle ear and was confined to bed. His wife was downstairs at the time equally immobile due to her breathing problems. They wanted to be able to communicate with one another and Bill, who was summoned by "Lordy", was asked how this could be accomplished. Bill immediately suggested installing an extension phone, a simple solution. His lordship, who at times could be tighter than a fish's armpit, was horrified at the thought of spending money and insisted that when he was a boy scout he remembered communications taking place between two people with the aid of tin cans and a piece of string. Bill's face was a picture of numbed incredulity at the outlandish stratagem laid before him. He tried several times to explain that it only worked in a confined area when the string could be kept taut and in a straight line. His lordship's bedroom, located up two flights of stairs and along several corridors, made that impossible. But Lordy would have none of it and we had to prove him wrong, much to the glee of passing staff who giggled and tittered as we unwound lengths of string around corners, down the stairs and into the drawing room where his wife sat with a tin can against her ear eagerly, but futilely, waiting to speak with her beloved husband. I can still picture the bizarre scene.

The most classic of all memories of my time at the stately home was when a serious fire developed inside the enormous chimney breast of the huge, open fireplace in the great hall. It had been slowly developing over a period of time and eventually burned out of control. It has to be said that his lordship never agreed to have the chimneys swept by professional sweeps. Instead, he had the estate workers cut a large branch off a tree to be lowered down the chimney by rope to the hearth below. This was Lordy's economical way of sweeping soot from a chimney.

This drama with the chimney unfolded while we were all out in the garden having drinks. I heard loud crashing noises coming from within the house; roofing slates had worked loose and were hurtling downwards. Smoke billowed from under the roof. I ran to report these startling events to our hosts and then went to the study to phone for the fire brigade.

As I left the study, the pair of them were sitting by the fire in the grand hall sipping drinks and reading their newspapers without a care in the world. We couldn't get them to budge. When the firemen arrived both had to be bodily carried out through the front door. That was when her ladyship gave the estate manager strict instructions to bring out all the contents of the alcohol cupboard, and two deckchairs, so they could resume drinking and reading their newspapers while Rome burned. Reporters from the local newspaper arrived on the scene and the next day there was a wonderful picture of the two of them reposing in comfortable surroundings encircled by dozens of bottles of booze as brave firemen tried in desperation to quell the blaze. The end result was considerable damage to the stately home that prompted our noble hosts to go on a world cruise. Repairs were carried out to the house whilst they were abroad and Bill and I stayed on alone to supervise the work.

His lordship's Scrooge-like conduct regarding monetary matters was graphically illustrated via a project involving the lake on the estate. He planned to establish the number and species of fish in the lake and, if suitable, offer anglers the opportunity to fish on the estate – for a fee of course. Buoyed by his brilliant idea Lordy invited representatives from the local council to conduct a survey of the lake's contents. Workmen set off a mild explosive charge to see what came to the surface to determine fish types and approximate stocks in the lake. But all that surfaced were hundreds of freshwater eels.

Though visibly disappointed his lordship was undaunted. He refused to be put off from trying to make money from the lake and modified his original idea to suit the changed circumstances. "Dip the eels in barrels of saltwater," he instructed. "That will kill them then we can sell them to buyers to make into jellied eels." At that time jellied eels were a great delicacy in London and parts of southern England and still are today.

Before the buyers arrived to collect the eels they had to be cleaned and it fell to me, and Bill by extension, to wash them. This was not something I looked forward to because I had an incurable phobia about anything that slithered, and the thought of handling a tub full of slimy creatures filled me with horror. Anyway, we gritted our teeth and got stuck into the slippery task with an early morning start in the scullery. Five of us spent all day struggling to pick up and wash dozens of these slippery creatures. Every time we grabbed one it would shoot out of our hands even though they were long dead. It was then I discovered that the expression "as slippery as an eel" was not without foundation.

His lordship had arranged for a company in Brighton to collect the eels to be smoked and sold. However, nothing more was said; as far as I know the eel enterprise flopped – or simply "slithered away".

Then there was the occasion when the old couple's entire family descended upon the stately home. I was taken aback when I saw so many people pitch up at the house; not just family members but also friends with hordes of screaming children in tow. There were around thirty visitors and all seemed set on enjoying a weekend of his lordship's hospitality at Lordy's expense. This particular occasion stands out in my mind because we were approaching New Year's Eve and on that very morning I was facing a big problem: a water leak had sprung in the ceiling and a river of water was pouring into the vast library and drawing room. The damage was horrendous with largescale discolouration from a leaky sewerage pipe. Not at all pleasant as anyone can imagine.

Our investigations revealed that each of the upstairs toilets were clogged with dozens of nappies and reams of toilet paper. It was obvious to me that the dear little children had been getting up to all kinds of mischief.

Understandably the old couple were not amused, nor was I. The damage was extensive and so unnecessary. Prior to midnight we had to call out Dyno-Rod to unblock the drains. How well I remember the brave young man who arrived to tackle the problem. He dug a hole outside the house to access the sewerage pipes and was soon up to his neck in it. His hair, which reached down to his waist, was matted with the most disgusting detritus imaginable.

Feeling incredibly sympathetic for the poor man's plight, I offered him a large mug of steaming coffee which he gratefully accepted with filthy hands. Over my shoulder I heard Bill mutter, "Make sure you drop the mug in the garbage when he's finished."

Soldiering on undeterred, our Dyno-Rod hero was at pains to assure us he actually loved his job: "There's nothing else I'd rather be doing madam," he said reassuringly, while smiling through the muck on his face. That's just as well, I thought to myself, as I could not, at the time, think of anyone else on the planet likely to demonstrate a similar passion for his particular line of work, especially on New Year's Eve.

The clock in the hall struck midnight shattering my thought process. Throughout the house the strains of *Auld Lang Syne* rang out. Bill and I looked at one another each hoping that family and friends would make their exit before too long so that we might enjoy a peaceful start to the New Year.

Bill and I stayed on with Lordy until he passed away. I sat with him to the very end and was able to place a single, red rose on his coffin as the undertakers removed his body from the house. Akin to when her ladyship died, it was decided I was best placed to sort out and dispose of clothing and other personal effects.

The night before his lordship died he called Bill and me to his bedside and thanked us for all the love and care we'd given him. He spoke of the joy Bill and I had brought to both his wife and himself. He knew he was dying.

His lordship's body was carried on a horse-drawn farm cart to the church for burial. Many wreathes lined the outside of the cart but I was quite pleased to see my lone, red rose was still on the lid of the coffin.

His sad passing not only marked the end of our adventure with the noble gentry that had brought much joy and fun into our lives, it signalled the end of an era of honour and old-world charm that is now a thing of the past. Subsequently, this lovely stately home was turned into a hotel. It was time to move on and discover what else fate had in store for us.

Memories of America

I suppose my introduction to working with animals in the fight against cruelty and neglect began when I went to live in America.

Along with Bill, three dogs and five cats, I left England in August 1978 to arrive in Hillsborough, North Carolina four thousand miles later. It was the start of what became a twelve-month stay with Hilda, my sister-in-law, in a wonderful part of the world where I would later meet some equally wonderful people.

Hilda collected us all from the airport and drove us to her house. As we turned into the driveway I recall our arrival was heralded by what could only be described as a pack of baying hounds giving full chase. I knew Hilda was fond of animals and that she picked up the odd stray or two, but I was somewhat unprepared for the sight that met my eyes. Dogs of all shapes and sizes bore down on us at high speed. Hilda acknowledged we were under attack but did not slow down. The car careered from side to side with Hilda tooting the horn and bellowing commands like, "Get out of the way, idiot," and "Get off the hood darn you; I can't see a darned thing."

I glanced at our own three dogs all shivering and shaking in anticipation of an impending free-for-all. The whites of their eyes were beginning to show; lips beginning to curl up at the edges in a challenging manner. The signs were familiar.

With a sinking feeling in my stomach I thought back to the expensive vet bills for rabies injections and pre-flight examinations; the air fare for each animal that varied according to the dog's weight; not to mention the cost of the travelling kennels, poodle parlour and porterage – the list was endless.

I began to wonder if our three townies would end up as the next meal for the hounds of the Baskervilles now displaying kamikaze tendencies by throwing themselves at our moving vehicle. Alternatively, we could contrive to blot our copybook before formal introductions took place if our dogs decided to strike first by engaging and crushing this overconfident mob and rendering them an untidy heap of bleeding fur. My mind was awash with options and I didn't like any of them.

My thought process was interrupted, however, when our car came to a screeching halt an inch short of the closed garage doors. It came as no surprise to see that the finely-patterned indentations on the exterior of the garage matched similar dents and scratches on my sister-in-law's car. I took that as a sign that either she had very poor eyesight or enjoyed the occasional game of Russian roulette. Further observation was required.

Our first few weeks passed by on wings of song; everyday was a voyage of discovery. Hilda's house, standing in seventeen acres of woodland with a large lake and categorised as "old colonial", reminded me of the iconic backdrop for the classic movie *Gone with the Wind*. And we were in Dixieland after all.

*

Our arrival in good old Dixie was in August the hottest time of the year, temperatures in the upper nineties with humidity to match. Fleas were a big problem for the dogs. The conventional tin of flea spray we used in the UK was ineffective. Instead, we dipped the animals the same way as a farmer dips his sheep.

Hilda had amassed around forty rescued dogs and as many cats. All were victims of cruelty and some cases reminded me of the British TV series *Emergency Ward 10*. Throwing cats from fast moving cars on the highway was a favourite means of disposal, I discovered, and many of our inmates had suffered this cruel fate.

Shortly after our arrival in the States a caller brought us five, one-day-old kittens. Apparently, a stray cat had arrived on her doorstep about to give birth and the lady, a kindly soul, had made mama puss as comfortable as possible in her garage. Moments after the kittens were born, mother cat died.

In desperation they were brought to us. I was dubious about their survival prospects because all five were very frail. But I was determined to give it a try. Sadly, one by one, they succumbed to pneumonia until only one remained. I redoubled my efforts. The last little bundle of fur seemed to have a will of her own. I sensed that no matter how tenuous her hold on life, she was going to fight all the way. I decided to do the same.

This marked the beginning of my personal involvement with animals in the United States; an involvement that would bring a whole new purpose to my life. Though extraordinarily tiny in size and weight that last kitten did survive. I named her Weeny-one. When we returned to England she came with us and lived happily for many years.

*

It is often claimed that American hospitality ranks among the best in the world. It certainly proved to be the case for my husband and me in the good old USA. Everywhere we went we were greeted with warmth and expressions of interest that made us feel more like old friends going home rather than strangers in a new country.

Our arrival was heralded in what I'd describe as "folksy fashion" by the local newspaper in Hillsborough, North Carolina, which ensured our telephone never stopped ringing for our first few days in this delightful southern state. The calls included invitations to share a meal or two and/or to take part in the ubiquitous "happy hour", which I discovered to be an indeterminable period of time, usually during the early evening every day when friends gathered to enjoy a drink or two (or three) as the heat of the day gave way to cooler, balmy evenings.

It was also the time of day when the raucous sound of crickets and cicadas reached an ultimate pitch as local residents' day-long activities wound down and became sublime moments of peace and relaxation as nightfall approached. All aided, I might add, by planters punch, mint julips and my sister-in-law's lethal offering of a Manhattan cocktail. It tasted harmless enough, quite pleasant in fact, but it packed a real punch leaving recipients with a not-too-loving memory for some time afterwards. Come to think of it, it was somewhat reminiscent of my sister-in-law herself.

It wouldn't be the first time I'd be left wondering if it was Hilda's love of brinkmanship, or poor eyesight, or sheer malice that was responsible for the gastric holocaust her alcoholic concoctions

247

caused. Suffice to say she was famously known for what can only be described as exceedingly happy hours and, later, some less happy recovery hours.

I think it's fair to conclude that most countries have their creatures great and small often indigenous within a particular location and North Carolina was no exception. For example, the brilliant red Cardinal, the state's national bird, is a most beautiful sight to behold. But there are also snakes, some deadly others harmless. The Copperhead is a devious reptile resembling dry twigs so I found it wise to wear protective footwear whenever plodding around in the garden.

Archibald, a member of my sister-in-law's expansive animal fraternity, was a large black snake about eight feet in length and quite harmless. He liked to spend most of his time lying across the driveway, so visitors arriving or leaving had to vacate their vehicles and carefully reposition the docile reptile or forever remain one side or the other of the driveway.

I became acquainted with Archibald when I opened the larder door one day. There he was, all eight feet of him, hanging from the rafters and swinging menacingly in my direction. I almost died of heart failure. I am not a lover of snakes and Archibald's sudden appearance reinforced my innate distaste for reptiles; Lordy's slithering eels being a case in point.

Choruses of cicadas provided another experience altogether; transparent, winged insects that dispensed a chorus of chirping sounds which I found strangely relaxing. Together with the glow worms, and other phosphorescent insects, night-time, for me, was a most pleasant experience.

I also found the chigger to be another memorable little fellow but not for the best of reasons. This highly sociable little chap is a microscopic mite that inhabits areas of long grass. But, if a chigger comes into contact with an unwitting walker it will burrow under the skin, favouring areas around the knickers elastic line and other unmentionable parts of the anatomy. It then causes an acute irritation that can drive its host crazy: The more you scratch, the worse the itch. I was told that many an unfortunate victim had to be dragged away in a strait jacket as a result of a chigger attack. There is no treatment; the irritation has to run its course. Little did I realise that I would soon witness first-hand the handiwork of this little critter.

It happened on a tour of the North Carolina countryside. I was invited for happy-hour drinks aboard a Winnebago, a vehicle I think best described as a cross between a giant-sized camper van and a luxury caravan. This particular Winnebago belonged to the Mayor of Hillsborough, a southern gentleman ("call me Fred") who seemed fascinated by my English accent. I could see his point when compared with the sometimes unintelligible, broad southern drawl I came up against. Anyway, by the time he arrived to collect us there were already eight other guests in situ all oozing with southern hospitality and alcohol.

Driving along the country roads, guests were sustained by a delicious concoction called piña colada expertly prepared by Fred's wife from a mixture of freshly-crushed pineapple, creamed coconut and Bacardi white rum poured over crushed ice. Absolutely delicious. Similar concoctions are available in the UK but I doubt they taste as good as the real thing.

We were treated to a tour of the surrounding countryside, including the magnificent Blue Mountains as Fred provided a running commentary that became increasingly effusive as the piña coladas kicked in. After a spirited (literally) drive we arrived at the highest point and, to my relief, emerged from the vehicle and into a delightful early evening in time to watch the setting sun transform the hills into a blaze of colour.

Lost in an alcoholic haze, Fred, by this time, was teetering rather ungainly on the rim of a sheer drop, his jaded complexion in complete contrast to the setting sun. Observing him from close quarters, it brought to mind the Leaning Tower of Pisa except Fred's leaning was multidirectional and had a rubbery look about it. As the setting sun slowly disappeared in the west, so too did our host. We witnessed his disappearance in horror, but our angst was brief and unfounded as he reappeared moments later furiously scratching his body, an unfortunate victim of a vicious chigger attack.

I should point out that this particular area of North Carolina is steeped in American Indian history and culture, explaining why Fred's dramaturgical reappearance seemed to the assembled throng to be akin to a spirited performance of an ancient Indian war dance. He appeared none-the-worse for his death-defying leap into the sunset thanks to his considerable intake of alcohol that had obviously numbed his senses.

As the evening wore on, he began scratching himself with an augmented air of urgency. He seemed unable to sit still for more than a minute at a time, which made watching Fred on the drive home quite an experience. His antics made me think of one or two modern jazz pianists who seem to spend their entire performances unable to decide whether to stand up or sit down at the pianoforte. As we turned into our driveway I realised with mixed feelings and some relief that it was the end of a beautiful day.

With some difficulty I managed to extricate myself from the rest of the party of well-meaning and well-oiled new friends at the same time uttering a prayer of thankfulness for my safe deliverance. As the Winnebago disappeared into the night I heard Fred shout back at me "Party pooper!" Clearly the chigger attack had not dampened his spirits.

*

This seems a good time to acquaint readers with some of the many characters that became new-found friends in our family of American animals. Hence, it's my pleasure to introduce you to Ahab, Fred, Snowball, Lucy Locket and Duffy – in no particular order but all quite noteworthy in their own special way.

Take Ahab, a white mongrel and victim of a reckless hit-and-run motorist who suffered horrendous injuries but displayed great courage and patience during his long journey back to full health. Ahab came to see himself as the leader of the pack, welcoming into the house a steady stream of new arrivals in need of our help. He seemed to reassure them in their hour of suffering and, when they were fully healed, showed them who was boss. The only trauma Ahab suffered was a hatred for cars and anything that sounded like one.

Then there was Fred the jailhouse cat. His story began when he was out courting one night and was brushed by a car, sustaining quite a few injuries including a broken foreleg. The local sheriff introduced us to Fred and asked us to take care of him throughout his recovery period. We also learnt that prison inmates at the local jailhouse had clubbed together to pay for Fred's veterinary treatment and food bills during his stay with us. Sometimes animals can melt hearts, particular those injured in one way or another.

We decided to isolate Fred in the bathroom so he wouldn't feel threatened by the other animals. The bathroom was next door to my bedroom and night-time was anything but peaceful for me as I had to put up with Fred stomping around on the stone floor, his injured foreleg heavily protected in a ceramic pot. Fortunately he recovered quite quickly. Before he left us, the prison inmates had another whip-round, desperate to keep their partner-in-crime a part of their fraternity. This time the money went on a small operation to a make sure Fred's courting days were a thing of the past.

Snowball was a beautiful white Alsatian injured after being dumped from a vehicle on a busy highway and left to die. Faithful to his owners (who didn't warrant such loyalty) Snowball remained at the side of the road where they had dumped him. He refused to leave, presumably hoping his owners would come back for him.

Each day we took food to Snowball at the roadside and, over a period of time, coaxed him to leave the highway and come home with us.

He lived with us happily for almost a year then one night he went missing. It seems he decided to return to the highway and the same spot where he was abandoned. When we found his body we discovered, sadly, he'd been poisoned.

Perhaps one of the bravest animals I ever came across was Lucy Lockett a kitten about eight months old. It had snowed for the first time in some seventy years and Lucy, being a stray and very cold, had sought refuge in a car engine belonging to the county sheriff. He had been out and about and his car engine was still warm and clearly a welcome sight to a near-frozen kitten.

The first we heard of this incident was when the sheriff contacted us around midnight asking if he could leave a casualty in our care. When the sheriff returned to his car and started the engine the kitten got caught up in the fan belt and was badly injured. The distraught lawman appeared before us clutching a blood-soaked cardboard box; he was extremely upset and desperate to have us save the kitten if we could.

It was a job for a vet and the nearest was thirty miles away. But before we could get started we had to dig out the car from snow piled up around the garage. We also anticipated a hazardous trip ahead of us, which turned out to be the case. When we finally got there, we found the vet was working unaided so I stayed on to assist him. The prognosis was not good: The kitten had lost one foreleg and its left hind-leg was hanging by a thread. She had sustained severe head injuries and the area around her stomach was severely skinned. Lucy had suffered an alarming loss of blood, severe trauma and the odds of her survival were poor.

We worked on her for around three hours and when Lucy came out of surgery I left for home. She was heavily sedated and on a life-support machine. It didn't look good.

A week later you can imagine our surprise and delight when the vet phoned to invite us to bring her home where she could be nursed back to health in loving surroundings. He felt that she had a fighting chance with a one-on-one relationship. Her rear leg had been sewn back on and was healing nicely. The head wounds were also showing improvement but the skinned areas needed constant creaming.

We kept her comfortable on thick towelling inside a portable cage, unable to move for a considerable time. Constant nursing was vital. Whenever she needed to evacuate her bowels or urinate she made a very peculiar moaning sound which signalled the right moment to change the bedding. Lucy became quite insightful and a very close bond developed between patient and nurse.

It was hard to believe that within three months of her horrific accident this tiny kitten was up on three legs and shinning up trees. Lucy's survival so thrilled and inspired the sheriff he decided to adopt her.

Another great animal character in my life was Duffy. While travelling to Durham one day for a luncheon engagement we passed what we thought was a dead dog at the side of the road. This was not an uncommon sight in America as dogs seemed to run in packs and were frequently caught up in road accidents.

On our way back from Durham we approached the spot where we had first seen the dog only to find he was now on the opposite side of the road. Pulling over to investigate further we found he was still alive though badly injured. Duffy had lost his right foreleg but he was an old trooper and smart enough to move from one side of the road to the other enabling him to live to tell the tale.

When Duffy recovered he fell in love with my poodle and spent hours following her around. It was all to no avail, but it brought some joy to his life in his twilight years.

*

Subconsciously I ranked a lady called Sarah Lumley as one of many characters I was both delighted and privileged to know during my time in America. Although of the two-legged human variety, for a change, she was the source of many interesting episodes in my life. When I met her she was already in her eighties. The holder of a bank balance that would make Rockefeller salivate, she liked to descend on us quite unexpectedly and always at the most inconvenient time, but always bearing gifts the likes of which could have earned her a place in the Guinness Book of Records.

This particular day she arrived armed with a handful of old corset stays and a heaped tablespoon of very rancid fat. Pressing the latter into my hand she whispered: "A little something for the doggies' dinners dear." Well, I have read the parable of the loaves and fishes but this offering was preposterous. Expressing my gratitude, and with a smile firmly in place, I surreptitiously dumped the fat in the nearest trashcan, while Sarah affectionately prodded and poked the few dogs that had not been swift enough to evacuate the building on her arrival.

Though in her twilight years, Sarah was still handsomely endowed, her shapely bosoms the envy of many. She and her husband lived locally and it was said they had fought like cat and dog for the past fifty years. I suspect their arguments were mostly about money – not the lack of it but rather Sarah's distrust of banks. She had an infuriating habit of stuffing bills in the most unlikely places, causing her family great concern.

Sarah arrived on the scene as we were busy persuading an abandoned and terrified cat to allow us near him. He had taken refuge on the opposite side of our lake, so we were making daily trips in a rowboat ferrying food to him in the hope we would eventually get near enough to win his trust.

So, armed with the cat's daily rations, sister-in-law Hilda left the house and headed for the rowboat. Sarah saw this and eyes glowing at the prospect of a boat trip abandoned the dogs - much to their relief. Without waiting to be asked she joined Hilda in the boat.

Halfway across the lake on the return journey I noticed to my horror that two of our goats had broken loose and were eagerly munching their way through Hilda's prized rose beds. They had managed to escape from the paddock and I knew it would require two of us to get them back. Dropping everything, I dashed to the lakeshore and relayed the bad news to Hilda who had all but completed the roundtrip. Forgetting that Sarah was in the boat, Hilda jumped out, inadvertently jerking the boat violently and tipping poor Sarah headlong into the lake. As Hilda and I raced over to the roses, we looked back just in time to see Sarah, in a blind rage, dragging herself from the lake. She was bent over like the Loch Ness Monster, bosoms sagging, her clothes clinging to her body in a most unbecoming manner.

It didn't take long for us to restore law and order with the goats. I was aware they were partial to nicotine, so I grabbed and lit up a handful of cigarettes and puffed smoke madly into their faces. It was a successful ploy and we were able to drive the goats back into the paddock.

Walking back to the house we suddenly remembered dear old Sarah. For all we knew she might not be as strong as we had thought, after all she was very elderly. But we need not have worried about her fragility. As we rounded the corner we came face to face with what could only be described as an apparition. There she was, still in her wet clothes, hanging out dozens of $100 bills to dry on the clothes line. I couldn't imagine where on earth the money had come from, but when I looked more closely at the old dear I realised in that moment that her bosoms, which had been the envy of so many, were also pegged out on the line to dry. Smiling, I turned to Hilda: "I think that is what's known as monetary deflation."

*

At home the phone rang. I picked it up and held it to my ear.

"Have you gotta few minutes to spare honey...I just gotta talk to someone. We've got this German shepherd puppy...thirteen weeks old and he's as big as a devil...yes he sure is a devil dog honey...my you do have a nice voice honey...and this dog is chewing up everything in sight. He chewed up the rugs and a blanket...and I've had that blanket for years honey...got kinda attached to it honey...he's even eaten all the wooden hangers in the cupboard honey. I tell you honey I knocked up a bird bath and had to move it out of the garden into a field 'cos that damned devil dog chewed it up into little pieces...and that bath cost me ten dollars honey...TEN DOLLARS! We love him dearly but, honey, he's making us as sick as parrots. My, it sure is nice talking to you honey...yes ma'am that dog is a devil in disguise. Why this Christmas some relatives came visiting...hadn't seen them for three years honey and they brought some gifts nicely wrapped...they sure were nicely wrapped honey. Well, honey, they put the gifts on the floor around the tree and that darn dog pooped all over them...well I tried scooping it all up with a shovel honey but that gift wrapper surely was one hell of a mess honey...I guess that it didn't help much that they didn't like dogs. Yes siree, somehow I don't think they'll be coming back...that dog is a real devil honey. His legs are as big as my arms honey and he's only thirteen weeks old...Who do you say you are honey? I sure do appreciate talking to you like this honey...Here we are in our eighties and can't get around without crutches honey and this dog is driving us mad honey. We're so sick honey...why we've put down fifty newspapers on the bedroom floor honey and that darned dog will poop anywhere but on them...even on the bed honey...I tell you honey I'm going back to boxers. I understand boxers honey but this critter sure is a devil. Now we saw your programme the other day...sure is wonderful what you are doing honey and we want to do a swap with you for a boxer honey...Well I do appreciate talking to you like this...who did you say you were honey...well it doesn't matter anyhow, but would you get Mrs Brody to call me back...I'm so sick of that devil dog."

Still holding the phone, I sat rooted in the chair for several minutes conjuring up a vision of a "devil dog". I hadn't succeeded in getting one word in edgeways throughout the entire phone call, which was just as well as I was convulsed with laughter. Thank goodness poor Mr Soyer, better known to his friends as great uncle Sylvester, was stone deaf.

Hilda knew him and his sister Violet quite well and had regaled me with many tales concerning the old boy's exploits. In his eighties he was still active and spent a great deal of time and love on his beautiful garden. Violet, also in her eighties, looked after him as best she could, but it was almost a case of the blind leading the blind. Both were crippled, he deaf and she partially deaf, and both had failing eyesight so were somewhat cut off from society and that's why they took every opportunity and excuse to talk their heads off with anyone who would listen. Hilda suggested that it would be a waste of time to telephone the old boy back as she saw no chance of being heard.

Besides, I thought it might be a good idea to have a look at this scary devil hound and see just how bad things really were. I suggested to Hilda that maybe we could persuade them that an elderly dog with a calm temperament might be better for them than a boxer. However much they liked the breed, a puppy needs a great deal of time and patience, not to mention training before it settles down.

Upon our arrival at their home my first impression was that I had arrived in a relatively tranquil environment. The garden was neatly tended, not a leaf out of place. I had expected to see holes in the lawn; borders dug up; curtains hanging in tattered shreds at the windows; evidence of war damage.

Not one sign of the anticipated holocaust was to be seen just a notice on the gate which didn't read "Beware of the Dog", as one might suppose, but instead read "Please go to the back door, we can't hear you knocking".

We did just that, and Violet greeted us like long lost friends. I don't think she realised she had never seen me before in her life but she gripped my hand in hers and beamed, "Now honey we don't see enough of you."

There was no sign of the devil dog but I knew he was around somewhere by the freshly laid newspapers scattered over the floor and the tell-tale puddles on the carpet.

Greetings over, Violet ushered us into the little sitting-room where great uncle Sylvester, fork raised, was poised to tackle a pork chop. Upon seeing Hilda he forgot his repast and greeted her so affectionately that I was sure that he thought her to be another of his long lost relatives. Before I could be introduced he embarked once again on the saga of the devil dog, breaking off once to say, "...you sure do have a lovely telephone voice honey."

I was slightly distracted by the sight of a large fly swat on the settee beside him but failed to grasp its significance until the door to the sitting room swung open and devil dog tumbled in, hotly pursued by Violet, brandishing an even bigger fly swat. "Devil dog" turned out to be a beautiful German shepherd puppy, large perhaps for his age but, like any puppy, full of fun and energy.

However it was an irrefutable fact that he was free-loading on a kindly couple of mugs as devil dog saw the situation. He knew he had the upper hand, and wasn't going to knuckle under as long as he could get away with murder. Twice we rescued the old folks' supper and in the end devil dog settled for a demonstration of fork-bending while Uncle Sylvester prattled on with his tale of woe. He enlarged upon the episode of the Christmas gifts with their highly decorated wrappers and confided that their visiting relatives disliked all animals and so Clipper "Mk 2", alias devil dog, had done nothing whatsoever to improve his image with them. Rather he had added insult to injury in a grand finale by eating all the Christmas gifts.

Time was pressing so Hilda took over the conversation: "Mr Soyer," she yelled, "perhaps we should find another home for Clipper and then maybe you could have another smaller dog – one that's already trained."

Hilda looked hard at Sylvester and sister Violet though with well-meant sympathy and understanding. But she was totally unprepared, as I was, for his strong riposte: "Get rid of him honey? Why we couldn't do that. He's a devil and he sure is making us sick as parrots but honey we love that little buzzard. Tomorrow I'm going over to buy wood enough to make him an outside house…not too big you understand, but not too small either. We sure do appreciate your coming over like this. It's real nice to have someone to talk to…and honey us sure don't see enough of you." Great uncle Sylvester turned to me and, pausing momentarily for breath, he added, "Who did you say you were honey…you sure have got a nice telephone voice…yes siree!"

Further conversational exchanges ended quite suddenly as Clipper Mk 2, alias devil dog, alias "that buzzard", stood up and with open defiance relieved himself in a very big way on the long suffering carpet.

"Well did you see that honey; clean papers over there and that devil has to poop over here? Well I guess it will scrape up honey…but I tell you honey that dog is a holy terror."

By this time we had slowly edged our way to the door hotly pursued by devil dog and narrowly avoided being side-swatted by Bonny and Clyde. At last we were on the "safe side" of the gate, home and dry and heading for the car with uncle Sylvester's parting words echoing in our ears, "Honey stick your hand through the gate and see if he'll bite you."

Somehow I felt that it would only be a matter of time before we would be treated to another instalment in the life of Mr Soyer, his sister, and that devil dog…yes siree honey!

A complete change

The time arrived for us to try something different in our lives; a significant course adjustment in aviation terms. Flying was now a thing of the past and, with retirement just around the corner, Bill and I needed a new challenge in our lives.

There was nothing to keep us in Sussex. Naturally our friends there were very much part of our lives, but living so close to the world of aviation, yet no longer having an active role to play, Bill, more so than I, would find it difficult to make the break to try something else. Flying was his life, as I have alluded to previously, and I felt he would find it difficult to adjust to anything outside the only world he'd known since joining the RAF at an early age.

Anyway, we decided to sell our lovely townhouse in Lewes and head north to the beautiful Yorkshire Dales where we both had roots. Bill's father originated from Aysgarth in Wensleydale where he lived before migrating to Canada as a young man. He married a Canadian girl and Bill was born in Vancouver in 1922 where he remained until his father, by then retired, decided to return to England to enjoy his twilight years.

I recall Bill relating a couple of interesting incidents that happened back in Canada concerning his father and maternal grandfather. Bill's father was employed by a bank and worked his way up to become bank manager, the youngest in Canada at the time. No one knows if his promotion had anything to do with his cautious nature, but he did take the precautionary measure of having a hole drilled into the bank's ceiling. The purpose, he told the bank's board, was so a security guard could be positioned there and have a ready-made hole through which to poke his shotgun in the event of a raid on the bank.

Grandfather, Bill said, was a fire chief in Vancouver in the days of horse-drawn fire tenders. When he retired the horses also retired and lived with him on a very large estate. By this time fire engines were motorised, yet every time the horses heard the frantic ringing of the fire engine bell they would jump the fence in their pasture and chase after the fire engine all the way to the fire.

Bill decided to return to England with his father just prior to the outbreak of the Second World War and immediately joined the RAF to learn how to fly, which he did with unbridled enthusiasm. It marked the beginning of an illustrious flying career that ended when he retired, reluctantly, in 1974.

As for my family, father was a Yorkshireman and my maternal grandfather was from the Yorkshire city of Bradford. All our family were North Country folk so there was no doubt in our minds that we should pack up and head for the Dales.

It was customary for us to spend our holidays in the Scottish highlands, stopping off in the Yorkshire Dales to visit Musgrave family members on our way north and again on the way south. Over the years Wensleydale came to hold a special place in our hearts; somehow we always felt we were going home. The Dales gave us a real sense of belonging and we had no reservations that this was where we wanted to be. So our next important move was to find suitable accommodation.

In response to our housing enquiries we received through the post details of several properties in the area that were available for viewing. So, packing our bags we joined the Great North Road and headed to Yorkshire to seek out our retirement home. The one property that had caught our attention and interested us most was outlined in the first brochure to drop through our letterbox, though I carried with me details on all the properties we intended to view.

When we arrived in Yorkshire we checked into the 17th century George and Dragon Inn in Aysgarth that was to serve as our temporary base from which to conduct our house-search. It was then I discovered in my haste to pack that I had somehow mislaid details of the first property – the one that interested us most.

Subsequently, we spent the next two days driving from one end of Wensleydale to the other; popping in and out of different houses but without any luck. We didn't find anything that thrilled us. It was always a case of too little or too much, nothing quite hit the mark. By now we were tired, frustrated and disappointed so we decided to head south the next morning. We felt quite dispirited.

When we arrived back in Sussex, and as I stepped out of the car, I accidentally dropped the AA book onto the ground and out fell a folded pamphlet containing details of the house we were anxious to view in Redmire village. Bill and I looked at one another wondering if this was some sort of sign. In any event, the next morning we jumped into the car and headed back to Wensleydale determined to locate West Cottage in Redmire and look it over. We found it and the minute we saw it we thought it was everything we wanted, all we had hoped for.

West Cottage turned out to be a pretty stone cottage with a huge garden to the rear absolutely ideal for all of our animals which had increased in number. Facing towards the beautiful village green with its magnificent maple tree, and surrounded by equally pretty stone cottages, we could not have asked for more.

When we explored the interior of the house we got a big surprise: At one time the cottage had been used as the village institute, and the ground floor was one enormous room suitable for meetings. There wasn't even a fireplace, just primitive heating appliances. A number of smaller rooms led off from the main area. Looking around, we both knew we faced a great challenge to get it into shape. However we were up to the task and moved into West Cottage on June 23 1984 duly taking up the challenge to get the place organised to our liking.

While the removal van was still outside the front garden, Bill and I noticed a small gathering of people. Some folk were holding jugs of coffee or tea and were leaning nonchalantly on our garden wall watching proceedings unfold. In that instance it seemed our arrival was the most important event taking place in the village. Compelled to go outside to see what the fuss was all about, immediately we became the focus of an unending stream of handshakes and introductions. It was a pleasant surprise with one small qualification: many in the assembled throng claimed to be our cousins, many times removed, and each person had a different surname. It made me feel I had better watch my p's and q's as I had no idea how many relatives I had by marriage, and I don't think Bill had either.

Even so it was a wonderful reception and we felt we had definitely arrived home where we belonged; that West Cottage had been waiting for us. In my experience, this lovely cottage was always a warm, loving home as well as my friend, my strength and my safe haven throughout the thirty-odd years I've lived within its stone walls. I can honestly say that West Cottage and Redmire have brought me such great happiness, peace and contentment. There is nowhere else I would rather live despite having been to some of the world's most interesting destinations.

If asked to describe the lifestyle in Wensleydale I would find it difficult to define. To me the Dales offer a world within a world; much like stepping back in time. Here, life trundles along in the slow lane. Wensleydale is somewhere you can walk over windswept moors knowing that nothing has changed in generations; one can almost touch the past. There is an air of stability even as the years come and go. And though we have all the advantages that symbolise the modern world, in Wensleydale we live one day at a time.

For me it has proved a great place to spend my golden years. Sadly, the younger generation often have to leave the Dales to find work. We can only hope that those who wish to return and are able to do so, will feel, as I did, that they had never been away. To my mind a sense of belonging best describes the intangible virtue of life and living in the Yorkshire Dales.

*

West Cottage was a dream come true even though it was still a work-in-progress before we could call it our home. But that was all part of its charm.

As a child I had become accustomed to moving from one army residence to another; all very fine properties in their own right but none we could ever call our own. To make us feel more at home my mother had insisted on acquiring our own furniture but, with a lot of our time taken up by overseas postings, it spent a great deal of time in storage.

When Bill and I got married and bought our own house in East Sussex, we settled for a brand new Georgian-style house. Though choosing furniture and furnishings had proved a great experience for me, acquiring West Cottage meant that at last I could try my hand at transforming into a home something formerly used as the village institute, and give it our own seal of approval. We began renovations by knocking out walls here and there and slowly, but surely, the house began to take on the look of a home...our home.

We transformed the ground floor area into an open-plan concept with a delightful dining/kitchen space housing a small kitchenette for dishwasher, fridge and cupboards. My AGA cooker had pride of place at one end of the dining area and worked extremely well.

Being partial to entertaining, I was able to enjoy the company of my friends and prepare lunch or dinner at the same time.

Restoration of the downstairs area was completed with the addition of a small cloakroom and a very large, open fireplace where we could burn logs all winter. Upstairs was less of a challenge: four bedrooms became three and one en-suite plus a guest bathroom. My mother, who by this time was eighty-one and a widow, came to live with us. Life for me, I would say, was complete.

Our first few years were filled with new experiences in addition to acquiring a number of interesting friends in the lovely village of Redmire where we both found the lifestyle a novel change from what we were used to. Life's daily routine was notably slower and I found it such a joy to wake up and have time to savour every moment of a new day.

Back then the village had fewer than eighty houses, a large number of them owned by Dales-bred folk. There were only a few children in the village so the local village school was shuttered and children were bussed over to Leyburn.

Of particular interest to us as newcomers were the three working farms associated with Redmire. A daily activity to look forward to was watching a large herd of cows, led by a goat, coming down from pasture for milking before returning to pasture. This happened twice a day. Many visitors passing through the village became fascinated by the presence of an accompanying white goat. I learnt from the farmer that one of his cows had refused to go anywhere without his friend the goat and this was the start of what became a daily routine.

All about us there were so many things to do and explore: wild and windy moors, quaint villages and atmospheric pubs, some seemingly miles from anywhere. Now we had all the time in the world to enjoy a variety of activities we once had to pack into a hectic holiday schedule.

The James Heriot TV series *All Creatures Great and Small* was very popular in those days and drew many overseas tourists to see where the episodes were filmed. James Herriot was a British veterinary surgeon and writer who used his vast experience as a vet to write stories about animals and their owners. But he was best known for his semiautobiographical works often referred to collectively as *All Creatures Great and Small* because the title was used in some editions and in film and TV adaptations.

At that time we had a large number of animals including some ten dogs, a similar number of cats, plus rabbits and hedgehogs, all rescued from situations of cruelty. We were running a veritable menagerie that had not gone unnoticed by the TV production team. Indeed, a number of our animals featured in some episodes of the TV series. When they were required to perform, Bill and I would drive the animals to the set of *All Creatures Great and Small* in the nearby village of Askrigg where the series was shot. There, the animals were taken from us on site; we were there simply to attract the attention of the dogs while they were being filmed. Little Emmerdale and Weeny-one, two dogs that came home with us from America, had roles in the series as did Minnie Mouse our white poodle. During filming, the days were long and it was usually early evening before we got home.

It was particularly interesting for Bill and me because we got to meet Christopher Timothy, Carol Drinkwater and other, well-known characters in the series. They were extremely nice people, unpretentious and totally unassuming. During the years they spent in the locality filming one series after another (and there were quite a few) the TV stars became "locals". The Bolton Arms, one of the pubs in Redmire, was used for filming during one particular series. This public house has remained relatively unchanged in every way; generations may come and go but the village pub never undergoes many changes. And it was absolutely ideal for the TV series.

In those days there were two pubs in the village, the other being the King's Arms dating back to the 18th century and used traditionally for the Redmire Feast, an annual event known as "Feast Sunday" held on the first Sunday following September 19. At one time it featured a week's celebrations of village activities but, by the time I got there, it had been reduced to a long weekend featuring a children's sports day on the village green followed by a fancy dress competition.

At the height of its popularity the event included two famous local sports played by villagers: quoits and wallops. Quoits was most often played in inn yards during summertime with horseshoes sometimes replacing the standard, large metal rings pitched by competitors. The idea was to land on or close to a metal spike driven into clay at the end of an eleven-yard pitch. One point was earned by whoever got closest and two points for a "ringer" (encircling the spike). Most of the men of the village took part playing in pairs and the winners received a fine copper kettle made by the local Shields family. The sport has been kept alive in Redmire and the winners still get a copper kettle though in miniature form.

Wallops, as readers may have initially imagined, was not a sport where participants knocked the living daylights out of one another. It was in fact reminiscent of the game of skittles though instead of bowls, sticks were thrown by competitors at nine wooden wallops arranged in three rows. Participants had to stand behind a chalk line nine yards away; ladies were allowed to stand six yards away. The sport died out some years ago.

The Redmire Feast finale was held on Saturday night in the pub when the elderly men of the Dales got together to sing in dialect all the local songs of long ago. They all had wonderful voices and there was an immense poignancy in their performances. I considered myself fortunate to see and hear them perform but sadly, within a year or two of my arrival, many had passed away or become incapacitated and unable to take part. There is still a sports day for the children on the green and the fancy dress competition survives but, unfortunately, the rest has gone. So too has the King's Arms.

In the thirty-odd years that I have been lucky enough to live in the village, there have been more houses built and, with the exception of a few of the old Dales' people, the old order has changed as seems the way of the world. However the village remains unspoilt and its allure prevails. This is something far more valuable than anything money can buy, engendering, as it does, a great sense of tranquillity which transcends all understanding.

On the day we moved into West Cottage I answered a knock on the door and came face to face with a local Redmire gentleman bearing a basket of freshly-grown vegetables from his garden. It was a surprise but a welcome sight indeed. We invited him to come inside for a cup of tea, which he agreed to do. During our chat, he offered us a piece of advice: "If you meet the village halfway, the village will come the rest of the way to meet you." This turned out to be very wise counsel that stayed with me throughout the years.

I also learnt from him that some cottages in the village had been sold off to people previously living outside of the Dales. The new owners, he explained, were usually folk who had visited the Dales on holiday, fell in love with the charismatic charm of the area, and then bought property with retirement in mind. Among villagers these people were characterised as "incomers"; sometimes accepted by locals, sometimes not.

I must say I found it difficult to come to terms with some of these incomers. In general they arrived brandishing an agenda seeking change in the village; to bring it more in line with life as they knew it in other parts of the country. What they failed to see was the whole *raison d'etre* for being in the Dales in the first place, which was to enjoy the simplicity and charm of its unique lifestyle. Why would anybody want to change this?

Obviously tainted by a "Tinsel town" lifestyle, these folk had a false sense of their own importance and were intent on showing the rest of us how it was done in the real world.

Big mistake. The local folk had no intention of taking this lying down, and rightly so. Their opinion was: Why come to the Dales if the lifestyle is the same as where you come from?

One couple of this ilk bought a house near the village green and, after only a few days, began exerting a misguided sense of self-importance. Previously an RAF officer, the man and his wife had discovered the allure of the Dales whilst on holiday. As soon as they moved into the village the man took it upon himself to write a letter to the village hall committee. He suggested they make him "Master of the High Green" so he could perform "daily patrols of the village green and keep the children off it." Everyone involved wondered what on earth he imagined the village green was there for in the first place? Needless to say his arrogant request was ignored and children continued to climb the splendid, age-old maple tree and follow traditionally childish pursuits on the village green.

However, as a result of his arrogance, his card was duly marked as they say in Yorkshire. The villagers hatched a retaliatory plan. It was well known in the village that one of the locals kept a horsebox permanently parked in a parking lot near the village green though it was no longer in service because his family had grown up and left the area. However the horsebox remained in situ and was now something of an ancient relic. Even so, it was viewed by the new incomers as an unacceptable annoyance, an eyesore.

274

The traditional parking area covered the entire length of one side of the green where stood two houses, one of which was owned by our retired RAF officer. At the time of his arrival the horsebox was parked on the farther side of the parking area outside another villager's house, yet it still constituted a real bone of contention between our retiree and the villager. The more one complained, the more the other dug in his heels.

The entire episode provided a fount of amusement in the village and daily bulletins were carried forth by the jungle drums to keep everyone updated with breaking news. The villagers got their opportunity when it came to light that the couple planned to go on holiday and, prior to departure, had issued the horsebox owner with an ultimatum to have it removed before they returned – or else.

In a manner of speaking, the would-be "master of the high green" got his wish: With the help of several villagers, including Bill, the horsebox was dragged from its traditional place at the far end of the parking space to the opposite end and parked right outside the house of the master of the high green.

When the pair returned from holiday the man was so incensed I thought he might have an apoplectic seizure on the spot. But the ruse worked: Within short order, he and his wife put their house up for sale and village life returned to normal. The village community rejoiced. I reminded myself of the wise words of advice from our first houseguest about meeting the village half-way. When that advice was first offered Bill and I agreed wholeheartedly. What we weren't prepared for was an invitation to a peas and pie supper in the village hall where we would "have a chance to put our money where our mouths were."

We had no option of course but to accept the invitation -- or was it a challenge? Everyone would be there, we were informed, and therefore it would be a great opportunity to pitch in and demonstrate our willingness to integrate into the community. Not quite knowing what to expect, we were both gripped by an inner fear, a bit like one's first day at school. And this was heightened when the buzz of animated conversation stopped abruptly the instant we stepped into the hall. The silence was palpable; I can hardly describe how conspicuous we both felt as we waited for a thumbs up or thumbs down from the assembled throng.

Like a knight in shining armour, our new-found friend emerged from the shadows to introduce us to the villagers. Though most people already knew who we were our presence was, in a sense, an initiation into the ways of village life. And we knew right away that we had done the right thing by pitching up. From that day forward we were made very welcome and, before long, gradually slipped into the ways of village life. I felt we had a slight advantage over others by having a name like Musgrave and because of Bill's family roots. But the fact remains we had to prove ourselves to the folk in the village irrespective of our heritage, and rightly so.

Another very interesting couple who retired to Redmire had their house built facing out onto the main road. In no time at all the new "incomers" had lodged a complaint with the village elders that cows passing up and down the road, going to and from milking, were depositing unwelcome cowpats outside their house. As previously mentioned there were three working farms in those days and herds of cows had taken the same route for years. I had to wonder which planet these folk had arrived from. In any case, when you consider the advantages in terms of soil enrichment, and the added benefits to one's roses, they should have been grateful to the cows and the farmer. In due course they got used to the routine but, sadly, an outbreak of foot and mouth disease a few years back marked the end of the herd's daily, itinerant regimen.

I once attended a talk given in the village hall by a lady who had also migrated to the village a few years before I did. She became my good friend and was well thought of by the local folk. Ronnie, that was her name, told me she would never answer her door to anyone before she had put on her make-up. I couldn't understand why as she really was a very good-looking woman with superb bone structure. That particular evening she was delivering a lecture on various beauty products and their advantages. The next morning at about eight o'clock, and before Ronnie had had a chance to put her face on, there was a bang at the back door. As her husband was ill in bed, she had to answer the door only to come face to face with one of the village ladies. She was a farmer's wife, in fact, very pretty and with the most beautiful skin.

Without any hint of a "good morning missus" or any formal introduction or reason for being there, she simply blurted out, "…well personally I have always used udder cream," and without another word she thrust a bucket of cows udder cream into Ronnie's hands and departed without a further word. After observing, first-hand, this lady's beautiful skin, I can strongly advocate the use of udder cream for anyone seeking to improve their complexion – it works.

Summer turned into autumn then winter, and our first Christmas in the Dales turned out to be a wonderful experience. We held a large party for all of our newfound friends and got invited to many parties ourselves. There was something so special about Christmas in the Dales: The silence of the countryside; cold, crystal-clear nights with moonlight reflected on frost-covered trees, and snowclad hills -- all creating a winter wonderland that supplemented the spirit of the season.

Village life had been that way for generations; hundreds of years in fact and remained relatively unchanged. It was a joyous occasion with a great feeling of spirituality and the wonderful assurance that things of greatest value cannot be bought.

On our first New Year's Eve in the Dales, Bill was invited to be the "first-foot" at Hogra Farm. First-footing is a tradition known more in Scotland and northern England than the South. We duly arrived at 10 o'clock in time to tuck into a buffet accompanied by copious amounts of alcohol.

The prescribed custom for this occasion was to wait until the clock struck midnight to ring in the New Year. Then, the first-footer (in this case Bill) who would be waiting outside the house in the cold, had to knock and enter carrying a piece of coal, a stick, salt and a wee tot to bring good fortune in the coming year to the house and all who lived therein. It was customary for a tall, dark-haired man (whenever one could be found) to play the role of first-footer. I suppose there are variations on this theme but that's how we did it in the Dales.

In my family, irrespective of where we were in the world, we always honoured the tradition of first-footing. My mother would clean the house from top to bottom on New Year's Eve; change the bedlinen, make sure all the washing was done and the fire cleaned out before midnight. Old ashes were always removed from the house ready for a new start for the New Year.

For our first New Year's Eve in the Dales we deemed it a great honour to be invited to perform this ancient custom. Bill was very tall but most of his hair had retreated long ago so the "tall, dark-haired man" prerequisite was dropped. He simply had to grit his teeth and do the best he could. And that's what he did. At five minutes to midnight he was ushered outside the house and into the freezing cold. His instructions were to listen for the spontaneous outbreak of *Auld Lang Syne* at the stroke of midnight then bang on the door to be let in.

By this time everyone was in an alcoholic haze and brim-full of bonhomie, Bill included. It was just as well as it was bitterly cold outside and snow had started to fall. On cue, Bill hammered on the door with an increased sense of urgency. In great haste, he stepped over the threshold, performed his duties to perfection then dashed off to the toilet to answer the call of nature. From inside the house I could only hazard a guess how cold it was outside.

However, if we thought the party was drawing to a close after Bill's re-entry we couldn't be more wrong. After yet one more round of drinks to toast the arrival of the New Year, we were hustled into our topcoats and, together with our hosts, set forth for the house next door to perform the same ritual...then on to the next...and the next.

We soon cottoned onto the age-old tradition followed in Redmire to first-foot at house 1 and then, with its occupants, first-foot at house 2 moving along from one house to the next and so forth. By the time we got home, several hours later, we were legless and utterly exhausted.

The next day, feeling very much like the-morning-after-the-night-before, we vowed that if we weren't able to get away for New Year we would get to bed by eight o'clock. Constitutionally, it was question of survival.

First-footing is another tradition that I am relieved to say has almost died out. With the demise of so many old folk from our early days, life in the village has undergone change. Sad, in many respects, but natural in the order of things. In all the years I've lived in Redmire as many as seventy of the original folk have died. And I must add that for me to live in one place for over thirty years is not only novel but also a great pleasure. Seventy friends no longer with us. That's an unbelievable loss and I am saddened to think that so many wonderful people who have walked through my life in the village are no longer a part of it.

I very much doubt I will ever again see the likes of such characters. But one thing I do know is my life became enriched by every single one of them and I will never forget them as long as I live. In their own individual way they took Bill and me to their hearts and for that I shall be forever grateful.

*

It is time to introduce readers to a dear lady called Gladys whom I suspect was one of the most colourful characters ever to reside in the Dales where she spent her retirement. An elderly lady, and one of our friends, Gladys was once headmistress at a school in Bradford and gained fame for her rather Victorian outlook on life. She was deaf as a post so inclined to yell at Force 9 which could, at times, be quite embarrassing. Yorkshire born and bred, Gladys was a splendid character with an insatiable passion for men despite being in her eighties. Simply put, she was man mad.

A regular member of the Aysgarth church congregation where we went on Sunday mornings, it wasn't long before Gladys latched onto Bill. Whenever I took my place in the choir, she would make a beeline for Bill. She loved to sit next to him every Sunday where she would bend his ear and flutter her eyelashes like a teenager.

Bill, of course, played up to her. Before long she was easing her feet under our table at every opportunity. We thought she'd be good company for my mother who was of similar age, but Gladys had eyes for no-one but my husband. A sugar mummy was all Bill needed right now, I thought to myself. My mother wasn't particularly impressed either. However we all tried to help Gladys believing her to be on her own and lonely.

I took her out for lunch on one occasion at a restaurant crowded with diners all happily chatting among themselves. Gladys, in a rather loud voice, was revealing to me her passion for wildlife, especially wild birds, and how she encouraged them to visit her garden. Midway through lunch, and quite out of the blue, she bellowed in a voice that could be heard in the next town, "…but my tits are all over the place!" The dining room was stunned into silence. I still recall hearing my own voice weakly saying, "Oh I suppose you mean the blue-tits in your garden Gladys, is that right?"

My remarks changed little; startled patrons were already falling about in bouts of giggles like unchaperoned schoolkids. Serenely unaware of what was going on behind her back, Gladys gave me a look that suggested I was borderline stupid before turning back to devour her poached salmon. On the subject of food, she exhibited an enormous appetite. I would say she loved food almost as much as she loved men; certainly she attempted to devour both in similar fashion.

Meeting her request, I took her to a pet shop in Leyburn to buy some fat (meaning grease) balls for her bird garden. Blue tits love fat. She insisted in going into the shop herself because, having sent me in when we first arrived, I had returned to the car with small ones – a good buy, I thought, at £1 for half a dozen. But not good enough for Gladys: she grabbed hold of my arm which held my recent purchase, and dragged me back into the shop. Looking directly at the man behind the counter she announced, in her Force 9 voice, "I have come to ask you if you have got big balls." Frantically I held up the net of six small balls behind her back and vigorously pointed a finger in Gladys's direction to attract the shopkeeper's attention. Thankfully he got the message. Satisfied, she emerged from the shop with her big balls of fat and a smug expression of accomplishment on her face.

I discovered to my amazement that Gladys had never had a day's ill-health in her entire life – not even a common cold -- and she was now in her eighties. She had, unfortunately, developed problems with a hip and had to have a hip replacement operation. Without any previous experience of hospitals she was quite excited at the prospect and even viewed it as some kind of adventure.

What made her day was being told that the women's surgical ward was fully occupied and she would be accommodated in the men's surgical ward. She beamed as her face took on the look of someone who had died suddenly and gone to heaven. Even more pleasing for her was the fact she was the only women in the men's ward. She beamed even more; there was a heaven after all.

I would say she thoroughly enjoyed her stay at Northallerton's Friarage Hospital and I know she was bitterly disappointed when she was discharged and sent home for a period of convalescence. Bill was there to greet her, which was her only saving grace.

In due course, she was scheduled to return to the same hospital for an operation on her other hip. Gladys was salivating at the thought. I can honestly say that if she had been booked to travel on the most exotic holiday in the world she would not have shown as much pleasure as she did relishing the thought sleeping in the men's ward.

In anticipation of fun times ahead, I was "commanded" to take her on a shopping trip to buy a couple of nightdresses at Marks and Spencer's in Darlington. She wasn't prepared to shop for them locally because "… I want honeymoon nighties…because the surgeon is so dishy."

Admission day arrived and she was chomping at the bit. Gladys was able to get around without a walking stick but, for effect, she greeted me at her front door hobbling on two sticks. I feigned a look of alarm: "What on earth happened Gladys?"

"Nothing has happened Eunice. I am going for my hip operation and I want to look the part," she replied winking at me. It was clear that nothing I said at that moment in time could separate her from her "stage props".

After arriving at the hospital we were ushered into the female surgical ward where Gladys was given a bed. Her smile gave way to a deep frown as she came to grips with what she considered a change in plan – her plan. Raising her hand and drawing herself up to her full height of five-ten she stepped forward to have a word with the ward Sister: "Listen to me," she barked as if talking to a delinquent schoolchild, "the last time I was in this hospital for an operation I was in the male surgical ward and I demand to go there immediately."

Sister was unimpressed and totally unmoved by Gladys's ultimatum. "Be quiet and get undressed please," she instructed in a firm, matronly manner.

One of the nurses had brought Gladys a cup of tea which she was drinking when Sister arrived on the scene. Spotting the half-empty cup she screamed, "…and you should not have anything to eat or drink!"

"Why ever not?" Gladys demanded at Force 9 causing Sister to take an involuntary step backwards.

"Because you are going down for your op in two hours' time."

Gladys glared at her. "Stuff and nonsense. When I had my last hip done I came in the day before the operation and could eat and drink."

"You are due for a gastroscopy in two hours…not a hip operation," Sister fired back.

I judged it time to step into the fray and head-off any further misunderstandings by explaining to the nursing staff that Gladys was due for a second hip replacement and certainly did not need a gastroscopy.

When the confused and slightly agitated hospital staff recovered from their numbed embarrassment one of them consulted their records. There were two patients with the same name and Sister had latched onto the wrong one.

"Get dressed," she said to Gladys with authority and unconcealed relief, "you shouldn't be here at all."

Smiling now, her complexion having regained some colour, Gladys turned for the door. She couldn't get out of the female ward fast enough. After depositing Gladys in the car I had to return to the ward again to collect her walking sticks but…surprise…surprise she no longer needed them. Her mind had moved onto other things. Gladys did get her second hip replacement but did not get a chance to spend time on the male surgical ward. The dear lady died at the ripe old age of 101 and in all those years her greatest passion remained the opposite sex, which proves much of it is all in the mind.

All the world's a stage

Word got around that I had enjoyed a musical background though I hadn't used my voice or acting skills for many years. Nevertheless, a few villagers approached me and asked if I would produce a village pantomime. There had been a regular drama group in the village at one time but went the way of many of the traditional activities now just distant memories.

I talked it through with Bill. He was very keen I should go ahead which surprised me considering how much he had always been against the idea of me getting involved in the performing arts.

By now Bill had slowed down noticeably, spending much of his life relaxing or fraternising in the various pubs in and around the Dales. He lacked enthusiasm and was finding it difficult to get by as flying was no longer a part of his life.

He loved being in the Dales but despite everything he enjoyed about country life, he was in every way a fish out of water – more appositely a pilot without an aircraft.

Bill did not have a hobby so conversations among friends always got around to flying. In many ways it might have been better if we'd remained among our flying friends but he didn't want that either. He had always harboured a desire one day to return to his father's roots; clearly there was a piece of his heart firmly anchored in the Dales.

Getting back to the panto request, I expressed my delight at being asked to do something for the village. Indeed, as someone fairly new to Redmire at the time, I considered it a great honour to be asked to return to the world of panto. Little did I realise at the time just where this would lead. As it turned out, not only did I produce the show, I decided to write the script as well. That way I was able to mould the characters around the people taking part and that was fun for everyone involved.

With rising enthusiasm I enlisted my friend Ronnie's help with the choreography. She was an excellent dancer with a host of good ideas for routines. She agreed to take on the role.

On the night of our first meeting I was amazed at the turnout. People came not only from Redmire but from nearby villages. Young and old alike; everyone wanted to perform, to get in on the act so to speak. We were certainly on our way to having a supporting cast of thousands.

Our first pantomime was *Cinderella,* performed in the village hall. It was a resounding success. People came from far and wide and every seat was taken for a whole week. From then on it was all systems go. The following year I had to write and produce another panto this time *Ali Baba and the Forty Thieves.* Our fame had spread; we were invited to take the production to Leyburn for a second week. The theatre was packed each night and we soon realised that from now on it would become an annual event.

We were also making quite a lot of money from the box office and from my scriptwriting, but none of it for personal gain as far as I was concerned. Each member of the cast made their own costumes and we had a volunteer crew of carpenters and artists constructing and painting the scenery. Everyone pitched in, something I found a sheer joy at the time.

We decided to form a company called the Yordale Musicals. Everyone wanted to do more than just one panto a year and it was agreed we should aim for a summer musical and a winter panto. The money from the panto paid for the musical rights for performances and the hire of the playhouse plus other expenses.

Ronnie skilfully handled the treasury side of matters. I was kept busy with production and scriptwriting as we introduced more musicals such as *The Sound of Music, Oklahoma, Carousel, The King and I, Showboat, Hello Dolly* and many more…ten in all before I retired. Ronnie and I had to take leading roles in all the shows in addition to our primary administrative and production tasks.

We had a few outstanding performers among our members but, in terms of vocals in the musicals, a higher standard was necessary to make the shows more professional. And this was something we always managed to achieve. I worked to a very high standard, accepting nothing but everyone's best efforts.

"We cannot expect people to pay to put their bums on seats unless we give a professional performance every time," I told the ensemble. "We owe it to our public and to ourselves." It may have sounded grandiose, but it was true.

With a background in music, particularly musicals, I wanted the very best from them -- and for them. Even though pantos were more slapstick and great fun, I still expected the same level of professionalism and they always rose to the occasion. We became well-known for our very high standards, something born out of everyone's dedication and something of which I will always be very proud. I began to deeply appreciate the candour in Shakespeare's observation that "…all the world's a stage, and all the men and women merely players…"

I spent ten years with Yordale Musicals bowing out for personal reasons when my marriage broke down and my mother died at around the same time. I needed a break from everything. But more about that sad and dark side of my life later.

I left Yordale Musicals to find time to recover from my personal setbacks. But, before long, I was approached by another village, near Bedale, to take over their pantomime group. New people?

New places? A fresh start? I became quite involved with them, promoting pantos I had written whilst demanding the same high standards from the new group.

We drew audiences from all over the north of England and a lot of my previous followers came to support me. Houses were packed each night for a whole week. At the same time I performed one-act plays for the drama festival at the famous Georgian Theatre in Richmond winning awards for a number of years for either best play or best performance.

I felt I was making up for all the lost years and enjoying every moment under the stage lights. I performed at music festivals all over the North and won awards in many of them singing in opera and musical categories.

After my marriage broke down I found great comfort in music. But reality kicked-in and I realised that, once again, I was coming to the end of another chapter in my life quite unaware I was destined to encounter many more twists and turns on the road that lay ahead.

Dark moments

The importance Bill attached to flying cannot be overstated though I had no inkling of the abject misery retirement would bring him and those around him -- especially my mother and me. Settled in the Dales, Bill and I were in a dream home in a dream location, but he lacked the one thing that gave him a reason to live – flying. Some readers may find it incomprehensible that a man with so much going for him could become so withdrawn and dejected. By way of a possible explanation, I would equate Bill's temperament to someone who had suffered a bereavement and was dealing with the tremendous sense of personal loss that follows when you lose someone (or something) you love more than anything else. Life, as Bill had always known it, suddenly ceased to exist. And personal remembrances of all he'd once been, and achieved as an accomplished aviator, were now a very painful set of memories clouding his mind day after day. He was like a rudderless ship without an anchor, adrift from its moorings. Worse still, he was in total denial.

My well-intentioned attempts to persuade him to sit down and talk it through rationally came to nought; the shutters came down, Bill clammed up and a self-induced bitterness took over. Neither I nor anyone else could help him because he was unwilling to talk about it. Uncharacteristically, he even encouraged me to go back to my musical pursuits – something he once frowned on. Bill was turning his back on reality by building an imaginary wall between us.

By this time I was deeply engrossed in rehearsals either for musical productions or pantos though I had to keep in mind my mother's need for a little help from time to time. She was now eighty-nine years old, fairly independent in most respects but, because of her failing sight and hearing, could not be left alone at home in the evenings in case she encountered any difficulties. At Bill's insistence I continued to exercise my musical proclivities and, as he no longer went out of the house during evenings, there was no need to be concerned for mother's safety. Also coming to our aid was a mutual friend who, similar to Bill, was partial to a game of Scrabble or tackling the *Daily*

Telegraph crossword. She seemed to enjoy her visits to West Cottage and the time she spent with Bill and mother while I was out rehearsing. It seemed to be a very happy and convenient arrangement but I was wrong. In fact I couldn't have been more mistaken.

One evening I returned home from rehearsals to discover that Scrabble and crossword puzzles were not their only recreational pursuits. On entering the house I was alarmed to find that apart from mother sleeping in her bedroom the place was empty. I checked our bedroom to find that Bill's wardrobe and drawers were laid bare; my husband's belongings had gone…along with my husband. There wasn't even a note of explanation; nothing to suggest or hint at any problem with our relationship.

It is difficult to describe my emotional state at that time. I do recall shaking from head to toe from a deep sense of shock and disbelief coupled with the nagging realisation that what I had considered a happy thirty-two years of marriage had now come to an abrupt and unhappy end.

My initial feelings of despair were further compounded after hearing from a mutual friend that Bill and his *femme fatale* had for six months been conducting an affair behind my back. A dark veil descended upon my life giving me a strange feeling of emptiness and loneliness.

Some folk might say a woman always knows when something romantically amiss is going on; when she's being cheated. I would quarrel with this. If you love and trust your partner as I did then there's never any reason to suspect wrongdoing. Some while after the event Bill did say I hadn't done anything wrong and he had no excuse for doing what he did to me. For that much I was grateful.

Reflecting on what had really happened to Bill I believe he was running away from the reality and challenge of his new circumstances. He wanted to turn back the clock; to hear someone say, "...over to you Bill, it's your turn to do the take-off..." But that could only be in his dreams. Moreover, we had shared an active life flying together so my presence presented a constant reminder of those heady days four and a half miles above terra firma. I was a link to his past and I know that each day he was with me he found it impossible to accept or adjust to a new lifestyle.

In his vexed state of mind he may have imagined that by running away with a woman unconnected to his past life, yet someone clearly interested in him, he would be able to find peace of mind. I came to realise later that wasn't the case and he did too.

At Bill's request I visited him in the early part of 2015. It was only a brief encounter but long enough for him to tell me I was the only woman he'd ever loved...still loves and will always love. In my heart, and to this day, I know this to be true.

Bill never married the woman who came between us and, according to him, never had any intention of doing so. During our little chat we made our peace. I have always loved him and I will till the day I die even though the shock of his sudden and painful departure resulted in my mother's death three weeks after Bill left the marital home. There has never been anyone for me except Bill; we were soulmates and I believe we always will be.

After the break-up of my marriage I walked a solitary path for twenty-three years during which time I learnt that sometimes, and often for good reasons beyond our control, partners are not always destined to complete life's journey together. Paradoxically, when I look back over all I've achieved in those years I am certain that had my marriage prevailed I would never have taken on so many of life's many challenges; personal endeavours I was predestined to tackle alone. Destiny is a powerful force and I remain firm in the belief that matters are taken out of our hands at times for reasons beyond our understanding.

Many people believe destiny is decided by the law of karma meaning that the "cause and effect" of "action and reaction" controls the destiny of all living creatures. It believe that's the case, but first we must establish our objectives in life because it provides a moral compass to guide us. Everything happens for a good reason. And no matter how winding the path we follow or how high the mountain peaks confronting us, we must be resolute and place our trust and faith in the belief that we are never alone. There is always someone in whom we can trust and place our faith.

I have plumbed the depths of trust and faith on a number of occasions especially when I practised clinical hypnotherapy. Later I will explain more about that chapter of my life.

Out of the darkness

My life was in turmoil; compass spinning wildly, pointing in all directions.

I had to deal with my mother's death and the break-up of my marriage. With no living relatives I didn't know where to turn for help. All I wanted to do was to go to ground, fall into a deep sleep and never wake up until it had all gone away. My mind went numb. I was unable to come to terms with the reality of what had occurred. For the first time in my adult life I had no clear sense of direction or mental strength to deal with the future. I was in a state of suspended animation not knowing what tomorrow would bring and not really caring.

Bereavement is normally associated with death but any sense of dramatic loss can cause emotional trauma. In my case, I was grieving the sudden departure of my husband; the startlingly dramatic break-up of my marriage and the loss of my beloved mother -- all at the same time. Yet it was also a time when good friends and the village of Redmire would come to my aid providing solid support in my hour of need. Everyone was so kind and understanding. Till the day I die I will remain grateful beyond words for all the love showered on me, not only from close friends but from people I barely knew.

I should point out that by this stage of my life I had become very well-known as a result of my musical leanings; everyone, everywhere seemed aware of my personal predicament and offered to help. As such, it was impossible to follow my initial urge to run away and hide. The village of Redmire drew ranks around me and became a large and supportive family. West Cottage, which had always meant so much to me, became my safe haven…my shelter from the storm.

Of course I also had my beloved dogs to think about. They were my friends and they gave me an excellent reason to get out of bed every morning and face whatever life threw at me. Animals, so much a passionate part of my life, helped me confront a new tomorrow. It was time for me to bounce back, to emerge from under the veil of darkness. Somehow I had to find inner strength to carry on.

Survival was my immediate goal so my first objective was to seek meaningful and rewarding employment. Aside from this I had also decided not to grant Bill a divorce. I had done nothing wrong, I told myself, and even though he had walked out on me to co-habit with another woman he was still my husband and would be until death us do part. I was the innocent party; Bill had no legal or moral grounds for divorce so he would have to wait out the mandatory five-year period before taking further action. That gave me time to regroup and plan my future to keep a roof over my head and support myself. I did not intend to move out of West Cottage or Redmire – it was, and still is, my world. I was back in the game, thinking clearly and reshaping my future. Once again my compass was set and steady.

Words of wisdom uttered by my mother years ago echoed in my ears: "…no matter which star you choose to follow Eunice my dear, if I were you I should first consider a reliable profession so you will have something to fall back on should the need arise." Mother was absolutely right, of course, and I felt grateful for having taken on board her well-intentioned advice by training as a nurse after leaving school. I thought my knowledge of catering could also throw up some possibilities. After all I had at one time catered for an eccentric English nobleman and his vinous wife and survived to tell the tale. Gradually I came to accept my changed circumstances and steeled myself to face life's challenges.

In the five years it took Bill to get his divorce I worked hard and became independent. Although I'd valued every moment of my relationship with him, I had, in a way, surrendered my individuality. It was time to re-establish my identity and my changed circumstances forced me to confront whatever challenges came my way. I was free to go wherever I wished and do whatever I wanted to do such as catering or nursing.

I chose nursing and began to train in clinical hypnotherapy at the Northern College of Hypnotherapy. Before I finished the course, the college was awarded Medical Board Accreditation. I qualified and was immediately invited to join the teaching staff where I lectured in Leeds and Newcastle. Later, I was invited to become a clinical lecturer on the subject. I felt I had entered my "recovery period". In fact it turned out to be a most rewarding interlude in my life.

As a qualified therapist I was able to conduct a private practice which I did from my home. I was also licensed as a counsellor in the area of grief and bereavement something I was able to relate to through personal experience. Even though I have retired I can still practice these skills if I choose to do so. For now, I am happy to be able to share with readers some of my experiences practising clinical hypnotherapy in the following chapter "It's all in the mind."

If life has taught me anything at all it is to keep faith in my own ability to achieve whatever I set my sights on, remembering that nothing worth having is easily achieved. A person's character is forged in the fires of experience: falling down is not important; what is important is how you pick yourself up and carry on.

My attitude always has been to grasp life with both hands and just get on with it. And that includes any opportunity coming my way if it fitted in with nursing or flying. I know I was blessed with the gift of music and not to use God-given gifts would be a sad indictment affecting my belief we should grasp life with both hands. I wasn't about to wait for a light to appear at the end of the tunnel; I went down there and lit the damn thing myself!

There is no doubt that I could have had a much more prominent musical life if it hadn't been for Bill's intransigence. But it was my choice: I wanted to fly and I wanted Bill. He would not tolerate both; he hated me being the centre of attention. When I met him in 1961 I had just appeared in *Kismet* at the Odeon Cinema in Folkestone and was lined up to play the lead in *Carousel* the following year. Bill put his foot down: I had to choose; music or Bill. I chose Bill.

Making a choice brings to mind a curious tale that greatly affected my life.

Ever since childhood I have been psychic. Suddenly I would wake up during the night with the knowledge that when I opened my eyes I would "see" the same scenario. What I "saw" was an image of a man dressed in a navy blue sweater and trousers held up by a wide, brown belt with a large buckle. He wore a cap, similar to a Breton cap, and was holding a large clock. The time on the clock was always the same -- nine minutes to two. It was an unpleasant experience that went on for a year and then stopped. Then again, after performing in *Kismet*, I awoke to the same experience and the same scenario.

Later I accepted an invitation to play the lead part in *Carousel* opposite the male lead role of carousel barker Billy Bigelow whose costume was exactly as in my visions. It was quite uncanny.

As I mentioned previously I had only just met Bill and he had made me choose between him and music. That was his ultimatum and I chose Bill. I never had the same vision again until just before I was due to appear in *Carousel* when it all started up again. The clock showed the same time – nine minutes to two.

It was during the time I rehearsed for that show that Bill walked out on me, though he later admitted it was no fault of mine.

Earlier I suggested that many people believe destiny is decided by the law of karma: "cause and effect" of "action and reaction". I am a great believer in karma. I also believe that when one returns to another life it is usually to have the opportunity to put right a wrong or at least have the chance to redress situations whether of your doing or someone else's. I have always believed that Bill and I were soulmates and Bill said the same thing when we first met. So, what could possibly have caused our marriage break-up that went beyond worldly matters?

Later, when I trained for hypnotherapy in 1998 I found the answer to my question. All students had to undergo past-life regression hypnosis and the senior tutor put all eight of us into hypnosis together for this experience. Each of us had to work through our own agenda – if there was anything to work through – during that session. That is when I got the answer to my question and this is how it happened: I experienced being in a sled-like carriage pulled by a single horse. I was dressed in Victorian-era costume...I remember the high-buttoned boots on my feet. Snow was everywhere and the sound of silence that comes with snow was very much a spiritual part of the experience.

I travelled across a bridge with tall and ornate Victorian-style lamp standards along either side. The lamps were noteworthy because of their ornamental workmanship. As I passed over the bridge I saw a large, grand building on the right hand side. It was an opera house.

Then the tutor's voice broke in, "...Look into the distance...is there anything or anyone there?" We were then left to our individual experiences.

As instructed I looked ahead and saw a man walking towards me. He was wearing a silk top hat and black opera cloak with a red lining. It was Bill.

The scene played itself out with me as the audience. It was apparent we were engaged to be married, but he was an American and determined to go back to his country. He wanted me to give up singing and go with him. I couldn't accept the offer and he left me there and then. Faced with a choice, I chose music over the love of a man.

I was aware that Bill had an inbuilt dislike of water and would never go by boat if there was an alternative. On the other hand, from being a small child, I had an inexplicable fascination for the history of the ill-fated *Titanic*. I loved to listen over and over to the story of this unfortunate ocean liner, addicted to the disaster in a way my parents couldn't understand any more than I. It may appear laughable but I imagined I was one of the doomed passengers on that ill-fated ship.

It was at that point in the session I realised Bill was the one on the *Titanic* and he drowned when it went down. Then it hit me: If I had spurned a career in music and agreed to marry him he would not have left so soon and would not have been on the ship.

When I returned to "full awareness" I was sobbing uncontrollably. For the rest of the day I couldn't pull myself together.

Driving back home from Leeds that evening I couldn't stop crying and I can't remember to this day how I got home. I do remember everything with clarity and I desperately wanted to know where that incident took place but I had no way of finding out. When I got back home I put on the TV as usual. To my amazement there was a travel programme being aired. I saw a troika being pulled by one horse that was travelling over the same bridge I had seen under hypnosis. It was snowing hard and there was the same "silence". The narrator said that there was an opera house to the right of the bridge. It was the same as in my experience, as were the tall bridge lamps distinguishable by their ornate design.

But where was it?

"...Saint Petersburg..." I heard the narrator say.

All my questions had been answered. I realised in that one moment I had a karmic debt to pay to Bill when I was faced with the same choice this time around -- love or music. This time I chose to give up music for the man. I had repaid the debt. That comforting thought has helped sustain me through many a dark hour.

Despite my personal upheavals, I consider myself to have been very lucky. Throughout all that has happened to me I have had incredible support and help from sincere friends who gave me strength to carry on under circumstances beyond my control and understanding. As a result my life was enriched not only by support from many wonderful people but also from the challenging nature of the adversities I faced. Let's be honest: What would life be like without the challenges it throws our way? The unforeseen circumstances we face in life give us the opportunity to grow and the way we deal with them makes us who we are. But first it is fundamentally important, I believe, to discover one's purpose in life and work earnestly to achieve it. Destiny commands that much.

Now I want to put the spotlight on clinical hypnotherapy.

It's all in the Mind

After qualifying as a clinical hypnotherapist in 2000 I was invited by The Northern College of Clinical Hypnotherapy and General Medical Board to become a member of the teaching staff. Years of enjoyment followed, not only lecturing on the subject at

Leeds General Hospital, Newcastle General Hospital and Sheffield University, but also running a private practice from my home.

Before I was able to get back into nursing I had to retake some exams, which I did while working as a cook in a vegetarian restaurant in Hawes. Once again, my catering experience came to my rescue. Afterwards I worked in the mental health sector at the Friarage Hospital in Northallerton. In 1998 I undertook a two-year degree course in Clinical Hypnotherapy at Leeds Infirmary then joined the teaching staff and went into private practice for the next ten years as well as working in a nursing capacity for terminal cancer care in a north-east England community based at Bishop Auckland.

I think it's reasonable to assume that not many people are aware that clinical hypnotherapy is widely used in dentistry and general medicine as well as in private practices to address a variety of human frailties. Phobias, weight-loss challenges, attempts to stop smoking, and a host of other conditions can successfully be dealt with and help people live a problem-free life.

Within the sphere of medicine and dentistry, numerous clinical conditions can be addressed by this form of therapy in terms of pain control, stress-related conditions, childbirth, and irritable bowel syndrome. It is truly a case of mind over matter...and there is no more powerful tool than the mind. Also, it has to be said that many doctors are in favour of the general use of clinical hypnotherapy.

Obviously, it is important not to confuse clinical hypnotherapy with "stage hypnosis", which is purely for entertainment purposes and must not be taken too seriously. A great many stage shows are designed to make fools of people for the enjoyment of others. Consequently, many folk who could be helped by clinical hypnosis are terrified that therapists will make fools of them. This is far from the truth. And it has to be said that no-one can be hypnotised against their will. Clinical hypnotherapy is used for the good of those who are genuinely in need of professional help to address certain conditions and bring about relief. I will illustrate this point with a few examples.

*

I have practised clinical hypnotherapy extensively for pain control purposes and marvelled how someone in constant pain can, through hypnotic techniques, perceive their pain to have eased. One of the techniques used in addressing this is called "time distortion".

We have another procedure called "glove anaesthesia", a technique used to numb the surface of the skin; a useful tool when changing painful dressings as in cases of severe burns. And childbirth can be made much easier using hypnotherapy techniques as quite a large number of pregnant women have discovered.

Certain surgical procedures can be performed without the use of anaesthetics and these have been demonstrated in the presence of medical professionals. I do recall watching a fascinating TV documentary on this a few years ago. And it is important to remember the Chinese have used such techniques for many years as part of traditional Chinese medicine.

At this juncture I will resist the urge to go on endlessly about the efficacy and benefits of hypnotherapy and, instead, reinforce the fact that it is all down to the power of the mind and the professional application of hypnotherapy.

*

From my experience during years of training other people in the field of hypnotherapy, there have been occasions when students, under hypnosis, have tapped into deep-rooted memories from a past experience. On one occasion, a female student, who had volunteered her services for a demonstration of what we call "past life regression", retrieved a memory from her subconscious mind which, upon investigation, proved completely accurate. Under deep hypnosis she identified herself as a man. Questioned further, she provided a full name, an address, and mentioned what year it was. She stated her occupation as coal miner. Once the therapist had identified with the subject the past-life gender, and name, the conversational exchange continued on that basis. Readers should appreciate that names have been changed for the sake of propriety:

"Well Fred, if you are married would you please give me the name of your wife?"

From the response I recorded his wife's name as Sarah, and that he had three children named Margaret, Mary and Hannah.

Then I moved Fred one year on in time and asked, "Where are you Fred?" That question was followed by a great deal of coughing; it was obvious Fred was unwell.

He went on to say he was ill in bed so, in order to remove the stress of the moment, I again moved him one year on in time. Nothing was forthcoming. It was then I realised Fred had died by that time, so I took him back six months. Fred responded but weakly; obviously he was dying. I asked him if there was anything he wished to do, or anyone he wished to see. He wanted to see his next door neighbour, also a miner and friend, who had helped during Fred's illness. He provided the full name of his friend. I indicated to Fred that his friend was with him and urged him to make his peace and express his thanks.

At this point I brought my student back to full awareness. She was feeling quite moved by the experience but otherwise fine.

Using the information we collected from the experiment the student went to the location where Fred said he lived and checked the town records in the archives. Records confirmed that a man, the one named during the experiment, had lived there with his wife and three girls and all names cross-checked. The man had died of a lung disease caused by coal dust (probably pneumoconiosis or black lung disease). All the dates were correct; there wasn't one item of conflicting information.

*

Students who are trained as therapists are encouraged to work in pairs after attending a demonstration. Then they practice on one another.

I recall one particular female student, a health worker, who attended the course. From the first day I couldn't help but notice that her head was tilted to one side. Concerned she might be suffering from a stiff neck I approached her. For no accountable medical reason, she told me, her neck had always been that way. No-one knew why and no-one had been able to do anything about it she said. It wasn't painful so she just lived with it.

During the course's one-to-one teamwork, the health worker's partner put her under hypnosis. However she started to panic when the lady began to show signs of distress and appeared to have breathing difficulties. At this point I took over and moved the lady back six months in time at which she regained a calmer demeanour. Apart from that there was no response. I then took her back nine months and asked for and received a verbal response. She was a man, I discovered, imprisoned in Durham's Northgate Prison in the 1800s, for murdering a child for which he was condemned to hang. Deep hypnosis had actually taken her through the trauma of the hanging, hence the breathing difficulties.

Brought out of trance, not only was this lady absolutely fine and showed no trauma at all, but, from that moment onwards, and as far as I know to this very day, no longer experienced neck tilt. The incident suggested this had been one of her past lives and, thereafter, she carried the trauma in her subconscious mind distinguished by the neck injury -- in this case a neck broken by hanging. There was now closure for this past occurrence and, as a result, no further problems with her neck.

*

At this point, and by way of further clarification, I should explain more fully how therapists work their craft with regard to past-life instances as characterised by the hanging example.

Once "past-life" has been experienced by the subject (in my example the health worker), the individual comes back to full awareness with a complete memory of that past-life experience.

Should further therapy be required, the therapist will begin by using a technique called "revivication" i.e. reliving the experience. That is the starting point. The therapist then gradually desensitises the patient to that "relived" event. Most importantly, the patient needs to be fully aware of what caused the problem they have lived with, even though in a state of complete ignorance. A problem can only be resolved when the root cause is established. And that is the true value of what is known as "past life regression". It is not necessary either to believe in life after death or to be religious.

This example brings to mind the case of a young man who had a fear of going down stairs. Going up wasn't a problem, but he had a definite phobia about going down.

In treating him I first put him under hypnosis in the usual manner…counting down 10, 9, 8, 7 and so forth to zero. But each time I did this he went to pieces for no apparent reason. I adapted my approach and successfully used a different technique to put him into trance.

Under hypnosis, and using something called "age regression", I counted him down from his actual age to when he was in his mother's womb. I found that at the age between zero and one he reacted adversely; and again at the age of three. I experienced the same emotional trauma from him on each occasion.

When he came back to full awareness, all he could visualise was a sense of falling – and fear. I asked if his parents were alive…and could he check with them if anything out of the ordinary had occurred at those ages.

The next time I saw him, he told me his mother, who lived in the United States, was amazed that he had asked about something that had occurred at such a young age. Nevertheless, his mother did confirm that when she was pregnant, and near full term, she fell down the stairs in her home. That accounted for one traumatic experience at age zero.

Later, at the age of three, two other things occurred. He was out with his nanny, strapped to her back in a sling. The nanny was scrambling with the family on a rock climb. The sling wasn't secure and snapped, tipping the young lad from her back. He rolled down the incline. Although uninjured he was distressed.

The second incident occurred whilst he was in his cot, one with drop sides. He had stood up, and one side of his cot dropped down tipping him out. His family never related these incidents to him because they figured he was too young at the time and would soon forget. Unfortunately the trauma did not go away but manifested as a fear of falling or going down [stairs]. Once that was revealed he lost his immediate fear because he now had a plausible explanation for it. In time, and with therapy, we eradicated the phobia altogether.

*

Joan, another patient of mine, had such a fear of heights she couldn't go upstairs, or climb a ladder, without feeling disorientated. In past-life regression she recalled being a small boy who was born blind. His job was to look after a goat herd in a locality where villages were constantly attacked by Afghan raiders. On the day when another raid appeared imminent, he was sent up the mountainside, along with the goats, as a safety measure. Unfortunately, he fell from the mountain and died.

This past-life memory of the incident remained in the subconscious mind. Because of a phobia for heights, under hypnosis I was able to release the memory of the incident. After that, and in a fully conscious state, Joan was able to understand that her fear was born out of something that had never affected her present life; that heights could not prove a danger to her at all. After treatment I took her up to the parapets of Bolton Castle in Yorkshire and she proved to herself that she no longer had a fear of heights. She is a very good friend of mine to this day and no longer suffers from the phobia.

*

I recall, with some amusement, a delightful and inspirational story about one of our hypnotherapy students, called Peter, who was blind yet determined to qualify as a therapist. It is indeed possible for a blind person to become a hypnotherapist but as most of us worked by observation it was a challenge in this young man's case to find another way for him to perform. There was added fascination because, as a blind person, Peter had more kinaesthetic awareness than a sighted person. It is the case that blind folk develop other senses such as hearing, touch, smell, etc., to a much higher degree when unable to rely on eyesight.

The way this young man worked his craft was by resting one hand on the patient's shoulder, with the patient's permission of course. Through touch, Peter could detect changes in the patient's breathing... whether it was faster or slower...generating greater or lesser body warmth, all of which indicated to him depth of trance. He was very successful as a student and for the rest of us it was a salutary lesson watching and working with him.

Peter's Labrador guide dog accompanied him everywhere he went and became a firm favourite of everyone else on the course. The dog patiently sat by him during lectures. From the start, we were all instructed not to feed the dog, a Labrador that had by nature an insatiable appetite. More importantly, the dog was on official duty and therefore expected to attend to Peter's every need.

As part of our refreshments we kept coffee on hand and a large biscuit tin on tap at all times. During coffee breaks the dog would dolefully look at the tin of biscuits longing for someone to do the decent thing and offer him one or two. But we didn't dare feed the dog because Peter, acute of hearing would, from a mile away, pick up the chomping sound of a canine eating biscuits.

The day of the exams dawned. Peter, being blind, had to sit the written exam in a separate room using a tape recorder under supervision from a tutor. The tutor posed the questions and Peter answered into the tape recorder. The other students gathered in another room to take the same written exam under my supervision. At the opposite end of the room we had the coffee and biscuit tin sitting on a table to which we all had our backs turned.

There was total silence through the examination. At the end, students began to discuss the exam and became conversationally engrossed in what each one had answered in response to the questions. Suddenly, the door burst open and Peter lurched in…minus his dog. It transpired that after the exam his tutor had left the room taking the tape recorder with her and leaving Peter to find his own way back to the lecture hall. She thought he'd be alright because the dog would guide him back. What dog? Panic set in…where was Peter's guide dog?

Not quite sure of what to do, we popped over to the coffee table to gather our thoughts. As sighted people, we immediately saw that the large biscuit tin was empty. It was brim-full when the exams began. Peter, being blind, and more concerned to find his dog, did not join us. Fortunately so, because skulking under the coffee table was one embarrassed-looking Labrador. One of our group tiptoed out of the room with a quiet and overfed dog and then declared, noisily and triumphantly, "He's here, Peter, he was in the corridor looking for you."

By this time all members of the group were laughing fit to fall over. Peter never quite believed the scenario as presented by us, but neither did he discover that his dog had stolen into the room and polished off a tin of biscuits. Luckily we had a spare tin in the cupboard.

When the time came for the presentation of diplomas, Peter proudly stepped forward to receive his award. And, because his dog was loved by all and had attended every lecture and practical demonstration throughout the two year course, the Labrador was also awarded a diploma for good and faithful attendance.

*

Many different reactions result from being put in to an altered state of hypnosis; sometimes there's sadness and tears, sometimes laughter and joy.

Take the occasion when a large and burly medic – a student on the course – couldn't stop laughing under hypnosis. Each time I spoke to him he became convulsed with uncontrollable laughter. And, after a while, so too were the rest of the class. In spite of his irrepressible giggling he carried out my instructions without hesitation while rolling around in his chair and even after he fell off and continued to roll around the floor. It wasn't just *my* voice, I'm happy to say. No matter how often he was hypnotised he reacted in trance exactly the same way to any voice. Sadly, he didn't finish the course.

*

The segment of training that deals with the eradication of unwanted habits is also quite interesting. A lot of people who volunteer for this demonstration may include, for example, those who desire to stop eating chocolates or quit smoking. In dealing with unwanted habits I favoured a technique known as "aversion therapy". It was effective but there were difficulties. In a demonstration, one had to be very clear and explain to the class that some of them might find themselves affected by the technique. This occurs because some people easily slip into hypnosis even though they are not the object (or subject) of the procedure. Listening to the hypnotic voice may be all it takes to put them into trance. I discovered that when dealing with such groups it was important to remember when bringing the prime subject out of trance to do the same for the others.

As I previously stated, this could be a very effective technique. I have a case that may serve to clarify the point; it concerns a friend's sister who had a thing about cheese. She gorged on it, consuming large quantities. This not only adversely affected her weight and cholesterol levels, but her health in general. In short, she was clinically addicted to cheese.

She asked me to treat her and I agreed. I warned her that the method I used was very powerful and involved knowing a great deal about real aversions, which she later experienced. We had two therapy sessions a few years ago. Since then she hasn't eaten cheese. She can look at, smell it, buy it for her family and even cook with it, but she no longer has any desire to eat cheese.

*

That was a serious example but "aversion therapy" can have its lighter side.

I remember one girl in the classroom while under hypnosis found herself in a place she couldn't identify under questioning because it was "too dark" she said. I suggested she listen for sounds that could be identified. At first nothing was forthcoming. Then she suddenly announced: "There is a hell of a stench of horse shit!" It turned out she was a highwayman waiting to rob a coach.

I think the funniest incident I encountered was, again, related to past-life regression and involved a rather prim-and-proper gentleman who signed on for the course. He was a stickler for dotting-the-i's and crossing-the-t's and I guessed that he would be a force to be reckoned with in his professional capacity as a businessman.

During the staged one-to-one practical hypnosis session, a young, fresh-faced male nurse was paired with this gentleman whom he put into deep hypnosis. I was supervising the session and noticed a cheeky smirk appearing on the face of our prim-and-proper gent.

"Can you tell me where you are?" I asked, curious to find out what was so amusing.

"I am in the saloon having a few drinks after a hard day's work on the ranch," he declared speaking with a broad Texan drawl. From further questioning we established he frequented the same saloon on a regular basis. Asked by the young nurse if there were any other people with him, he began reeling off a long list of women's names.   It became clear that they were all "ladies of the night". Then he declared he was particularly fond of one lady called Lucy.

By this time the young, male nurse's neck and face was turning beetroot red with increasing embarrassment. With panic-stricken eyes he turned to me for help. I pressed him to keep on asking questions.

"Do you have a favourite lady?" he prompted the man to answer, somewhat nervously.

All students, by now, had stopped whatever they were doing and coalesced around the one-to-one exchange that had taken centre stage. They were riveted by the total change of character of the gentleman under hypnosis. Whereas he, under trance, had no idea of what was going on.

"Yep, I sure like Lucy best of all," he fired back with unbridled enthusiasm. "She charges a dollar a session...dollar-fifty with a feather boa, but I'll be darned if she ain't got the hairiest minge I've ever seen!"

The young, male nurse was beside himself with angst and all the other classmates were falling about the floor in fits of laughter. I judged this to be an opportune moment to bring back the poor man to full awareness before we found out what other forms of entertainment Lucy kept in her extensive repertoire.

All experiences considered, I deem hypnotherapy to be a fascinating subject and, used wisely, an effective way to bring much needed help to many people under a variety of conditions. I loved every moment of my teaching years during which I met a large number of interesting people. And I continue to rejoice in the thought I was able to help train many students who have since gone on to practice their clinical hypnotherapy skills for the benefit of people in need.

Life in Redmire

When I look back on life I don't cry or even regret what happened; I smile and even laugh because it did happen.

For over thirty years it has been sheer joy and a great privilege living in the charming village of Redmire at the very heart of the picturesque Yorkshire Dales. To coin an overused cliché, but true in my case, much water has flowed under the bridge since my arrival. Yet it seems like only yesterday that West Cottage became my home.

Many people may claim that nothing stays the same forever and, up to a point, that has to be true. But, in my experience, Redmire has remained reassuringly steadfast throughout the years though my personal circumstances have undergone change with the tides of life. Different people may come and go, after all that is the way of communities, but the quaint village of Redmire retains an indefinable quality that exemplifies its strengths, and long may it prevail.

During quieter moments, when I think about the past I also think of Redmire and a host of interesting characters spring to mind. Sadly not all are with us any longer, but their imprints are enshrined in the sands of time.

*

One gentleman who comes to mind, a retired farmer now in his eighties, has left me with many lasting memories. He brought so much colour into my life. I must say I respect him for his open candour: if he is curious about something or wishes to check on anything he is forthright with his questions, rather than choosing to select from a dozen available variations on a theme i.e., village gossip.

We became acquainted one afternoon when he knocked on my door: "I heard you would like to have a grey cat," he said, gently cradling a tiny grey kitten in his arms. He was retiring from farming, he told me, and quitting his farm to live in a cottage on the opposite side of the village green to me. He didn't want the kitten left to the unfortunate fate faced by so many farm cats, so I ended up with this little grey bundle of fluff that grew into a magnificent cat called Grebo.

Joan, a good friend I have already mentioned, often joined me for a morning coffee which, in the summer months, we would take sitting in the front garden in full view of passers-by. Afterwards, for reasons I can't quite recall but may have had something to do with soaring summer temperatures, we switched to my back garden for our coffee breaks. In a village where everyone knows everyone else's business this seemingly insignificant change in routine did not go undetected by many villagers, including my farmer friend.

Whilst we were enjoying coffee in my kitchen which overlooks a little lane leading to the rear garden, Joan and I had a visit from Dick, a great friend and occasional helper. I could see from the big smile that lit-up his weather-beaten face that he had something of great importance to impart.

"It appears your farmer friend is asking about your whereabouts," Dick confided, taking quick glances out of the kitchen window. "It seems he hasn't spotted you in the front garden at your usual coffee time."

I immediately thought our farmer friend may be wondering if Joan and I had fallen out with one another though, at this juncture, I should caution readers that Dick can be a great tease, a talent he manages to project with a poker-straight face.

"I think your farmer friend is quite concerned at not seeing you drinking coffee in your front garden. He thinks something is amiss."

"What did you tell him?" I asked, slightly fearful of what might come back in the way of a reply.

"I told him that because of the warm weather you and Joan had taken to having coffee in the rear garden where you could sunbathe topless."

My fear was justified. Stifling the urge to laugh out loud, Joan and I peered out of the kitchen window just in time to catch our farmer friend running a sub four-minute mile down the lane, at the same time craning his neck to see what he could see. Joan and I could only imagine his bitter disappointment.

In another Redmire incident of similar magnitude, Dick became conversationally engaged with a fellow villager, a lady on this occasion. For over twenty years Dick had worked for me in his spare time doing odd jobs that sometimes taxed my physical abilities.

Apparently, the lady had button-holed Dick and asked if he was working for me. Not entirely happy with Dick's affirmation, she informed him she could see exactly what he was getting up to if she stood on the bed in her spare room and trained her binoculars on him. I didn't know whether to laugh or cry so I remained tight-lipped. I was old enough to be Dick's mother. As in previous village incidents my sense of humour came to my aid. I shudder to think what she imagined she would see but I guarantee it wouldn't be enough to steam up her high-powered field glasses, that's for sure.

*

Whilst on the weighty subject of high-powered binoculars, I am reminded of three enterprising ladies who lived in Redmire; two being distant relatives of husband Bill. My mother was once very friendly with one of them and often visited the lady's house a few doors down the road. Together, they would drink cups of tea and have a good old natter as they whiled away the time. With my mother sitting directly before her, this lady would proudly deliver her observations regarding mother's every movement for the day, and for every day that had passed since her last visit. Mother would be "clocked out" when she left the house and "clocked in" again when she returned. Armed with her binoculars this lady would sit in an armchair, side-on to a window with net curtains, where she could observe all movements on one side of the road. It may have been a throwback from her wartime duties as an air raid warden.

Another lady, a few doors further down the road, did likewise. And the lady on the opposite side of the road used her binoculars to watch the other side of the road. Each day, at a prearranged hour, all three ladies met to compare notes and swap information. This is just another snapshot of village life; that's how it is…not one iota of harm in it…simply the way it is and has been for many years. They were all lovely people with the kindest of hearts and I wouldn't have missed the opportunity to know any of them.

*

A very fascinating and well-known character in the Dales was Colonel Crump a Second World War veteran and active member of the horseracing fraternity around Middleham where he lived. This colourful North Yorkshire village is also the site of the much-visited 12th century Middleham Castle, at one time the childhood home of King Richard III.

On one occasion, Colonel Crump, a long-term customer of a bespoke gentleman's tailors and outfitters in the nearby town of Leyburn, stood outside of the shop talking about horseracing to the shop-owner, a friend of mine, when he was approached by an all-male contingent of Japanese tourists.

"Tell me where is Middleham Castle," the group leader asked, addressing the colonel in broken English.

"Listen lad, you found your own bloody way to Pearl Harbour," Colonel "Grump" muttered, "so find your own bloody way to Middleham Castle!"

*

Unrelated to this unsavoury example of the colonel's lack of political savoir-faire, but nevertheless a character with the stature of a navy battle cruiser, was a certain American lady from the great State of Alaska. She breezed into North Yorkshire for a holiday, fell in love with the Dales (and James Heriot) and married a local shepherd whose tall, thin frame presented a severe - though humorous - contrast to that of his wife's.

Referred to as "Baked Alaska" by all who knew her, she joined our performing arts group and though she was rather unkempt, as well as being built like the pocket battleship *Admiral Graf Spee*, she had one of the most strident singing voices I have ever heard. When I say she "joined" our performing arts group I really mean it was impossible to keep her out. For obvious reasons, and for the safety of others in the production, I always tried to hide her in the back row of the chorus but, somehow, she always managed to inveigle her way to the front.

I was stumped as to what to do with the lady at least, that is, until we decided to put on a performance of *Show Boat*. That gave me a brilliant idea. I took her to one side, painted her black all over and gave her the speaking role of the mammy servant. She was made for the part, something I discovered first-hand when I stumbled across her in our local grocery store where she was staging a one-woman performance. There she was, large of presence with voice to match, wheedling her way towards the checkout.

"I have never had as many showers as I've had this week," she hollered at no-one in particular in a queue of bored and disinterested shoppers. "Normally I bathe once a year," she confided, "but this black stuff is shit to get off!"

That wasn't her only glowing performance: On another occasion, again in the checkout line of the same grocery store, she zeroed-in on a heavily-pregnant woman in front of her who had one toddler on her trolley and two more hanging on either side.

"There's a cure for that," Baked Alaska declared in a loud voice that would stop a buffalo at forty paces. "It's called contraception," she said pointing towards the kids.

One thing she did approve of was sheep; she loved them. She lived in a caravan but was constantly urged to move on because local farmers did not want her on their land. She tended to treat the sheep as her children allowing them to sleep inside the caravan with her while her inconsequential hubby slept in a tent outside. Not surprisingly, the marriage did not endure.

Later on she told me she had found a "fancy man" who had plenty of money and bought her beautiful things. He was the proud wearer of a capacious wig – he walked under it to be more accurate.

"I promised to take him to Alaska," she told me on one occasion. "But only if he got a new wig and a decent set of false teeth."

"Baked Alaska" was a unique character who, sadly, died of a sudden heart attack when she was in her late thirties or early forties. Her bulk may have contributed to her premature demise.

The amazing thing about this extraordinary lady was to subsequently learn that she was stepsister to American singing star Barbra Streisand; her father had married Streisand's mother. It came to light that her father had told "Baked Alaska" she would be welcome in the United States if she lost weight, a challenge she was never to fulfil.

*

In and around the Dales we had other forms of talent of a more tangible form; artistically gifted men and women. The wonderful Marie Hartley MBE was a well-known writer, artist and historian with a great passion for music. On many occasions Marie arranged concerts simply because she wished me to sing operatic arias for her. A remarkably persuasive woman, loved by all who knew her, she died in 2006 at the ripe old age of one hundred. I was with her, in a nursing capacity, the night before she died and feel greatly privileged to have been there toward the end of her long life.

*

A magnificent photographer, Ann Holubecki on many occasions exhibited old photographs of villages in the Yorkshire Dales along with images of people in the 1800s. Her prize collection of historical photographs and delightful modern-day photographs drew interest from far and wide. Ann was a great friend of mine for many years. Significantly, in the year 2000, she photographed everyone outside his or her property in Redmire and wrote a short piece about each person and their life. The result is a wonderful, lasting legacy of the village and its inhabitants. When this warm-hearted and quite lovely lady died in 2013 it was a great loss to Wensleydale. But she will never be forgotten.

*

Another interesting lady called Isabelle McGregor, born and bred in Redmire, wrote an inspiring work on Redmire's history called "Redmire: A Patchwork of its History". A schoolteacher by profession, Isabelle had a passion for local history particular the scenic village of Redmire.

*

Also born and bred in Redmire, Ian Spensley has produced several excellent books on the history of lead mining including "Mines and Miners of Wensleydale". His latest book, a work-in-progress, documents the history of generations of families in the Dales.

*

Then there is the incomparable Piers Browne, a noted landscape and seascape artist who has exhibited paintings throughout the UK, Iceland, Malibu in California, and Munster in Germany. Piers, a wonderful character and dear friend, is much loved by all who know him. He also has a fine tenor voice and once composed an opera based on Wensleydale.

*

Without question, the Dales have spawned a wealth of retired writers, artists and musicians – *tout à fait* a rich tapestry of talent. The sheer beauty and magic of this enchanting countryside, and the peace that has prevailed almost unchanged throughout generations, continues to draw creative people to its heart.

When I look back on my life in the village I can't help feeling that my journey along life's road, which brought forth many different experiences of places and people throughout the years, aided my personal development in every conceivable way. Now in my twilight years, I am blessed with so many wonderful friends and animals and I know that my soul has been enriched by the gift of so much friendship and love. When I look around me I know, without a shadow of doubt, I have come home.

Naturally, I often think of what the future might hold; not from the point of view of worrying about it because, as I have stated on more than one occasion, I believe I follow a predetermined path.

What I do know from my days writing and performing in pantos and musicals "it ain't over till the fat lady sings." And even though one's body may have succumbed somewhat to the "sagging syndrome" requiring increasingly innovative measures to defy gravity, the show must go on. It would be wonderful, of course, if we could jump into the dryer for ten minutes and come out wrinkle-free and several sizes smaller. But I don't believe that is predestined in my case. Wrinkles apart, I find it even scarier when my insides begin to emulate the same noises made by the coffee machine in my kitchen.

These days I have opted to simply put up with the "sagging syndrome" and not worry about shopping for products for fast relief and/or incontinence problems. At my age I have the right to be myself; say what I think and do what I feel like doing. I am developing the same mind-set of the 104-year-old lady who, when asked what she considered the best thing about reaching such a grand old age, replied, "No peer pressure!"

To a certain extent she reminds me of a friend of mine, no longer with us, who constantly bleated and moaned about his various aches and pains. As he was in his mid-nineties I thought he was entitled to complain so I encouraged him to do so. Sadly, he suffered from spinal problems that restricted his mobility. Formerly an airline pilot, he also had difficulty hearing anything short of a jet engine at full pitch. Not surprisingly he took a hotchpotch of medication for this and that, which sometimes left him feeling dizzy and subject to the occasional blackout, coupled with poor circulation and the occasional memory loss. All that aside, he was irrepressibly proud of the fact he still had a driving licence.

I too have mobility problems occasioned by arthritic complications. To ease my pain I was advised to engage in light exercise, like swimming. I know it was well-intentioned advice but I had to explain that by the time I manage to bend my arms and legs, twist and turn my body to remove my clothes and don a bathing costume the swimming pool will be closed, the lights turned off, and everyone well on their way home. Writing about my inadequate attempts at exercise reminds of that oft quoted line from the *Ex Files* novel by Jane Moore: "If God had wanted me to touch my toes, he would have put them on my knees!" My point precisely.

327

I confess there are times I do feel old but I don't tempt fate by following every time-honoured convention such as attending friends' funerals. Whenever I do attend one, I feel I'm being bumped up a place in the queue. So, no thank you, I can wait my turn.

However to put my present situation into perspective I enjoy being my age because a) there are so many good things I can still find to interest me during the course of one day, and b) I can't do much about it anyway. Therefore I try to stay positive irrespective of what life throws my way. And if I can see the funny side of life that's a tonic in itself. To sum up: I am inclined to grasp each moment of today and make the most of every tomorrow.

To all who have reached that certain age and don't know what tomorrow will bring, I wish to leave you with an old folks' prayer that always brings me comfort: "Grant me the senility to forget the people I never liked; the good fortune to run into the ones I do like, and the eyesight to tell the difference."

But what does the future hold for me you may (or may not) ask?

I now have the opportunity to write, which is something I have always wanted to do but never had time. More importantly, with a lifetime of adventure behind me, I hope I have a story to tell that my friends, at least, will find interesting.

Moreover, I feel blessed with the return into my life of a good friend who has known me since I was in my twenties. Frank was our best man when Bill and I married and I am godmother to Frank's son Steven.

I consider Frank to be a very capable writer who has inspired and encouraged me to write this book and, with his help, I hope we have succeeded in producing something of interest that may even be seen by others as motivational. All I know for sure is that life, for me, has been a wonderful adventure and, who knows, perhaps a new journey is about to begin...one more path to wander along and explore.

*

Last thoughts...

Someone said prayer is not a "spare wheel" that you pull out when in trouble, but it is a "steering wheel" that directs the right path throughout.

Each day brings another twenty-four hours, enough time, in my experience, to make everything possible again. Throughout my life I have lived in the moment knowing that I will die in the moment, so I take one day at a time...and travel one path at a time praying my hands remain firmly on life's steering wheel...Eunice Musgrave

---

Printed in Great Britain
by Amazon